FUNDRAISING AND PROMOTIONS
FOR SPORT AND RECREATION PROGRAMS

THIRD EDITION

DR. WILLIAM F. STIER, JR.

Distinguished Service Professor
Kinesiology, Sport Studies and Physical Education
College at Brockport
State University of New York
Brockport, New York 14420

AMERICAN PRESS
BOSTON, MASSACHUSETTS
www.americanpresspublishers.com

Copyright © 2011 by American Press
ISBN 978-0-89641-491-4

All rights reserved. No part of this publication may be reproduced, stored in a retrieval system, or transmitted, in any form or by any means, electronic, mechanical, photocopying, recording, or otherwise, without the prior written permission of the copyright owner.

Printed in the United States of America.

DEDICATION

This book is dedicated to my wife, Veronica Ann—for her continued loving encouragement and unselfish support—without which this book, my 25th, would not have been possible. In addition, I wish to dedicate this effort to our five children, Mark, Missy, Michael, Patrick, and Will III; and, our ten grandchildren, Samantha, Joshua, Katie, Mike, Jessica, Jackson, Dalton, Daphne, Dahlia, and Alycia.

And, a special dedication to Francis J. Waickman M.D., a physician, a husband, a father, a teacher, a leader, an administrator, a role model, an innovator, a scholar, and a dear friend.

ACKNOWLEDGEMENTS

I wish to acknowledge and thank the numerous sport administrators and coaches throughout my career who have been willing to unselfishly share their ideas, strategies, tactics and success stories in the areas of fundraising and promotions. I must also acknowledge the contributions of both my undergraduate and graduate students at the College at Brockport, State University of New York, with whom I field-tested this 3rd edition during the past two years. I indeed have been blessed with exceptional students in the pursuit of their own careers and I have learned much from their inquisitive minds, challenging questions and appropriate suggestions.

Finally, I am much appreciative to Marci Taylor who served as the supervising editor for this project on behalf of the publisher, American Press. Ms. Taylor provided meaningful suggestions and input relative to the final version of this 3rd edition which you are now holding in your hands.

Special thanks to Brian L. Robbins (Artist/Designer) and Richard Black (Director: Design and Production, College at Brockport) for their efforts in creating many of the figure, tables and appendices that are used throughout the book.

Contents

	CHAPTER 1
1	**UNDERSTANDING SUCCESSFUL FUNDRAISING, PROMOTIONS AND PUBLIC RELATIONS IN THE 21ST CENTURY**
1	Chapter Highlights
2	Introduction
4	Definition of Terms
	Fundraising Activities
	Promotional Activities
	Public Relations
	Publicity
	Constituencies
	Publics
6	Relationships between Fundraising, Promotions and Public Relations
7	Promotional, Public Relations and Fundraising Perspectives of Sport
9	Ingredients of Successful Sport and Recreation Programs
19	Developing Competencies in Fundraising, Promotions and Public Relations
10	Graduate Degrees in Fundraising and Philanthropy
11	Keeping Things in the Proper Perspective
16	References
18	Discussion Questions
	CHAPTER 2
19	**FUNDAMENTAL ELEMENTS AND RESOURCES OF FUNDRAISING AND PROMOTION**
19	Chapter Highlights
20	Fundamental Processes or Components of Management within Any Organization
21	Essential Administrative Processes—PPPOSDDCoRRRFEB
	Planning
	Prioritizing
	Problem Solving
	Organizing
	Staffing
	Directing

	Decision Making
	Coordinating
	Reporting
	Recording
	Risk Taking
	Facilitating—Supporting
	Evaluating
	Budgeting
27	Resources, Tools, and Assets Available to Support
	Fundraising and Promotional Activities
28	Available Assets and Resources
	Available Time (to work)
	Personnel (internal/external and paid/volunteer)
	Equipment and Supplies
	Facilities
	Web Presence and the Internet
	Software Applications
	Reputation
	Image
	Status—Level of Competition
	Money
	Atmosphere, Climate, and Environment
	Services
	Associates
	Other Assets and Resources
36	Essential Characteristics and Qualifications of Fundraisers, Promoters, and Public Relations Professionals
38	Basic Skills
38	Technical Skills
38	Interpersonal Skills
39	Conceptual Skills
40	Commitment and Dedication Skiills
41	Image Skills
42	Leadership Skills
42	Adaptability Skills
43	Vision Skills
43	Professionalism Skills
44	Being a Renaissance Person
44	References
46	Discussion Questions

CHAPTER 3
47 BOOSTER CLUBS AND SPORT SUPPORT GROUPS

- 47 Chapter Highlights
- 48 History of American Sport Booster Clubs
- 50 Justification for the Existence of Support Organizations—Sport Support Groups
  - Why Sport and Recreation Programs Need Additional Financial Support
- 55 Support Groups for Sport and Recreation Organizations
  - A Single Support Organization or Multiple Support Organizations?
  - Challenges to be Faced when Instituting Changes
- 58 Creating a Wholesome, Productive Atmosphere within Sport Support Groups (SSGs)
- 59 Creating and Organizing a Support Group (SSG) or Recreation Support Group (RSG)
  - A Single Support Group or Multiple Groups—An Important Consideration
- 61 Seven Steps in the Establishment of a Quality Support Group
- 64 Membership Terms of the Board of Directors and the Corps of Officers
- 66 Financial Considerations of Support Groups
- 67 Whether to Incorporate or Not—That is the $64,000 Question
- 67 Benefits to the Members of the Sport Support Group
- 68 Specific Gifts Accruing to Donors Contributing to the Sport or Recreation Program
- 70 Controlling Potential Negative "Outside" Influences
- 71 Handling the "Three O'clock Booster Wonders"
- 72 References
- 73 Discussion Questions

CHAPTER 4
75 THE IMPORTANCE OF PLANNING IN FUNDRAISING ACTIVITIES

- 75 Chapter Highlights
- 76 The Importance of Planning
- 77 Appropriate Strategic Planning
  - Essentials of Planning
- 78 The Plan—What It Is and What It Is Not
- 78 PIA—Planning in Advance
- 78 Initial Steps
- 79 Before One Starts—Important Early Decisions to Make
  - Planning by Means of the Program Evaluation Review Technique
  - The Ten Commandments of Fundraising
  - NASPE's Position Paper—"Implementing Fundraising Project in Public Schools when State Funding is Cut or Nonexistent"
- 83 Attempting to Influence Opinions of Others—Use of Centers of Influence
- 84 Determination of Needs

85	Realization of Goals and Objectives
86	Liability Considerations—Fundraising and Promotional Activities
88	Risk Management for Preventing Exposure to Negligence Charges
89	Insurance Considerations—Fundraising and Promotional Activities
90	Applicable Federal and State Tax Laws—Fundraising and Promotional Activities
90	Permits, Licenses and Permission
	Restrictions on Selling and Distributing
	Licensing Transient Retail Merchants
	Exemptions from Licenses and Permits
	Alcoholic Beverages and Fundraising Projects
93	Results Orientation
95	Collecting and Storing Data for Decision Making
	Hard Data Collection
	Soft Data Collection
97	References
98	Discussion Questions

CHAPTER 5
99   THE WHO, WHAT AND WHY OF FUNDRAISING

99	Chapter Highlights
100	Philanthropic Activities
	Problems with Would-Be Charitable Requests
	Determining the Percentage of Money Raised to Actually Go to the Worthy Cause
	Corporate Giving
	Sources of Charitable Contributions
	Contributions to Educational Institutions
	Using Grants as a Funding Source
105	Types of Donations
106	Timing of Fundraising Efforts
	One-Time Events
	Repeatable Activities
	The Annual Event
107	Categories or Vehicles of Giving
	Endowments Provide for Long-Term Support
	Deferred/Planned Giving Programs
	Deferred/Planned Giving Programs—Proceeds from Life Insurance
110	Who Contributes
	Facts to be Considered in Soliciting Support
112	Known Characteristics of Givers (Briggs, 19834; Cole 2000)
115	Why People Contribute

	Advantages to Advertisers, Contributors, Supporters and Sponsors
	"Guilt and Glitter" Syndrome
117	Team Concept for Direct Contributions—One Type of Implementation
	Successful Record Keeping
120	Criteria for a Successful Sport Fundraising Activity or Promotional Project
	Conducting an Audit of Public Relations, Promotional, and Fundraising Activities
123	Steps in Assessing Promotional and Fundraising Activities
124	Why Fundraising and promotional Efforts Fail
125	References
126	Discussion Questions

CHAPTER 6
127 STRATEGIES AND TACTICS OF RAISING MONEY

127	Chapter Highlights
128	Developing a Conceptual Approach
129	Two Approaches to the Raising of Monies
	Donating versus Buying "Something"
131	The Feasibility of Raising Funds
134	Sources for Generating Need Resources
	Securing Permission to Engage in Fundraising Activities
139	Restrictive Philosophies
	State Laws and Department of Education Rules Restricting Fundraising at Schools
	Clearinghouse for Fundraising Activities
	Picking up "Nickels," "Quarters," or "Dollars"
	Limitations as to Who May Be Solicited
142	Concentrate on the Projects that will Produce the Most Benefits
143	Soliciting and Getting Potential Donors to Actually Contribute—Getting the Job Done
	Types of Consumers
	The Major Motivating Factor (Hot Button) of Prospects
151	The Quiet Phase of Major Fundraising
155	Asking for the Money or a Donation
157	Self Promotion in a Professional Manner
	Conveying the Perception of Individual Competency
	Perceptions Do Count—Whether Accurate or Not
	Managing by Being Seen—MBBS (Stier, 1999)
159	References
160	Discussion Questions

CHAPTER 7
161 SINGLE PERSON CULTIVATIONS

161 Chapter Highlights
162 Four Models of Fundraising
163 Single Person (Face-to-Face) Cultivation and Appeals for Resources
   Person-to-Person Solicitation or Single Person Cultivation
   Alumni Outreach Efforts—Endowment Outreach Efforts
   Cultivating Prospective Major Donors—Big Ticket Donors
   Utilizing the "Solicitation Kit" as Part of the Sales Approach
   Door-to-Door Solicitation and/or Selling
   Using Youngsters as Salespersons
   Sales Tax and Selling Merchandise for Non-Profit Organizations
   Direct Mail Appeals
   Acceptable Return Rates for Direct Mail
   Creating a Mailing List
   Using Computer Software to Managing a Mailing List
   The Sales Piece
   Direct Mail via the Piggyback Strategy
   Telephone solicitation
178 References
179 Discussion Questions

CHAPTER 8
181 PROFIT CENTERS FOR FUNDRAISING

181 Chapter Highlights
182 Profit Centers
   Types of Profit Centers
183 Success Breeds Success
184 Ticket Sales
   Establishing a Plan of Attack in the Structuring of the Ticket Operation
   Decisions Relating to the Method(s) of Selling Tickets and the Pricing of Tickets
   Establishment of Special or Group Rates (Discounted)
   The Use of Free Tickets
   Promotional Activities Associated with the Advertising and Marketing of Tickets
189 Concessions
   Operational aspects of Running Concessions—Points to Consider
   Picking Concession Food and Drink Items—Points to Consider
   Determining Pricing Schedule and Cost of Sales—Points to Consider
   Promoting the Concession Area—Points to Consider

	Gross Profit Potential for Various Food Items—Points to Consider
196	Program Sales and Other Printed Pieces
197	Merchandise, Product Sales
	Selecting Merchandise
	Use of Team Mascots, Logos, and Colors
199	Pricing of the Merchandise
	Marketing, Promotional and Advertising Strategies for the Sale of Merchandise
200	Car Wrapping and Moving Billboards
201	Parking
201	User Fees for Facilities and Services
202	Vending Machines
	Technology and Vending Machines
203	Premium Preferred Seating and Luxury Boxes
204	Parking Condos
205	References
206	Discussion Questions

CHAPTER 9
207 THE ESSENCE OF CORPORATE SPONSORSHIP AND BUSINESS PARTNERSHIP

207	Chapter Highlights
208	The Relationship between High Expenses and the Need for Corporate Sponsorships
209	The Beginning of Sport Sponsorship
	The "Corporate Olympics"
211	How Corporate Sponsorships Work
212	Types of Sport Sponsorship Agreements
212	Corporate Sponsorship Agreements and the Idea of Exclusivity
	Non-exclusive Sponsorships
	Semi-exclusive Sponsorships
	Exclusive or Sole Sponsorships
	Outright Ownership of the Event or Program
214	Corporate Sponsorships and Recreation Programs
	Effectiveness of Sponsorship Agreements with Recreation Programs
214	High Schools and Corporate Sponsorships/Partnerships
	Television and the High School Sports Market
	High School Corporate Sponsorships and the Soft Drink Industry
	Advertisers vs. Sponsors
	Advantages Accruing to Sponsors of the Buffalo Bills
	Food and Beverage Companies as Potential Sponsors
	Selling a Sport or Recreation "Product" of "Service"
220	The Challenge of the *Naming Game*

	Name Changing of Facilities
	Selling the Naming Rights to Parts of a Facility
222	Determining the Value of the Naming Rights to the Donor
	Pricing Structure of Benefits Associated with Corporate Sponsorships/Business Partnerships
223	References
226	Discussion Questions

CHAPTER 10
227 CREATING CORPORATE SPONSORSHIPS AND PARTNERSIPS

227	Chapter Highlights
228	Why Corporations Desire to Become Sponsors
	Official NCAA Corporate Sponsors
	How Sport Entities Could Improve Their Relationships with Sponsors
230	Corporate Sponsorships with the Media
230	Evaluating and Selecting an Appropriate Sponsoring Organization
	Doing One's Homework
231	Finding a Suitable Sponsor—Soliciting Organizations, Businesses or Industries
	Approaching the Key Decision Maker (Power Person)
	Working with Franchises and Franchisers
	Questions to Consider when Approaching Potential Sponsors
234	Controversial Sponsorships and Sponsorship Agreements
	Potential Problems with Sport Sponsorship (and Granting of Name Rights)
236	The Sponsorship Proposal
	Packaging the Sponsorship Proposal
238	Components of an Effective Sponsorship Presentation
	Information/Data to be Provided in the Potential Sponsor
	Information Needed by Sponsors
	Quantitative and Qualitative Information for the Sponsor
241	Meeting the Potential Sponsor's Needs
	Failing to Satisfy the Corporate Sponsor
	What Corporate Sponsors Look For in a Partnership with Sport/Recreation Entities
243	Financial Considerations of Sponsorships
	Benefits Provided to Sponsors
	Giving Away the Store—A Major Mistake in Fundraising
	Tradeouts
	Gifts-in-Kind
	The Financial Picture Associated with the Naming of Buildings
247	Sponsorship Deals with Colleges and Universities
	Securing Sponsorships for "Olympic" (Non-Majors) Sports

248	Sponsorship—Philanthropy or Business Investment
	Viewing Sponsorship as an Investment—Not Merely Philanthropy
250	Slippage among Sponsors
	Objectively Measuring the Effectiveness of the Sponsorship Experience
	Renewing Sponsorship Agreements
252	References
254	Discussion and Review Questions

CHAPTER 11
255 FUNDRAISING STRATEGIES AND PROMOTIONAL TACTICS

255	Chapter Highlights
256	Implementing Special Promotional and Fundraising Activities
	Coaching (Piggybacking) Fundraising Activities with Other Events
	Combining Two or More Fundraising Activities Together
258	Taking Holiday Seasons into Account when Planning
259	Categories or Promotional and Fundraising Activities
260	Sales
261	Gambling—Contests (Games) or Chance with Prizes
	Restrictions on Gambling Activities in the State of New York
	Overcoming Major Obstacles and Objections to Gambling
	50/50 Drawing
	Raffle
	Reverse Raffle
	Pseudo Give-Away
	Lottery/Sweepstake and Sport Pools
	Casino Nights
	Bingo
266	A Sampling of Special Fundraising and Promotional Projects
273	Pre-Game, Half-Time and Game Day Activities
275	Banquets and Luncheon Activities
	Food and Beverage Related Fundraising and Promotional Activities
277	References
279	Discussion Questions

CHAPTER 12
281 ORGANIZING SPECIFIC FUNDRAISING PROJECTS—USE OF A TEMPLATE

281	Chapter Highlights
282	Using he Fundraising-Planning Templete in Planning a Fundraising Project
	Two Purposes of the Fundraising-Planning Template
283	Creating a Template Conceptualizing in Detail the Complete Fundraising Projects

xv

285	Examining Potential Fundraising Projects in Light of One's Own Situation
	    There is more than One Way to Do Anything
	        Questions to Ask Yourself in Assessing and Planning a Potential Fundraiser

289	References
289	Discussion Questions
291	**APPENDIX A** **SAMPLE BY-LAWS GUIDE FOR BOOSTER CLUBS**
301	**APPENDIX B** **MEMBERSHIP PLAN FOR AN ATHLETIC SUPPORT GROUP**
303	**APPENDIX C** **ATHLETIC FUNDRAISING REQUEST FORM**
307	**APPENDIX D** **INDIVIDUAL SPORT MASCOTS FOR A SINGLE ATHLETIC PROBRAM**
309	**PHOTO CREDITS**
311	**INDEX**

PREFACE

INTRODUCTION — THE GOAL OF THIS BOOK

The 3rd edition of this book has been written specifically for those who desire to gain a greater insight into the strategies and tactics used in the world of sport and recreation fundraising. The material in this book encompasses three distinct yet related areas (fundraising, promotions and public relations) that almost all administrators and coaches will find themselves involved, to some extent, in almost any sport situation.

The information included within this third edition is based on the practical experience of the author who has had over 35 years of successful experience serving in a variety of managerial and administrative roles, including secondary and college/university athletics director, municipal recreation manager, fitness club manager/director and country club owner/manager.

SPECIAL FEATURES OF THE BOOK

There are a number of unique features presented in this book. The *first* is the presence of **225 Principles** strategically placed throughout all 12 chapters so as to enhance and reinforce the basic tenets of *fundraising, promotions and public relations* as applied to the world of sports. These principles are presented throughout this book so *that they may serve as guidelines for possible action and relate to, and are applicable to, almost any sport or recreation situation, in any community, in which one might find oneself.* The principles are based upon both sound administrative and management theory as well as upon successful practical experience in the real world of sport developed and refined over a period of years.

A *second* unique feature included in this book is the presence of *Chapter Highlights* that are provided at the beginning of each chapter. These Highlights summarize the essential information found within each chapter. A *third* unique feature that centers on the *Discussion Questions* found at the conclusion of each chapter. These questions provide an opportunity for the reader to review one's knowledge and understanding of the material presented in the chapter. The *final* unique feature is found in chapter 12 and centers around the presentation of a ***Fundraising-Planning Template***, an important tool in the planning and implementation of any fundraising/promotional project.

It is the author's hope that readers of this book will (1) develop a sound understanding of the components of the fundraising, promotion, and public relations associated with sport and recreation programs, (2) be able to adapt or borrow ideas and tactics outlined in this book and elsewhere; and, (3) be capable of planning, implementing, and assessing any number of fundraising and promotional projects resulting in increased financial resources as well as genuine enthusiasm and support.

1 UNDERSTANDING SUCCESSFUL FUNDRAISING, PROMOTIONS AND PUBLIC RELATIONS IN THE 21ST CENTURY

Signage at football stadiums is a mainstay
of fundraising and promotional efforts

CHAPTER HIGHLIGHTS

This chapter will emphasize:

- The terms: *fundraising*, *promotions* and *public relations*
- The need for financial support of sport and recreation programs
- The importance of fundraising for sport and recreation programs
- The difference between attitudes and opinions
- Why fundraising is both an art and a science
- The four major objectives of any successful fundraising project or event
- The "Father" of public relations
- The relationships between *fundraising*, *promotions* and *public relations*
- That there are few *totally new* techniques for raising funds

- The importance of taking care of the "home front" before branching out into fundraising and promotional activities
- Why only those things that are promotable should be promoted
- Why fundraisers must be able to adjust and adapt in their efforts

INTRODUCTION

Sports and involvement in and within sport as well as recreational activities—as participants or spectators/fans—has never been more popular in the United States than at the present time. And this popularity has no end in sight. However, accompanying this increase in popularity, participation and fandom has been an increase in the cost of providing, conducting and maintaining meaningful sport and recreation type activities (and all that that involves) for the enjoyment of all. Recreational leaders, coaches and sport administrators are painfully aware of the fiscal crunch facing almost all organizations that provide sport and recreational opportunities, activities and programs. This is true whether such activities are provided within the structure of an educational setting; a youth sport organization, a recreation department, a fitness/well center or some other non-profit or for-profit entity (Stier, 2009).

Sport and recreational programs continue to have ever-present financial needs that must be met if these programs are to continue to exist and to meet the needs of those individuals, groups and communities whom they purportedly serve. Such programs, regardless of their structure or mission, remain dependent upon securing adequate financial and moral support for their ultimate survival. Without adequate funding of sport and recreation programs, whatever their intrinsic value(s) might be, the programs are ultimately doomed to failure or, at best, a significantly diminished impact in our society. Thus, the securing of financial and moral support has long been recognized as one of the prime responsibilities (and challenges) facing modern day recreational leaders, sport administrators and athletic coaches (Stier, 2010).

In fact, in today's society, the ability to secure adequate funding is considered an essential, an indispensable skill or competency in the overall operation of any sport or recreation program. The sport or recreation leader who is a competent fundraiser and promoter is viewed as a highly valuable asset to any organization. As a result, fundraising today has become, through necessity, a fact of life for those of us in sport, recreation and leisure programs.

A truly successful fundraising project or event is one that satisfies four major objectives. *First,* it must be financially successful. The objective is simple and straight forwards. You need to generate resources, i.e., make money or gain assets that can be used to support your organization's many worthwhile activities. *Second,* the event generates enthusiasm for the fundraising project itself. *Third,* the project helps to foster and reinforce a positive image of your organization as well as its supporters through the exposure, promotions, publicity and public relations associated with the activity itself. *Fourth,* the event generates genuine support for the overall efforts and goals of the sponsoring organization and its leadership.

This book enables the reader to gain insight into a variety of ways by which sport and recreation programs may be successfully advertized, promoted, publicized and financially supported at all levels, under different circumstances and in varying situations. It is important, however, to recognize that one does not deal exclusively with the topics of *fundraising, promotions and public relations* for recreation and sport programs without also examining, to some extent, other aspects of organizations, management and administration.

Thus, the topics of *fundraising* as well as *promotions and public relations* will be examined from the perspectives of the sport and recreation administrator/manager, athletic coach, members of the community as well as booster and support organizations. The major emphasis, however, will be on (1) goal setting, (2) strategies, (3) techniques and tactics, (4) planning methods, (5) implementation efforts typically associated with such efforts, and (6) the evaluation of one's overall endeavors.

> ***PRINCIPLE # 1: There are fundamental principles than are applicable to all fundraising efforts***

With a thorough understanding and appreciation of fundamental principles, guidelines and real-life examples pertaining to *fundraising, promotions and public relations*, the basis of a realistic and significant body of knowledge in these areas can be formulated. This body of knowledge will facilitate (1) the development of an appropriate level of competency and technical skills, (2) the capacity for appropriate risk taking, (3) the skill in terms of the decision making process itself, and (4) the ability to prevent, resolve and solve programmatic situations that might face the fundraiser. In terms of risk taking, it is important that one is capable of assuming reasonable risks in light of worthwhile gains. Successful sport and recreation managers cannot survive for long if they assume the role of an ostrich and *keep their heads in the sand.*

Possession of appropriate knowledge, understandings, and the ability to make correct and timely decisions and interpretations are absolutely necessary in sports and recreation fundraising, promotion, and public relations. By observing these fundamental principles, readers should be able, in a variety of situations, to make appropriate and timely decisions, judgments and adjustments in the real world of sport and recreation management, out there on the so-called *firing line.*

After reading this book you will have a sound understanding of the essential elements and components of the fundraising, promotion, public relations and publicity processes associated with sport and recreation programs. And, best of all, you will also be able to adapt, adjust and/or borrow ideas and tactics outlined in this book and then to plan, organize and implement any number of fundraising and promotional projects that will net your organization increased enthusiasm for your activities and organization, genuine support for your overall efforts and goals, a more positive public image, and additional resources.

DEFINITION OF TERMS

Although the terms fundraising, promotions, and public relations are often bantered about quite freely within sport and recreation circles, there is frequently a lack of clear understanding of what is meant by each. Additionally, there are other terms to be understood that have a significant impact upon the successful management and implementation of sport and recreation programs and their fundraising, promotional and public relations efforts. These include the following:

Fundraising Activities

Fundraising efforts are those activities aimed specifically at generating additional financial resources (*defined as: money, services and/or tangible goods*) to support one's programs and organization, generally for a charitable, not-for-profit and/or worthy cause (Stier, 1995a). Generating such support is both a science and an art. It is a science in that there is a systematic application of generally accepted principles, guidelines and knowledge that support these efforts.

PRINCIPLE # 2: *There is an art and a science to fundraising and promotional activities*

Fundraising may also be viewed as an art due to the positive results emanating from the creative application of these same principles, guidelines, and knowledge associated with the fundraising efforts. This creative application involves borrowing and adapting ideas and adjusting activities to suit one's own particular circumstances.

Promotional Activities

Promotional activities involve actions associated with and related to the marketing and selling of ideas, images, services, and products to the constituencies and members of the general public for purchase, adoption or acceptance. Promotional activities help *create and reinforce attitudes and opinions* as well as motivate changes in (or reinforces) behavior regarding the sport and recreation program and those involved in and/or associated with the program.

Sport promotional efforts and activities are closely related to the associated activities of fundraising, marketing, and merchandising. An essential ingredient for successful promotional activities in sports and recreation is adequate communication with publics, constituencies and potential consumers.

> **PRINCIPLE # 3:** *Promotional activities help create and reinforce attitudes and opinions and motivate changes in behavior*

Public Relations

The overall goal of public relations is to gain support from and/or to create a favorable impression upon various constituencies or segments within the society (Bucher, 1987). Public relations are the sum product of on-going, multifaceted, never-ending activities in which an organization engages. It is these activities that may create an affirmative awareness and a positive, favorable image in the eyes of target constituencies and various publics toward specific personnel, a particular activity, an event, an organization or a program. Generally speaking, public relations activities and promotional efforts are different and distinct in that the organizational activities or products in promotions are explicitly planned or stated and are time and date specific, while in public relations they are not necessarily so (Stier, 2000a).

> **PRINCIPLE # 4:** *Everything that is associated with the organization and program (everything that we do and don't do) has an impact upon what we call public relations*

Edward Bernays, who was the nephew of Sigmund Freud, is considered to be the "Father of Public Relations." Bernays utilized his uncle's psychological concepts in mass markets and was credited with building public relations into a major industry. In fact, he was so successful and powerful that Spain's Francisco Franco, Germany's Adolf Hltler, and Nicaraguan dictator Anastasio Somoza sought him out as clients, he turned them all down. He died in 1995 at the age of 103. He is credited with numerous books, including *Crystallizing Public Opinion* and *The Later Years: Public Relations Insight 1956-1986* ('Father of PR' Dies, 1995).

Publicity

Publicity is a segment or subset of public relations. As such, publicity has more immediacy in terms of objectives and goals *through* public relations (Mason and Paul, 1988). It has a specific, short-term message about a certain activity, event, person, or program. And, publicity has as its primary purpose to inform (sometimes educate) and to create a general awareness of a particular program with various segments of the community. The primary objective of publicity *is to draw attention* to a specific person, program, sport, recreation activity, institution or function. It is important to note that the effectiveness of publicity tends to be associated with the type and degree of impact that continuous public relations efforts have on others.

Constituencies

Constituencies are those individuals, groups, and organizations that have some association or potential for some type of connection, some affiliation, some relationship, with the sport or recreation organization, its activities or program, and/or its personnel. Additionally, constituencies may refer to those individuals or groups *within* the sport or recreation programs themselves as well as outside the confines of these programs.

Public(s)

A public is a group of individuals drawn together by some common factor. These factors might be a common interest, being from a specific geographic area, or possessing a common feature such as age, religion, sex, occupation, race, nationality, politics, income, social status, affiliation, or educational background.

Honoring the coach of a national championship team

An individual can be categorized as belonging, simultaneously, to more than one public (Jensen, 1992, Brooks, 1994). Within any geographic area there are multiple publics that could be associated with or related to a particular sport or recreation program or activity.

RELATIONSHIPS BETWEEN FUNDRAISING, PROMOTIONS AND PUBLIC RELATIONS

Individuals who are involved with recreational programs or competitive sports, whether at the youth sport, scholastic, collegiate or professional levels, find themselves involved, at least to some degree, with what is commonly referred to as fundraising, promotions, and public relations, and to a lesser extent, marketing. This is true whether or not one is an athlete, a coach or one associated with the managerial or administrative aspect of sport or recreation entity.

Fundraising tactics, promotional activities and public relations efforts are closely intertwined. All have a direct impact upon the success or failure of a sport program. There needs to be successful coordination and integration of all three areas within the total administrative structure of the entity, be it a school, a college, a university, a recreational organization, a sport program within industry or business, a youth sports program, or a semiprofessional or professional team. One also needs to think in terms of staff, specific tactics and the potential participants when contemplating or planning a fundraising, promotional or public relations effort.

Whenever fundraising strategies in recreation or sport programs are implemented, those people involved in the programs, *must* by definition, at the same time, be heavily involved with the public relations aspect of sports and in promotional activities. Fundraising cannot be undertaken without involving public relations and the promotion of the so-called "product"—the sports/recreation activities, the participants, and the staff.

However, promotional activities can be undertaken without attempting to raise monies. This does not mean that promotional activities are never associated with fundraising efforts. To the contrary—frequently, promotional activities and fundraising activities go "hand-in-hand" with each supporting the other. It depends upon the purpose for which the promotional activities are planned and implemented, whether members of the organization also simultaneously engage in fundraising projects or activities along with promotional efforts.

In a similar fashion, public relations may involve activities that have nothing to do whatsoever with the raising of financial resources. And, as with promotional activities, public relations may be closely associated with fundraising, depending upon the goals of the organization and the purpose for which public relations efforts are being implemented.

> *PRINCIPLE # 5: Fundraising, promotions and public relations serve as the foundation of many sport and recreation programs*

Thus, it is the area of generation of financial support, i.e., fundraising, which by definition involves both public relations and promotional activities. One cannot be involved in fundraising without simultaneously being engaged in public relations and in promotional activities. In general, fundraising, promotions and public relations serve as the foundation of many sport and recreation programs and thus form the core areas presented within this publication.

PROMOTIONAL, PUBLIC RELATIONS AND FUNDRAISING PERSPECTIVES OF SPORT

The interrelationships of the essential ingredients for generating funds, conducting promotional activities and implementing a positive public relations effort is illustrated in figure 1.1. When one views the overall sport or recreation program from a global perspective, promotional, public relations and fundraising activities may be classified under the following six categories.

1. Working with members of the media (radio, television, print, WWW)

2. Creating publications, photos and printed materials for advertisement purposes (programs, schedule cards, posters, pens, displays, calendars, billboards, etc.)
3. Selecting of physical objects (premiums)—to distribute, sell, give, exchange, etc.
4. Instituting physical improvements (facilities, equipment, supplies,) and image enhancing efforts
5. Implementing operational and home event activities (policies, procedures, practices, and priorities)
6. Utilizing image enhancing activities and involvements (association with other organizations and/or projects which lend respectability)

Efforts in raising money, as well as promoting aspects of a program, are arbitrarily classified under the following four categories.

1. Single person cultivation and appeals—seeking money, services and products; person to person, or door-to-door, or via telephone
2. Sponsorships and corporate (business) partnerships
3. Profit centers—concessions, parking, store sales, tickets, clinics, camps, and sales of merchandise and services, etc.
4. Use of promotional type activities and special events—designed to raise money, increase attendance, improve image, and provide recognition for team members, coaches, boosters, sponsors, activities, programs and the organization itself.

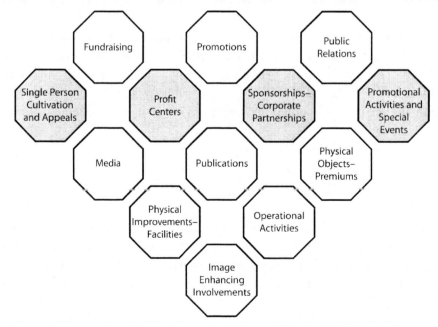

Figure 1.1 Promotional, Public Relations Activities, and Fundraising Tactics/Strategies

INGREDIENTS OF SUCCESSFUL SPORT AND RECREATION PROGRAMS

Four essential ingredients support a successful sport or recreation program, regardless of the level of its sophistication. Schematically, such a program might be likened to a table with four legs. The top of the table represents the total success of a sport or recreation program, supported as it is by four strong legs. The four legs, the essential supporting ingredients that form the foundation of the successful program, are (1) the participants, i.e., the users of the program's activities; (2) the administrative and support staff; (3) the actual sport or recreational programs, experiences and opportunities; and, (4) the fundraising, promotional, and public relations activities associated with the personnel, activities programs, and the organization. If any of these supporting ingredients are absent, or not at full strength, the tabletop begins to tip, and may fall completely. The consequences can indeed be significant and far-reaching, for all elements associated with or related to the sport or recreation entity. That is, the total program suffers and fails to reach its actual potential, a fact that can be looked upon as failure.

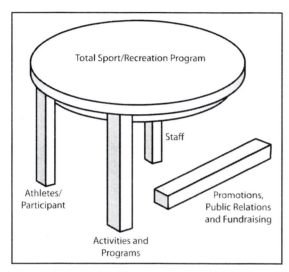

Figure 1-2. Essential ingredients supporting an athletic program

DEVELOPING COMPETENCIES IN FUNDRAISING, PROMOTIONS AND PUBLIC RELATIONS

Expertise and competency within the realm of fundraising, promotions and public relations type activities remains essential for the sustained and successful operation of any worthwhile program in the sports or recreation arena (Stier, 2000b). Since it is important for coaches, administrators, and even some volunteers and boosters to develop such managerial skills, it behooves those involved in sport and recreation programs to make good faith efforts to master a basic working knowledge as well as maintain at least a minimal level of competency in terms of fundraising strategies, promotional activities, and public relations efforts.

The world of sports and recreation within the United States seems to continue to be in a constant state of flux. As such, it becomes obvious that in terms of fundraising, promotions and public relations there exists a need to continue to learn and to be able to adapt to the changes and innovations taking place within these areas of sport and recreation management.

Today, more than ever before, it is necessary for those involved as a coach, athletic administrator, recreation manager, or sport volunteer/booster to maintain a posture of openness and of receptivity to change. This is especially true when it comes to self-improvement and grasping the body of knowledge supporting the generation of fiscal support as well as the promotion and publicizing of the sport and recreation programs.

This acquisition of cutting-edge knowledge, enrichment of ideas, expansion of creativity, improvement of competencies, and enhancement of skills may be realized through both traditional educational experiences, informal and formal in-service education efforts, as well as from actual practical experience. Such in-service education activities might include attendance at formal clinics, meetings, conferences, seminars, and workshops, as well as the reading of professional literature, such as this book.

> ***PRINCIPLE # 6:*** *There is a need to learn and to be able to adapt to the changes and innovations taking place within sport and recreation management—especially in terms of fundraising, promotions and public relations*

The final objective—insofar as the processes of fundraising, promotions and public relations are concerned—for the individual involved in a sport or recreation program, is to maintain a proper perspective, to develop an up-to-date knowledge base, and an awareness of tactics and strategies that may be utilized in:

1. The expansion of the financial support of sport or recreation programs
2. The promotion of sport or recreation activities or programs
3. The increase in public exposure of specific sport or recreation programs and the sponsoring organization

GRADUATE DEGREES IN FUNDRAISING AND PHILANTHROPY

There is an ever present need to possess up-to-date professional training and education in the area of fundraising (Hall, 2010). The importance of professional fundraising in our society today is rapidly gaining recognition, especially in the world of sport and recreation management. In addition, an ever growing number of colleges and universities are offering specific courses in fundraising, promotions and public relations in an effort to enable interested individuals to gain sufficient knowledge, skills, competencies and experiences with which to meet the challenges associated with the management of for profit and not-for-profit organizations and businesses, including those related to sport and recreation. Many of these courses are part of the sport management or athletic administration curricula offered at the many baccalaureate, masters or doctoral programs throughout the United States, and in other countries as well (Stier, 2001).

In fact, Lesley College, in Cambridge, Massachusetts, offers a full 43–credit master's degree in *Fundraising Management*. The 13 courses that make up the advanced degree program includes a 24–credit core curriculum, a 15–credit specialization, and a modular one-credit offering involving curriculum orientation and self-assessment and planning for the integrative learning experience, and the three–credit integrative learning experience. Students are able to obtain a Certificate in *Institutional Development and Fundraising Management.*

The type of courses that are offered in the master's degree program in fundraising at Lesley College include: Marketing Management; Financial Management; Prospect Research; Planned Giving; Strategic Planning for Non-Profit Organizations; Fundraising and Philanthropy; Capital Campaigns; Boards, Trustees and Manager Relations; Proposal Writing and Government Funding; Corporations and Foundation Giving; and, Management of Non-Profit Organizations.

Winners of special contests view the game from a special seating area (couch)

Other institutions offering graduate degrees/programs (master's level) as well as certificate programs in fundraising include, but are not limited to (1) Columbia University (Master of Science in Fundraising Management), (2) The University of Denver (Master's degree in leadership with a specialty in fundraising and philanthropy), (3) Indiana University–Purdue University in Indianapolis (The Center of Philanthropy/Fundraising School: a 3-day seminar program), (4) New York University (Master's degree in fund raising and grantmaking), and (5) Bay Path College (Master of Science in Strategic Fundraising and Philanthropy).

KEEPING THINGS IN THE PROPER PERSPECTIVE

PRINCIPLE # 7: *Fundraising and related activities are a means to an end, rather than an end in itself*

For those individuals who are involved in fundraising it is very important to keep one's efforts in the proper perspective. Too often it seems those in sports are enamored by the prospect of involvement with fundraising and related (promotional and public relations) activities. They perceive themselves, whether they are on the youth sport level, the secondary level or the collegiate level, as being another Don Canham, former athletic director at the University of Michigan, who had a national reputation as one of the most proficient and successful sport (NCAA Division I level) marketers, fundraisers and promoters in the country. They see themselves raising BIG DOLLARS (millions, billions, if not trillions) for their own athletic or recreation programs. They are too frequently quixotical in nature with respect to fundraising and related involvement for their own programs.

As a fundraiser, one must keep both feet on the ground. There is a constant danger of becoming infatuated with the "activities" themselves, with the supposed glamour and excitement associated with such fundraising, promotional and public relations activities. However, fundraising is not an end in itself. Rather, such efforts are simply a means to an end, the gaining of the wherewithal with which to have a meaningful and satisfying experience for those involved in the sport program.

Great care must be taken before deciding to promote an event, achievement, organization, activity or person. That which is to be promoted must be of value and must be able to be viewed as being of value by others, especially those to whom the promoting efforts are directed. Thus, one of the keys to successful promotion is to identify that which has the greatest potential for being promoted successfully (effectively and efficiently) among the various publics and constituencies (Stier & Schneider, 1999).

PRINCIPLE # 8:   *Take care of the home front before branching out*

A common fault of sport and recreation staff members, coaches, athletic directors and recreation leaders, is the failure to take care of the so-called home front, that is, the primary responsibilities for which one is hired. The director, manager, leader or coach should not spend so much time and effort on fundraising activities, publicity tasks or promotional efforts that other administrative or day-to-day responsibilities suffer. This is especially true in those situations in which fundraising is not a high or official priority on the sport manager's, athletic director's, recreation leader's or coach's list of job responsibilities.

Granted, on the NCAA Division I level, the direct involvement of both athletic directors and coaches in fundraising is often expected and frequently required. However, in many high schools, small to medium size colleges, professional sports and recreation departments, the prime responsibility of many of the staff *may not be fundraising*. There may be other tasks and responsibilities associated with the internal operation of the sport or recreation program that are deemed to be of a higher priority by one's superiors. In the above scenario, the sport managers, athletic administrators, recreation managers and coaches may be placing their respective positions in jeopardy if too much time and effort are devoted to fundraising and promotional activities to the obvious detriment of the more essential duties associated with their positions. This is especially true for those duties that are assigned a higher priority in the minds of their superiors.

There is an old sport axiom that states that one should find out what one's boss thinks is important, what one's boss wants you, the staff member to do—and then do it. This is sound thinking in terms of allocating one's own priorities within any organization. It is foolish to devote a significant amount of time, effort and energies toward a particular goal if that goal is not viewed as being important by those higher up in the organization, that is, one's boss(es). Since fundraising, publicizing and promoting of programs, activities and organizations can be very time consuming and challenging, it would be foolhardy indeed to specialize in these activities unless such a commitment was not only approved by one's superiors but actively encouraged and even mandated.

> **PRINCIPLE # 9:** *There are few things that are really new in fundraising and promotions*

There really aren't many new "things" in the world of fundraising and promotions—typically only adaptations. This is not to say that there are never new "things" that creative people don't dream up and perfect. However, usually things that are considered new are merely adaptations of other tactics, strategies and techniques.

An athletic director was once complimented on the numerous new ideas he was instrumental in bringing to the athletic department since he had arrived a few years earlier from another university. The response by the AD to this statement was that ". . . it isn't that I am doing anything really **new**, it is just that I am doing things that are **new here** or **different here**."

The point is that although fundraising efforts, public relations activities, and promotional ideas or tactics may be new *in a specific setting* or *circumstance*, these same activities, tactics, techniques and ideas probably have been previously implemented elsewhere, in some form or another, innumerable times. Frequently, the only things different are the circumstances in which the fundraising and promotional activities take place and the actual people who are involved in the implementation and evaluation process.

Nevertheless, sometimes there are some aspects associated with a particular fundraising, publicity or promotional effort(s) that are so unique or unusual that these elements make the effort significantly different from what has been tried or implemented in the past. In this respect, there really is something new in the effort, even though the new effort or strategy or tactic or project may have had its genesis in the far distant past. Look at the new or latest technology as well as numerous other scientific advancements/adaptations that have enabled creative individuals to put new twists and variations into projects and breathe new life into projects that have been around for years and years.

For example, the advent of high speed printers, copy machines, fax machines, more powerful computers, various types of software, cellular phones, video cameras, wide screen

TVs, digital cameras and VCRs/DVDs (just to mention a few) have all had a significant impact in terms of how organizers presently view various fundraising projects, publicity strategies and promotional tactics. Similarly, the abilities to create and update web pages as well as to create blogs have played and are playing a significant role in organizations' ability to continually communicate with vast audiences for any number of purposes.

> ***PRINCIPLE # 10:   Successful sport administrators take advantage of modern day technology to communicate as well as to promote and fundraise for their organizations***

And, such social networking web sites such as Twitter, Facebook and MySpace, as well as web search engines such as Google, Yahoo, Wikipedia, WebCrawler, AltaVista, Dogpile, and most recently Microsoft's Bing, provide innovative and varied opportunities for the sport and recreation administrator to fundraise for their programs and organizations as well as to promote, advertise and publicize same. Modern day technology serves as an invaluable tool for the professional sport or recreation administrator.

The fundraising project explained by Stier (1997, pp. 180-182) called "A Nite at the Races" [www.aniteattheraces.com/; 3043 Jupiter Park Circle, Jupiter, Florida 33458-6012—1-800-252-7373; 561-747-3900] is not new in one sense. But, in another sense, it is new and the factors that make it new, that make it possible to be an excellent fundraiser, is the availability of large screen TVs, VCRs and easy to use video tape as well as DVD players and CD/DVD disks—*in contrast to the use of the old fashioned 16 mm movie projector*. In essence, this fundraiser generates money through betting at the "races," however, the races in this instance are those provided by a VCR that shows taped races (or DVDs to be played on a DVD player) for those in attendance. Using horse racing (or dog racing) is not new in terms of fundraising efforts but using taped (DVD disc) races to be shown via a VCR (DVD player) over a large screen TV is—thus, this fundraising effort can be viewed as a new type of project.

In terms of utilizing new elements in one's fundraising, one only has to look to the selling of Olympic souvenirs containing athletes' DNA. Some of the official Olympic souvenirs that were advertised, marketed and sold at the 2000 Games in Australia contained or were "marked" (identified by) DNA taken from several of the Australian athletes. With the advent of this new technology, developed by Los Angeles-based DNA Technologies, all types of souvenirs, from hats to socks, could be promoted and marketed to the general public. Officials at the Winter Olympics in 2002 considered the possibilities and advantages of using DNA strips for some of their souvenirs (Vergano, 2000).

Some years earlier, in 1996, the Salvation Army took advantage of technology when it began to equip its trademark "red kettle" with credit card machines that enabled donors to charge their contributions on the spot. During a test market of the new devices it was found that while cash donations typically involved a handful of coins, donations via credit cards averaged around $25. At the test sites it was found that donations had increased some 35 percent (Balog, 1996).

It is important to determine what has previously been tried and accomplished, successfully as well as unsuccessfully, within one's own organization and one's community. It is equally important to examine what has been attempted elsewhere—everywhere and anywhere!!! Stier (2005) indicated that successful leaders and managers look at what has been done elsewhere (successfully) and adopt, adapt and adjust those successful tactics, strategies and efforts to fit one's own situation and circumstances. Don Canham (1986), the former athletic director at the University of Michigan, once suggested that the challenge facing administrators is not to think up totally new or original ideas or activities, but to be creative in the implementation of those things that have produced results elsewhere.

There need be no embarrassment for attempting to adapt a fundraising effort, publicity idea or promotional strategy that has proven to be successful and productive elsewhere, to one's own specific situation or circumstances. In fact, it is often the sincerest form of flattery. The crux of the matter is simple. Will the project, tactic or effort be worthwhile, and in the end, truly successful? *The proof of the pudding, so to speak, is whether the end result is successful.* Success itself is often determined by the circumstances in which one finds oneself.

> **PRINCIPLE # 11:** *Don't reinvent the wheel if you don't have to—learn from others, i.e., "borrow, beg and steal" ideas from others*

The individual fundraiser or promoter, whether relatively new to the exciting world of promotions and fundraising or a tried and true veteran, can always learn from the successes and failures of others. Of course, you must be able to determine which fundraising programs, activities and projects are suitable and are appropriate to use in your own situation. This borrowing and adapting of strategies, ideas, and methods from others is a most productive method of examining what is feasible in one's own community and work environment.

The ability to recognize reality is important. It is necessary to take stock of the particular situation in which one finds oneself and recognize where one's program sits within the pecking order of worthy causes. For example, there are inherent differences in terms of what can be accomplished in youth sport programs, in high school programs, in small college programs, in the so-called big-time university programs and in the realm of professional sports. The same can be said in terms of different kinds of recreation programs, both public recreation programs (in different size communities) and corporate recreation programs that are provided for their employees by large corporations such as Kodak, Xerox and General Motors.

A small liberal arts college cannot attempt to successfully emulate exactly the fundraising activities of the University of Michigan, the University of Texas or Stanford University with all of their resources and inherent advantages (image, reputation, history, money, alumni support, etc.). Similarly, a small, rural high school in Utah cannot attempt to mimic exactly what a large secondary school, located in a large metropolitan city, such as San Francisco or Chicago, attempts in terms of fundraising, publicity and promotional activities.

However, this does not mean that there is no room for following general fundraising, or promotional principles. Time proven and successful tactics and techniques used elsewhere can be adapted and adjusted to fit in with one's own situation. For example, there are various types of raffles, sales efforts as well as golf outings, which have been successfully utilized through the years to generate various amounts of financial support for different types of sport and recreation programs. The key to the successful implementation of these traditional fundraising activities is the ability to BORROW, to ADOPT, to ADAPT, and to ADJUST the actual activity (in this case the raffle, sales effort or golf outing) to fit with the local circumstances, situation and environment. This effort to effect change, adaptation and adjustment is the key to the success. The same can be said of publicity strategies and promotional tactics.

The ability to follow general principles or guidelines in terms of fundraising, advertising, publicity and promotional activities for one's sport or recreation program is one of the more important factors in determining the success or failure of any fundraising effort. Similarly, the likelihood for success in generating monies and garnering increased support and acceptance can be enhanced by adapting the planning, implementing, and evaluating aspects of any fundraising effort to be compatible with the sports organization's particular situation and circumstances.

In all that one does, but especially within the areas of promotional activities and fundraising, one must remain an optimist. In the promotion of any recreation or sports activity, in the raising of financial support, and in the *selling* of any product, service or idea, one is in constant danger of rejection and failure. Throughout all that one does, it is necessary to remain an eternal optimist.

The difference between an optimist and a pessimist is how one views the circumstances that exist. Two people, an optimist and a pessimist, viewing a bottle with liquid up to the halfway mark will respond differently. The pessimist takes the viewpoint that the bottle is half empty. However, the optimist looks at the same bottle, with the same amount of liquid, and considers it to be half full. It is all in the way things are viewed. For the publicist, promotional strategist and fundraising practitioner, being an optimist and having confidence in one's ability, are significant advantages in the performance of one's job.

REFERENCES

Baylog, K. (1996, December 23). Salvation Army rings out for plastic. *USA Today,* p. 1-B.

Brooks, C. M. (1994). *Sports marketing.* Englewood Cliffs, NJ: Prentice Hall.

Bucher, C. (1987). *Management of Physical Education & Athletic Programs* (9th ed.). St. Louis: Times Mirror/Mosby College Publishing.

Canham, D. (1986). Fundraising. *Athletic Director & Coach, 4*(3), 4–6.

'Father of PR' dies. (1995, March 13). *Democrat and Chronicle*, p. 2-B.

Hall, H. (1-3-2010). Lack of training contributes to scarcity of qualified fund raisers nationwide. *The Chronicle of philanthropy*.
http://philanthropy.com/free/articles/v19/i20/20002101.htm

Jensen, C.R. (1992). *Administrative Management of Physical Education and Athletic Programs* (3rd ed.). Philadelphia: Lea & Febiger.

Mason, J.G., & Paul, P. (1988). *Modern Sports Administration*. Englewood Cliffs, NJ: Prentice Hall.

Stier, W.F., Jr. (1995a). Obtaining goods and services can be a fund-raising strategy. *Athletic Management, VII*(5), 17.

Stier, W.F., Jr. (1995b, June 19). The Future of Fundraising and Promotions in International Competition. Presentation made at the Ontario Hockey Association, London, Ontario, Canada.

Stier, W.F., Jr. (1997). *More fantastic fundraisers for sport and recreation*. Champaign, IL: Human Kinetics.

Stier, W.F. Jr., & Schneider, R. (1999). Fundraising—An essential competency for the sport manager in the 21st century. *The Mid-Atlantic Journal of Business, 35*(2 & 3), 93–103.

Stier, W.F., Jr. (2000a). Fund-Raising and Promotion Secrets for the Busy Athletic Director. PROCEEDINGS—National Athletic Business Conference. WI: Madison. Athletic Business.

Stier, W.F., Jr. (2000b). A fundraising and promotional primer for sport: Part two. *Applied Research in Coaching and Athletics Annual, 15*, 12–147.

Stier, W.F., Jr. (2001). The Current Status of Sport Management and Athletic (Sport) Administration Programs in the 21st Century. *International Journal of Sport Management, 2*(1), 66-79.

Stier, W.F., Jr. (2005, November 1). Politicizing, Marketing and Promoting Physical Education and Sport—A Necessity for Survival. Presentation made at the *United Nations' International Conference for Sport and Education in Bangkok, Thailand*.

Stier, W.F., Jr. (2009). *Fundraising projects for sport, recreation, leisure and fitness programs*. Boston, MA: American Press.

Stier, W.F., Jr. (2010). *Coaching: Becoming a successful athletic coach*. (3rd edition). Boston, MA: American Press

Vergano, D. (2000). Olympic souvenirs contain athletes' DNA. *Democrat & Chronicle*, 3-C.

DISCUSSION QUESTIONS

1. Explain why involvement in fundraising and promotions can be thought of as being both an art and a science. Also, provide real life examples relative to fundraising efforts and promotional activities being both art and science.

2. Differentiate between publicity and public relations while providing clear examples of each in the real world of sport and recreation.

3. List and explain, with appropriate examples, the four broad categories that all fundraising and promotional activities can be arbitrarily categorized under.

4. Explain why fundraising should always be the means to an end rather than an end in itself. Discuss the possible negative consequences of failing to follow this philosophy.

5. How can today's sport personnel take advantage of modern technology to be successful in promoting and fundraising for their programs? Provide specific examples.

2 | FUNDAMENTAL ELEMENTS AND RESOURCES OF FUNDRAISING AND PROMOTION

When promoting sports on a college campus it is most helpful to have the leader of the institution demonstrate visible support for the program—President John Halstead [The College at Brockport, State University of New York] participating in the coin toss at a home football game.

CHAPTER HIGHLIGHTS

This chapter will emphasize:
- The 14 fundamental processes of management in any organization
- The importance of looking organized as well as being organized
- Resources, tools and assets that sport managers should have at their disposal in the fundraising and promotion of their programs
- Effective time management techniques
- The importance and the roll of various types of personnel associated with fundraising

- Various web sites applicable to fundraising and promotions
- The differences between image and reputation
- Accomplishments and achievements within the sport entity that can affect fundraising and promotional efforts
- How atmosphere, climate, and the environment can affect one's efforts in raising funds and promoting programs
- Why the waste or misuse of money is a double whammy in fundraising efforts
- The essential skills of a successful fundraiser and promoter
- The importance of interpersonal skills for the sport promoter and fundraiser
- Why today's sport fundraiser needs to be a renaissance person
- The reasons why the so-called bar has been raised in terms of expectations of sport fundraisers and promoters

Quality and effective examples of fundraising, promotion, and public relations do not happen by accident. Today, as never before, there is a real need for quality organization, management, and administration in the support of activities under the umbrella of what is commonly referred to as sport fundraising, promotion, and public relations (Stier, 2009). There is also a need for both a systematic approach to whatever one attempts to do, as well as a need for consistency and continuity, both in terms of quality and quantity of one's efforts and actions (Stier, 1992). A common criticism leveled at those in sport and recreation is that there is generally a lack of consistency in the quality of fundraising and promotional efforts. Such individuals are often looked upon as being a "flash in the pan" with no real staying power, lacking credibility, and having no real substance in the arena of fundraising, promotions and public relations.

FUNDAMENTAL PROCESSES OR COMPONENTS OF MANAGEMENT WITHIN ANY ORGANIZATION

What are the fundamental components or processes associated with good sport management, of competent recreation administration, and of successful fundraising, promotional and public relations efforts? As early as 1937, Gulick and Urwick (1937) delineated seven essential or basic tasks comprising administration and management. These essential processes were represented by the acronym POSDCoRB representing (1) planning, (2) organizing, (3) staffing, (4) directing, (5) coordinating, (6) reporting and (7) budgeting.

PRINCIPLE # 12: *There are 14 fundamental processes that every manager or leader must utilize in working towards one's objectives and goals*

However, in an effort to be more specific within the umbrella of sport and recreation management and specifically fundraising, promotions, and public relations, Stier (1994) supplied three additional processes of (1) recording, (2) facilitating or supporting, and (3) evaluating to the seven tasks originally enumerated by Gulick and Urwick. Then, in 1998, Stier added one additional process, that of prioritizing, thus creating the acronym of PPOSDCoRRFEB.

However, subsequently, Stier (2004) added three additional processes. These processes include (1) problem solving, (2) decision taking, and (3) risk taking. Thus the acronym today has become *PPPOSDDCoRRRFEB*, figure 2.1.

ESSENTIAL ADMINISTRATIVE PROCESSES—PPPOSDDCoRRRFEB

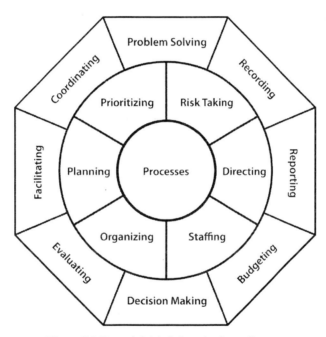

Figure 2.1 Essential Administrative Ingredients—
PPPOSDDCoRRRFEB

1. Planning
2. Prioritizing
3. Problem solving
4. Organizing
5. Staffing
6. Directing
7. Decision making
8. Coordinating
9. Reporting
10. Recording
11. Risk Taking
12. Facilitating
13. Evaluating
14. Budgeting

Planning

Planning implies determination of special needs, as well as goals and objectives. It is the creation of a road map (Ensor, 1988). Planning is one absolute, essential ingredient—the foundation that determines whether future actions will be meaningful or merely examples of aimless activity.

The components of planning consist of (1) deciding what is to be accomplished, (2) who will be involved and who will be responsible, (3) when the activities should be completed, (4) where the activities will take place, (5), under what conditions they are to be done, (6) how they are to be achieved, and (7) how the efforts and results are to be assessed, i.e., evaluated. In the absence of planning, one is caught in the perpetual trap of aimlessly wandering around. Planning helps delineate not only what the realistic objectives might be but also aids in the establishment of priorities. Planning also helps identify and utilize the available resources within specific time restraints.

Similarly, planning takes into consideration the tools or resources available to those involved in fundraising and promotions. Planning is the anticipatory phase of the process and involves activities undertaken prior to the actual fundraising and promotional efforts. Of course, once actual fundraising and/or promotional activities are initiated, continual monitoring of the plans remains necessary for the successful completion of those activities that comprise the overall fundraising, or promotional project(s).

Prioritizing

The ability to "put first things first," that is, to do the more important things before tackling the less important tasks, is a matter of establishing *and* following priorities. With all of the numerous and varied tasks and challenges facing the sport and recreation manager on a daily basis, it is imperative that some sort of order be established in terms of what is to be addressed or handled first, and then second, third, etc. The ability to be able to consistently prioritize tasks greatly reduces wasted efforts and can greatly facilitate the realization of important objectives and goals. "Failure to prioritize one's efforts finds the allocation of one's time, effort and other resources being directed aimlessly rather than on those objectives that will result in positive consequences" (Stier, 1998, p. 160).

Problem Solving

One must be able to identify potential and current problematic situations so that one can take appropriate and timely steps to prevent, resolve or solve these same situations. Problems are always going to crop up and it is imperative that the prudent fundraiser possess the ability to anticipate many of these problems so that difficulties may be averted, or in the worst case scenario, when problems do indeed crop up, at lease minimize any the negative consequences emanating from these difficulties.

Organizing

To be able to organize effectively and efficiently is to successfully allocate resources and place in proper perspective all of the components essential to the overall success of one's efforts. To place onto the top of the table, so to speak, all of the ingredients or factors that one must take into consideration, in the proper sequence in which they are to be utilized, symbolizes the epitome of organization. "The first fundraising rule is to get ORGANIZED" (Palmisano, 1984, p. 22). Within the world of the sport and recreation leader, it is important to not only be organized but also to give the image of being organized. All too often it is the image (or lack thereof) of being organized that is as important (almost) as reality.

> **PRINCIPLE # 13:** *One must not only be organized, but must look organized*

Staffing

Human resources, individual people, are at the core of any effort to achieve meaningful success in generating funds for any worthy purpose. Working with a wide variety of staff personnel (both paid and volunteer) on an individual basis, as well as in small and large groups, is an ever-looming challenge to the person having responsibility in the areas of fundraising, and promotions. Proper staffing is absolutely essential.

Without adequate staffing, both paid and volunteer, one's efforts are necessarily severely limited. However, mere numbers are not the answer. The key in terms of staffing is securing the services of highly motivated, dedicated, and trained individuals. Staffing also involves the appropriate training and retraining of staff members who need such assistance.

Finally, the staffing process involves recognition of the skills and capabilities (as well as the limitations) of individual staff members (individually and collectively) and the proper placement or matching of such staff with appropriate areas of responsibilities. It is absolutely imperative that the sport or recreation leader be willing and capable in the assigning of staff members to appropriate tasks depending upon the skill level, motivation, experience and potential of each individual person. One of the worst sins an administrator can commit is to assign an otherwise motivated, professional, and qualified staff member to a task for which the individual is not suited, either by temperament, training or experience.

Directing

Directing refers to the task of providing guidance and direction to personnel within the organization, as well as to so-called "outsiders," whether they are groups, organizations, or individuals. Directing qualified staff members as well as "outsiders" to appropriate tasks is a highly desired trait. The process of directing involves not merely the telling of others to do specific things but providing appropriate guidance and assistance to the person being directed—so that the person will be able to successfully assume the responsibility and/or complete the task at hand. It is this ability to provide meaningful guidance (direction) to others that is so highly prized in any manager. Within the areas of fundraising, promoting and public relations, with countless activities taking pace, this ability of directing others towards both small and large goals is especially valued and appreciated.

Decision Making

Fundraisers must literally make hundreds, if not thousands, of major and minor decisions relating to the planning, implementation and assessment of any fundraising program. These decisions take place prior to, during and after the actual fundraising operation take place. The ability to make timely and correct decisions is imperative for the successful fundraiser and promoter. Decisions must be made in terms of personnel, resources, goals and objectives as well as various strategies and tactics.

Coordinating

Matching the so-called tools and resources (assets) available to the fundraiser or promoter with the challenges and tasks at hand is an important coordinating challenge. *To successfully juggle all of the varied, but yet essential, components of a fundraising operation or promotional effort requires skillful coordination.* Yet, to be able to coordinate all of these components or essential elements without "dropping the proverbial ball" is frequently the determining factor between the success and failure of a manager or administrator.

Frequently, one needs to coordinate dates, deadlines, needs of others, available tools, resources, etc. Without such coordination, there is confusion and the successful generation of meaningful funds and/or media (public) exposure for the sport or recreation program is as much a result of good luck as anything. Juggling many things at once seems to be a perquisite of many fundraisers and promoters. While this can seem to be unproductive, the very nature of fundraising and promoting often necessitates the doing of many things at once. Thus, coordinating these often separate, distinct activities on behalf of many individuals and groups calls for skillful coordination—within a specific time frame. The fundraising process has been likened, with some accuracy, to a puzzle with many individuals attempting to put the puzzle parts together. It remains the responsibility of the fundraising administrator or promoter to coordinate everyone's actions and activity so that, eventually, the pieces start to fall into place and what emerges is the completed and coherent picture puzzle.

Reporting

Accountability is of prime importance in the fundraising and promotional arenas. The basic component of accountability is reporting, which refers to keeping others, various constituencies, one's superior(s) and one's own staff fully informed and abreast of all developments. Reporting involves the ability to succinctly and yet completely keeping others adequately informed of important facts, trends, and happenings, etc., in a timely fashion. And, reporting necessitates skill in (1) written (pen/paper, computer, etc.) communications, (2) body language, and (3) in verbal interactions with others. It is important to follow the administrative Golden Rule when effecting communication, i.e., always follow the chain of command when working with individuals within a hierarchical organization. Finally, it should be noted that adequate reporting is typically not possible without competency in the area of keeping excellent, accurate and timely records (see **recording** below).

> **PRINCIPLE # 14:** *Accurate and timely record keeping is imperative for any productive organization—future decisions are made in light of such assets*

Recording

In today's society, record keeping is one of the foundation blocks to success within any organization. The keeping of meticulous records facilitates the accountability challenge facing all sport and recreation managers. One needs to accurately record what transpires so that an accurate perception is obtained of exactly what has taken place. This recording process also enables one to more accurately assess whether what took place in the past was positive or negative and further assists in the planning process for future activities under the umbrella of fundraising, promotions and public relations (Stier, 2010).

There are innumerable records of all types that must be kept by the competent sport or recreation manager. With the presence today of computers and other related communication and recording devices, there is really no excuse for not being able to keep such records within any well-managed organization, group or business. The key to record keeping is to decide what type of information is to be recorded and maintained (and in what format and for how long) and then making the commitment to record the data in a manner that can be easily retrieved and made use of. For, in the final analysis, if the records that are kept are not used in a proactive, productive fashion, all of the time and effort expended in recording the data would have been wasted. In determining the type of records to be maintained, managers typically look to the data and information that will prove beneficial in making future decisions, making adequate assessments and evaluations of past efforts, and to predict future trends (in light of past experiences).

Risk Taking

Fundraisers must be comfortable in taking risks, reasonable risks. This is because they all too frequently must make decisions and take actions that, if not well conceived and well thought out, might well result in disaster, all in front of others, both inside and outside of their sport or recreation entity. The goal is to take steps to minimize the seriousness of risks that need to be taken through wise planning and strategic organization. Nevertheless, the ability to undertake reasonable and appropriate risks is an essential part of being a successful fundraiser and promoter.

Facilitating—Supporting

The process of facilitating for the sport and recreation manager in terms of fundraising and promotions refers to being able and willing to assist others in their tasks and to making the tasks "doable" by providing assistance in any way that is feasible and appropriate. To facilitate means to operate in the so-called HELP MODE, providing adequate support mechanisms to the entire fundraising operation, promotional endeavor or public relations effort, as well as to those individuals involved in the process. There must be *willingness* as well as the *ability* to provide meaningful support—moral, personnel, financial to the program, to the process itself, and to the staff associated with the fundraising activity and promotional effort.

Evaluating

Assessing the effectiveness and efficiency of one's efforts is essential in any organization. To know where one has been, where one is currently at, and where one is going is the objective. And, this cannot be accomplished without an evaluation. It is important to think of evaluation as an on-going activity, program or process rather than as a one-time effort.

Thus, determining criteria by which success and failure can be judged or determined is essential to the assessment or evaluation process. It is important that both the individual doing the evaluation and those individuals being evaluated clearly understand the criteria by which one is being assessed. When assessing the success or failure of an event, a program or an effort, it is also important to have a clear idea or image of what is acceptable in terms of objectives and goals and what is unacceptable; and hence, what should be changed in the future.

Essentially, evaluation aids in the determination of what should be done next and what should be changed, if anything, by examining how successful past achievements and performances rate in light of predetermined criteria. Evaluation is an approved form of hindsight, with a purpose (Stier, 1996a).

Budgeting

It is important to provide proper financial support and to allocate monies to specific areas and tasks that have significant, direct and sometimes immediate impact upon the ultimate success of the fundraising operation. Since it often does take money to earn or raise money, one of the cardinal sins of fundraisers is to waste or not properly use what financial resources that are available for the task(s) at hand, i.e., to generate additional monies. An appropriate budgeting process assists in the proper allocation of resources (dollars) in ways that are the most productive.

Every sport manager and recreation administrator is involved in the budgeting process to some extent. It is important that the accomplished and successful leader be able to achieve three things in the management of one's sport or recreation program or organization: (1) to secure adequate funding for one's program through the regular budgetary process of the organization, (2) to frugally administer whatever financial resources that the organization has made available in the pursuit of established and recognized objectives and goals, and (3) to generate sufficient outside resources (financial assets), when there is a need for such resources in addition to the normal budget available from the organization itself, so as to be able to plan, organize and implement a successful program or activity.

> *PRINCIPLE # 15: A respected, expertly run and fiscally responsible organization will find it easier to secure outside monies via fundraising and promotions*

RESOURCES, TOOLS, AND ASSETS AVAILABLE TO SUPPORT FUNDRAISING AND PROMOTIONAL ACTIVITIES

Every sport manager and recreation leader is concerned with the assets or tools that are available to use in pursuit of objectives and goals. What are these tools, resources and assets, especially those that can be used in support of the areas of fundraising, public relations and promotional activities? Generally speaking, the assets that one has as a leader, manager or administrator may be classified into one or more of the following categories:

1. Time
2. Personnel
3. Equipment
4. Supplies
5. Facilities
6. Web Presence and the Internet
7. Software applications
8. Reputation
9. Image
10. Accomplishments and Achievements
11. Status—Level of Competition
12. Climate, Atmosphere and Environment
13. Services
14. Associates (people)

15. Other . . . (anything that facilitates the fundraising tactics, promotional efforts or public relation processes)

> **PRINCIPLE # 16:** *The manager must recognize those tools and assets that can be made available and that can be put to good use in the various fundraising and promotional projects and efforts*

Selling Christmaas trees can be an annual seasonal fundraising effort

It would be wise for the sport and recreation administrator to recognize that the above list may be viewed both as objectives (desirable to be obtained) as well as resources, tools or assets that can be used (when available) to generate additional resources and/or to realize objectives and goals, depending upon the situation and circumstances one finds oneself in at any given time.

AVAILABLE ASSETS AND RESOURCES

Available Time (to work)

Time is truly a most valuable asset for any organization. Attempting to do too much in too little a period of time is an open invitation for failure. There must be made available an appropriate amount of *quality* time to carry out the fundraising project, promotional scheme or public relations activity. Time is just as much a tool as money, facilities, and staff.

Time management skills are essential for the sport promoter and fundraiser. Time, being finite, is one resource that must be guarded most carefully lest it slip through one's fingers. Wasting time is an act that can easily take place even without our consciously realizing it. An important factor to keep in mind is the *amount of quality time spent on task(s)*. It is the amount of quality time spent that determines the effectiveness and efficiency of one's efforts, which in turn has a direct effect upon the realization of the objectives and goals of the mission, i.e., one's eventual success or failure.

Time is one of the greatest assets an individual or organization can possess. And since there are only 24 hours in a day, it is how these available (but limited) hours are actually utilized that matters. Let's face it; most people waste far too much time. And hence, their efforts are diluted and their effectiveness diminished, if not negated completely. Coaches, athletic and recreation administrators, and sport boosters are no exception. Through efficient time management and the recognition, setting and following of priorities, the sport fundraiser or promoter is able to increase the effectiveness and efficiency of the efforts that are initiated. Time is indeed a valuable tool for any fundraiser and promoter. A lack of time or failure to utilize time appropriately most assuredly invites failure.

Personnel (internal/external and paid/volunteer)

Having adequate personnel, both in terms of the number of individuals and in terms of their capabilities and competencies, is an additional requirement for any successful fundraising and/or promotional effort. Lacking adequate personnel (actual numbers as well as individuals with specific skills) within one's organization or staff to support and sustain a successful fundraising or promotional project, the manager or administrator is faced with the task of looking elsewhere to obtain the services of skilled, trained, and experienced personnel. The key to success is to be able to draw upon sufficient personnel, individuals who are motivated, trained, hopefully experienced, capable, and interested in being involved in the effort or the project.

When considering the topic of staff, it is important to consider individuals in terms of (1) *one's own staff* (internal) or (2) *staff of another organization* or entity (external). Some staff members may be individuals who work directly for your organization and report to administrators and managers within the sport or recreation organization itself. Or, staff members may be outside personnel, external to your organization. These could be individuals who work for themselves as independent contractors (see below). Or, they could be individuals who work for another entity or organization, and this organization in turn supports your sport or recreation efforts.

Further, staff or personnel may be further classified under three categories. The *first* type of personnel includes those who are *paid staff* (on the payroll) of the sport or recreation organization. The *second* category includes *volunteers*, individuals who work for you and the organization due to the goodness of their hearts. The *third* classification of staff who can perform work for the sport or recreation entity are *independent contractors*. These are individuals who are hired and paid by a third party (company or business) or who work for themselves as an independent business person but who perform assigned tasks for your organization (Gray, 1995; Jones, 1996; Wong, 1996).

For many, many sport and recreation managers, it is the volunteer staff members who form the core of the productive staff working on fundraising and promotional projects. Nevertheless, it is important for the skilled manager to recognize the distinctive differences between internal and external personnel as well as paid and volunteer staff. Such individuals frequently have different needs and requirements due to the nature of their relationship to the organization, its programs and activities. Thus, it behooves the wise and prudent manager to deal with and to treat these various staff members in different ways.

Equipment and Supplies

Under this category falls the multitude of items that are essential for any business or organization—both hardware and software. Included are such items as typewriters, computers, copiers, fax machines, phones, cellular phones, paper, signs, merchandise, premiums, tickets, automobiles, etc. Technology is especially important in today's (and tomorrow's) world of fundraising, promotions and public relations. The modern advances in equipment and technology are occurring so rapidly in our society that managers must keep up-to-date lest they attempt to solve 21st century problems and challenges with 20th century solutions (ideas, tools and strategies).

Facilities

The facilities that are available for fundraising and promotional activities will vary as much as individual booster organizations or sport programs vary. Under this category would fall office space, indoor and outdoor sporting and recreational facilities (gymnasia, natatoriums, weight rooms, dining halls, conference rooms, ball diamonds, etc.), as well as other facilities that may be rented or borrowed by the sport or recreation organization.

Web Presence and the Internet

A great tool for the modern sport administrator or recreation manager is the World Wide Web. Computer literacy and the use of the Internet are expected by those sport personnel who have responsibility within the areas of fundraising, promotions and public relations.

The use of the WWW has grown tremendously in recent years. As late as 1997 it was reported that although computers were used in 98% of the NCAA Division I athletic programs, only 43% of the Division I athletic departments were utilizing the Internet to help promote and publicize their sport programs. And, at that time, only 37% of these same athletic departments even had a web page (Farrell & McCann, 1997, p. 12). Today, it is estimated that almost all Division I athletic departments (and most Division II and III schools as well) have a presence on the WWW by means of a web page that is used for a variety of purposes, including promoting and publicizing various sports program (Stier, November 30, 2000).

> **PRINCIPLE # 17:** *A sport or recreation organization without a presence on the WWW is shooting itself in the proverbial foot*

There are numerous sites on the WWW that deal with fundraising, and promoting various types of organizations, programs and activities. Many of these sites have pertinent information that sport and recreation administrators can take advantage of in their efforts to generate additional resources as well as to promote and publicize their programs, activities and organizations. Some examples of web sites devoted to fundraising are provided below.

1. http://www.fundsraiser.com
2. http://www.fund-raising.com/frindex.html
3. http://www.fundsraiser.com
4. http://www.fundraisingdepot.com/
5. http://www.easy-fundraising-ideas.com/
6. http://www.teammarketing.com
7. http://www.fundraising-ideas.com
8. http://www.fundraiserhelp.com
9. http://www.afpnet.org/
10. http://www.fasttrackfundraising.com/

Software Applications

Keeping abreast of the latest in software applications is absolutely essential for the sporty promoter and fundraiser. With the ever-present changes that are taking place in the world of computer and software applications, it is the wise individual who remains at the cutting edge of software that can make one's job of fundraiser and promoter easier. Appropriate software can prove to be an invaluable tool/resource for the fundraiser.

Reputation

What people think or feel about a person or program without firsthand experience with that person or program is referred to as *reputation*. The reputation of a sports or recreation program (from a distance) is that which makes others think or feel a certain way about that entity and what it stands for, i.e., its worth. *A reputation is a perception gained without actually having a first hand experience with the person or program.* Possessing a general positive reputation can enhance fundraising, as well as promotional activities and public relations efforts.

PRINCIPLE # 18: *A reputation is a perception gained without actually having a first hand experience with the person or program*

Members of the general public, as well as internal or external constituencies, are more likely to support a recreational or sport program that has a sound reputation and is thought of in a positive light. The same holds true of an individual. People in the community are more likely to support that individual (and that person's activities and organization) if others view this individual in a positive light, that is, if the person has a positive reputation.

The reputation of any program can be determined by a host of factors, such as the quality of the activities sponsored and how others view the staff (both paid and volunteer). Frequently, it is the news media that has a very real and significant role in conveying the image (accurate or not) of a person, an activity, a program or organization to the general public by means of newspaper stories, radio blurbs and television coverage. However, the reputation of any organization, program or even a person, is usually not determined by one single factor. Rather, a whole host of factors go into creating a reputation. Similarly, reputations are usually gained over a period of time rather than resulting from a single experience or instance.

Image

What people think and feel in reaction to what they see is referred to as the *image* they have of someone or something. A program's image is the impression(s) or view(s) created when other individuals have an opportunity to view the sport or recreation program up close, first hand. Although reputation and image are closely associated, the difference between the two is that a sport or recreation reputation can have an impact upon individuals who have had no personal contact with the program itself. On the other hand, an image is usually created by first hand, personal association or dealings with the program or the staff affiliated with the program or the program's activities.

Like reputation, the image (real or perceived) that others have of any program can have a profound effect upon whether individuals and groups will respond positively to the promotional activities of that program and support the fundraising effort. An image may be created deliberately or accidentally. That is, an image of an team; a sport, recreation program or of a specific sport program can be determined or shaped by the way the staff and participates are dressed, by the manner in which home event activities are organized, by the cleanliness of the facilities, and by the way the athletes behave (on and off the field or court), etc. An image is more immediate. It can be created by a single experience, episode or a series of experiences or happenings. Accomplishments and Achievements

Accomplishments and achievements in sports, both for individuals as well as the organization itself, can have a positive and long lasting impact upon various segments of the public and various constituencies. Past achievements, therefore, can be utilized as a tool in that such accomplishments make others more receptive to having their ideas or perceptions either reinforced or changed as well as being more in a "help" mode toward the organization and its staff and programs. Everyone wants to be associated with a so-called winner. Witness the number of people wearing the sweatshirts and hats and other paraphernalia of successful sport teams. A wise fundraiser, a prudent promoter, an effective public relations professional will utilize an organization's or sport team's accomplishments as a tool with which to open doors of potential contributors or untapped constituencies.

Status—Level of Competition

The status held within the athletic arena or sport world can be a decisive and helpful tool. UCLA, with its status as one of the major educational and athletic institutions in the United States, and a member of the NCAA Division I, enjoys a certain status by virtue of its membership in the most competitive Division of the NCAA. It also enjoys a certain status because of its historical past within both the academic and athletic arenas. The institution enjoys this status by virtue of its involvements and associations (past and current) in sport, its successes in sport at the highest level of competition, its tradition, its reputation, its image, its facilities, its staff, etc.

Utilizing this status as a tool only enhances the likelihood of additional gains in terms of fundraising projects, promotional activities, and public relations efforts. Such efforts will tend to be more successful, with less effort and resources expended, merely because the focus of the fundraising and promotional activity is UCLA itself. The same can be said of certain secondary schools and smaller colleges and universities, as well as many youth sport teams and recreation organizations. The status and high esteem of a sport or recreation entity is often self-perpetuating (at least for a time). In other words, the status of a program enables that program to maintain the level of success or even achieve greater successes because of its status. As a result of such successes, the status is further enhanced—and the cycle is perpetuated again, and again and again. The challenge for any sport organization or recreation program is to do what it takes to achieve relatively high status, which in turn facilitates further enhancement activities that leads to further improvement or reinforcement of the high status.

Money

The old adage "it takes money to make money" (Palmisano, 1988) still holds true today. Money itself is a very, very important tool. However, the absence of money should not be a deterrent to successful fundraising or promotional activities. Other techniques, strategies, and tools can be used in lieu of actual dollars. For example, "trade outs" (see chapter 13) are an effective means of securing products and services from others without having to pay cash for these products and services. The end result is that the sport program obtains the needed products and services without spending money.

PRINCIPLE # 19: *One must never misuse or waste money in an effort to generate additional funds*

Nevertheless, hard, cold cash remains a most valuable tool or resource. Adequate cash flow provides much needed flexibility for any organization. It enables the program or activity to secure services and products on an almost immediate basis. The crux of the matter is to use this valuable resource in a timely, efficient and effective fashion. Nothing is more disheartening and discouraging than to misuse such a valuable tool as cash. After all, the objective is to raise monies for the sport or recreation program. When monies used in fundraising efforts are not used in the most productive manner, the result is a double whammy—money already on hand is wasted and anticipated monies are not generated to the extent expected. This is an unforgivable situation in which to find oneself as a manager or administrator.

Atmosphere, Climate, and Environment

There are intangible aspects of any recreation or sport program, such as the atmosphere, climate and environment surrounding either the total operation of the organization or some segment of the total, which can serve as powerful tools or assets. Or, in some instances, they can be equally powerful hindrances. The atmosphere, environment or climate affecting such programs can be viewed as either internal or external to the organization itself.

An *internal climate, environment or atmosphere* is exemplified by the working conditions in which the internal staff and those involved in the fundraising and/or promotional efforts find themselves. A friendly, open atmosphere, environment and climate can contribute to the overall progress of the fundraising project, as well as facilitate the interpersonal relationships of those involved with the project. The absence of a positive work environment creates a needless hindrance to the successful completion of any fundraising or promotional attempt lessening the motivation of those involved and sometimes even destroying morale.

> ***PRINCIPLE # 20:*** *Circumstances, environments and situations out of our direct control can often determine the success or failure of fundraising efforts or promotional projects*

One type of *external atmosphere* is the *financial* climate or environment in which the fundraisers and promoters find themselves at the time when the fundraising activity or promotion, etc., is to take place. For example, in a healthy economy when there is a healthy financial growth within the community, it is certainly easier to have funds contributed to worthy causes. However, the converse is true. When the economy is on a down turn, when it is faulty, when there are high interest rates, when a major employer is leaving the community, when the stock market is on the decline, when there is a recession or a fear of a recession, and when money is generally "tight" in the community—it is very, very difficult to fundraise on behalf of a sport or recreation organization or program. During these times of financial constriction, fiscal hardship, the task facing the fundraiser is much more difficult due to the lack of a healthy economic atmosphere, climate or environment.

Another type of external environment is the *political* climate existing within the community. When the head football coach has just been named "man of the year" by the local service club, the climate or environment is conducive for the generation of financial support for that football program. When the girl's basketball team at the local high school wins the state championship or when the wrestling team at the area college/university returns home with the national NCAA championship trophy, the time, the atmosphere, the setting, the climate, and the timing is ripe for positive consequences to result from a fundraising effort, either on behalf of an individual team and/or on behalf of the total athletic program.

Conversely, it is not advisable to kick-off a major fundraising effort or promotional campaign for the football program when the head coach and the president of the football boosters are being officially and publicly charged with fiscal mismanagement. Such a negative political climate will only impede the fundraising efforts.

Services

There are a variety of services that those who are involved in fundraising, promotions and public relations may take advantage of. Such services may be categorized within two areas. *First*, those who are available from within the organization itself. And, *second*, those services available from outside, from other sources or from other organizations. There is a wide range of services (both external and internal) that may be made available to the fundraiser or promoter. Some examples are printing services, duplicating services, tax services, transportation services, medical services, consulting services, legal services, and cleaning services—just to mention a few. These services become significant tools that the sport administrator or manager may exploit even if they are not available free or at a reduced cost.

Associates

People with whom the individual sport administrator or leader is acquainted can function as significant resources or assets. This is nowhere more evident than in the areas of fundraising, promotions and public relations. Associates, especially those people who are held in high esteem by other individuals and constituencies, can serve as "tools" or assets by lending their presence or prestige (becoming *centers of influence*, to the fundraising efforts or projects. And, these people whom the sport or recreation leader or manager knows may be tapped for their experience and areas of expertise to help in any number of different ways. Thus, the cultivation of associates becomes of paramount importance in establishing a firm base of support and creating resources that may be turned into real assets to be used in fundraising and/or promotional projects.

Other Assets and Resources

Generally speaking, anything that can assist the fundraising or promotional process may be considered to be a tool, an asset or a resource (McKenzie, 1988). Undoubtedly, there are many other resources that, from time to time, might prove to be of significant help to those interested in generating monies and support for sports or recreation programs or segments thereof. It is up to the personnel involved in the overall scheme of things to look around and ascertain whether there exists sufficient tools and resources, as well as potential for success, prior to embarking upon a specific fundraising program promotional project or public relations effort.

Searching for hidden prizes in the infield entices fan involvement

ESSENTIAL CHARACTERISTICS AND QUALIFICATIONS OF FUNDRAISERS, PROMOTERS, AND PUBLIC RELATIONS PROFESSIONALS

The ultimate goal, in terms of sport administration and recreation management, is to obtain as broad a base of internal and external support as possible, both financial and moral, given the resources, limitations, and circumstances which exist. Hopefully, through good strategic planning, possession of a high level of competency, and the implementation of successful promotional tactics and effective fundraising efforts, this goal can become a reality.

In the not too distant past, almost anyone and everyone "associated" with sports considered themselves to be "expert" in the areas of fundraising, promotions and public relations. However, this is rapidly changing, if it has not changed already. The definition of an expert is no longer "an individual who travels 50 miles with a briefcase and a Power-Point slide show." Today, there is greater recognition that truly successful efforts in these areas require more than merely an interest, a desire or even an honest effort.

There is a need for a significant degree of professionalism and a rather high standard of excellence in the areas of fundraising, promotions and public relations. In fact, this need has never been greater in sport and recreation than today. Gone are the days, if they ever existed, when any well meaning individual (a "good old boy" or a "good old girl") could step onto the "firing line" and experience meaningful and sustained success in these areas. Presently, there is an urgent demand for greater sophistication, more extensive knowledge, better planning,

Chapter 2: Fundamental Elements and Resources of Fundraising and Promotions   37

more accurate assessment, more effective implementation, and honest follow-up than ever before. The age of *accountability* is upon us in the world of fundraising, promotion and public relations.

Sport leaders, whether they are called managers or administrators, are being judged, as never before, by higher standards. Standards have been set by successful sport leaders as well as by professionals outside of sport and those within the general field of fundraising (development), promotion and public relations. The result is that there now exists greater expectations placed upon those individuals attempting to promote the world of sports and attempting to increase the funding base of sport and sport related activities and programs.

> *PRINCIPLE # 21:* **The "bar has been raised" considerably in terms of expectations that the sport manager or leader must satisfy in the areas of fundraising, promotions and public relations**

Sport and recreation fundraisers and promoters must be confident, must have self-esteem, and must project these qualities to others without being overbearing or insufferable in any way. As a result, they walk the proverbial tightrope between being an obnoxious prima donna and being a well meaning, dedicated, skilled professional expending efforts to achieve specific goals within an overall plan of attack.

In the examination of the fundraising, promotional, and public relations activities of any sport or recreation program, there are ten essential areas in which minimal skills or compe-

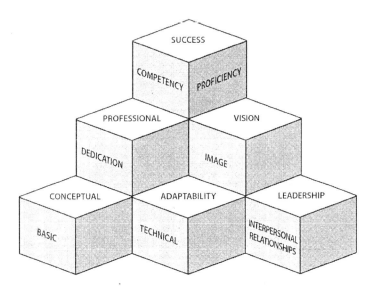

Figure 2.2 Essential Skills and Competencies

In the examination of the fundraising, promotional, and public relations activities of any sport or recreation program, there are ten essential areas in which minimal skills or competencies are necessary for the successful administrator. These competencies are an absolute MUST for the personnel involved, if the stated objectives and goals are to be realized in a timely fashion and at an acceptable quality level. They include (1) basic skills, (2) technical skills, (3) interpersonal skills, (4) conceptual skills, (5) dedication or commitment skills, (6) imagery skills, (7) leadership skills, (8) adaptability skills, (9) vision skills, and (10) professionalism skills. See figure 2.2.

BASIC SKILLS

Those skills that are considered basic include those that are elementary or absolutely essential for any reasonably educated, trained and experienced professional to possess if that person is to experience success in today's world of business. Included within this initial category of skills are those used in writing, speaking, listening, reading, understanding or comprehending that distinguish the educated individual from the uneducated within our society.

TECHNICAL SKILLS

Technical or mechanical skills may be viewed as "... an understanding of, and proficiency in, a specific kind of activity . . . involves specialized knowledge, analytical ability within that specialty, and facility in the use of the tools and techniques of the specific discipline" (Katz, 1955, p. 34). Technical skills are those that involve technological or semi-high tech areas that form the foundation of promotional schemes/activities, fundraising tactics and strategies, and public relations efforts.

These skills include, but are not limited to, competency in typing, graphics, printing, photography, computer literacy, selling, accounting, phone usage, etc. Mastering these technical skills is not dissimilar to the coach mastering the X's and the O's, the technical tactics and strategies, of a sport.

INTERPERSONAL SKILLS

John Donne (1623) wrote that "no man is an island entire of itself, every man is a piece of the continent, a part of the main"—a concept which the sport or recreational fundraiser and promoter should remain well aware. In our society we are quite literally forced, for our daily survival, to be able to work in a variety of circumstances and for a multitude of purposes with other human beings. This is certainly a maxim within the sport and recreation arenas.

Chapter 2: Fundamental Elements and Resources of Fundraising and Promotions 39

> **PRINCIPLE # 22:** *One must be able to work well with others in a variety of settings and circumstances, both on an individual basis and in group settings*

To understand others and to be able to work effectively with them is a highly prized competency (Katz, 1955). Perhaps in no other area of sport or recreation is the need to work with people more essential than in the world of fundraising, promotions and public relations. It is essential that the professional involved in these tasks be able to work effectively and efficiently with other people (positive human relations), on a one-to-one basis, as well as within a group setting. In reality, this competency is too frequently lacking in individuals working within the umbrella of fundraising, promotions, and public relations, even at a minimally acceptable level. The consequence is that failure is the end result frequently experienced in what is a "person to person" or "people" business because of a lack of expertise in working with human beings, i.e., with people.

CONCEPTUAL SKILLS

How one views the total picture of one's recreation or sport program is very important. Having an appropriate and accurate perception of (1) the overall mission, (2) the strategies and tactics involved in working toward established goals, (3) the available resources and limitations, as well as (4) the specific objectives and global goals of the sports program or activity, is not only highly desirable but absolutely essential. One must be able to understand the needs of the total sport or recreation program, as well as the role of each of its components, and be able to make important decisions in an effective and efficient manner. In terms of a school athletic program, the athletic director must be able to have a realistic picture of exactly where all of the sports (not just the sport of football) fit within the total athletic program in respect to the school's goals and objectives and in terms of both resource allocation and priorities. Ditto with the recreation administrator who has overall responsibility of a large number of different programs and activities serving the needs of many different groups and constituencies.

> **PRINCIPLE # 23:** *Possessing a global view of the organization and its needs and assets allows the manager to make wise decisions*

The same analogy can be made in the areas of fundraising, promotions, and public relations. That is, those individuals involved in such activities, under the umbrella of the sport or recreation program, must understand, appreciate and support the role of their total programs, as well as each of the components of their respective programs, in respect to priorities, resources, limitations, missions and goals. Failure to have such a firm, clear grasp leads one to aimlessly struggle, to "spin one's wheels," to go off on tangents, and to inadequately utilize resources in an ineffectual and inefficient manner. People need direction and guidance, without which the recreation worker, coach, administrator, or booster member flounders, wastes valuable energies, time and resources, and, eventually experiences failure.

COMMITMENT AND DEDICATION SKILLS

The ability to consistently demonstrate true dedication and commitment to the task(s) at hand is an invaluable skill. A sport person must, by the very nature of one's involvement in sports and by the very nature of the beast (sport), be willing to expend an exceptional (even, at times, extraordinary) amount of energy, effort and time in the performance of one's job in promoting, raising monies, and creating positive public relations for the sport program or activity (Stier, 1986). Being able and willing to make a significant time commitment is certainly an asset. However, merely spending time and effort at a task is only part of the challenge. There must be, in addition, quality work accomplished during the time spent on task. Effort alone will not suffice. Practice alone will not make perfect. Perfect practice makes perfect. It is the bottom line, the end results, which are all too frequently the measure of one's success.

PRINCIPLE # 24: **Spending time and effort at a task is only part of the challenge—there must be quality work accomplished during the time spent on task—effort alone will not suffice**

Paying attention to details is vital. Mackay (1988) stated that while managers need to delegate they also need to pay strict attention to detail—a fact that is not necessarily in conflict with the idea of time management. Everyone has the same amount of time. It is what we do with it that makes one person different from another. It is the quality of our work (time spent on task) that differentiates the successful manager from the average person.

Quality work coupled with an adequate quantity of time spent at a task may equal a meaningful outcome in terms of goals and objectives sought. Nothing guarantees success. However, without being dedicated and willing to make a commitment in terms of the amount and quality of time one spends working for goals, one is doomed to failure (Stier, 1996b).

It is also most helpful to have an understanding spouse (and children) when it comes to committing oneself to a series of tasks or to a goal. Being able to be truly committed and dedicated and to spend the necessary time on task, without having to face undue criticism at home, is a very significant asset. Having an understanding family willing to support the recreation leader's, coach's or sport administrator's efforts to achieve success in sport promotions and fundraising is invaluable.

IMAGE SKILLS

> ***PRINCIPLE # 25:** The perception of what is real, in terms of a person, activity or program, is as important as the reality of the situation itself*

How one is perceived by others, whether that perception is accurate or not, is of the utmost importance. Sometimes the perceived image or reputation is more important than the reality of the situation. What an individual is can be termed *reality*. What others think of the same individual are *perceptions*.

Perceptions held by others may have no resemblance to reality. In another instance, perceptions may have some resemblance or a great deal of resemblance to what is real. Nevertheless, the perceptions are formed by a variety of factors, some within one's control and others outside a person's control. It is the task of the sport or recreation person to work within such a climate and conduct oneself so that the perception(s) closely resembles reality in terms of the quality of the people involved, the quality of the program or activity and the quality of the effort supporting this program or activity.

Recreation and sport personnel, at all levels, should be able to consistently and adequately present the most positive image or picture possible to as many individuals and groups or publics as possible. Through this effort, which is what public relations is really all about, the correct and positive image of the program can be effectively disseminated to and successfully received and internalized by numerous publics and constituencies.

The image we project as professionals within a sport or recreation organization is created and reinforced by a multitude of factors. These include, but are not limited, to the following:

1. Physical appearance
2. Activities
3. Motivation
4. Speech
5. Clothing worn
6. Communications skills
7. Mannerisms
8. Work ethic
9. Habits
10. Attention to detail
11. Associates—organizations, groups and/or individuals

There is an old saying that is appropriate in the discussion of imagery skills. It says: "What you are speaks so loudly I cannot hear what you are attempting to say." It is necessary that administrators and managers, as well as boosters and supporters, pay more attention to their personal and professional image, to the quality of their activities, and to the perception that others have of them. For, in reality, such an image plays a significant role in creating perceptions that are held by members of various constituencies. And, it is these perceptions that have an effect, either positive or negative, upon how the sport or recreation person (and one's programs and activities) is (are) viewed, treated, and supported by others.

LEADERSHIP SKILLS

> *PRINCIPLE # 26: Being an effective leader is a matter of actually leading rather than merely having the title of "manager" or "administrator"*

Being a good leader is a prerequisite to being a good sport manager or recreation administrator. Being in a leadership position, which all managers are, means that others are motivated to follow, to act. Being a good leader places the individual in a position where one must be capable and willing to guide the actions of others and to remain in a facilitating role in terms of those individuals who report to the administrator or manager. It is important to recognize that one is an effective leader not merely because one holds a title of "administrator" or "manager" but because others have confidence in the leader's ability, judgment and character and are motivated to action because of their belief and confidence in the leader.

ADAPTABILITY SKILLS

Possessing adaptability skills means being able to deal with changing circumstances and situations as they affect one's job situation—and things do change, all the time. It means being able to adjust and modify one's action, one's plans, and one's mode of operation. One must be flexible in today's society if one is to remain an effective and efficient manager or administrator. If there is one thing for certain in this society that we all live in is that there will be change. There will be changes in personnel, in resources, in expectations, in objectives and goals, as well as a whole host of other things. The successful manager is one who is able to be flexible, to adjust to the changing times and yet still reach the established goals.

Today, involvement in fundraising, promotions, and public relations within the world of recreation and sport has become, by necessity, a challenge, and a daunting task. A task to be completed by those who are knowledgeable in using generally accepted principles or guidelines, adapted to fit one's own particular situation or circumstance. *It is this ability to adapt facts, information, ideas, principles, and guidelines to fit one's own individual circumstances, resources, and needs, that distinguish the successful sport fundraiser or development officer from the would-be imposter.*

> **PRINCIPLE # 27:** *One factor that distinguishes the successful sport fundraiser or promoter from the would-be imposter is the ability to adapt and adjust facts, information, principles and guidelines to fit one's own individual circumstances, resources, and needs*

VISION SKILLS

A competent manager need to possess vision in terms of having the ability to look to the future and anticipate how future changes might affect one's own situations in terms of programs, organizations, activities, etc. Nothing remains stagnant in our society, at least not for very long. Leaders involved in areas of sport management and recreation administration need to possess a vision for the future so that they can position their organizations and programs to exist in the future, with whatever changes that the future might hold. Being on the cutting edge of one's profession is an integral part of having a vision for the future and being able to help one's organization meet the challenges of that future.

> **PRINCIPLE #28:** *If there is one thing certain in this society—it is that change is inevitable*

PROFESSIONALISM SKILLS

Being a professional means doing those things that professionals do, that is, acting like a professional. It is imperative that managers not only be professional in all that they do (in terms of their behavior and their image) but that they be deemed to be professional by others with whom they come into contact. Being professional means that one is current in the field, reads widely, is knowledgeable (an expert), attends professional conferences, makes professional contributions (presentations at conferences, meetings as well as writing for publication), and exhibits positive personal and work characteristics necessary and appropriate for the position and the field.

BEING A RENAISSANCE PERSON

Sport managers and recreation administrators need to become *renaissance individuals* in their roles of leaders and directors of sport organizations and recreation programs (Stier, 1999). Individuals involved in fundraising, promotions, and public relations must also be considered *renaissance persons*. **A renaissance person is defined as an individual who is an expert in at least one area, preferably two, and who is nevertheless knowledgeable in many other areas.**

> *PRINCIPLE # 29: Successful fundraisers and promoters are renaissance individuals, both personally and professionally*

Thus, someone who is involved in fundraising for a sport organization needs to be an expert in that specific area. The person might also be an expert in planning and implementing promotional activities as well. However, this same individual also needs to be knowledgeable in many other areas, such as public relations, dealing with people, finances, communications, computer graphics, etc. The concept is simple, individuals involved in sport management and in the activities of fundraising and promotions, etc., need to be well rounded in terms of their specific skills and competencies and capable of drawing upon a wealth of experiences, their own and others, in the organizing, implement and evaluating of such efforts.

REFERENCES

Donne, J. (1623). Devotions upon emergent occasions. *Meditation # 17*.

Ensor, R. (1988, September). Writing strategic sports marketing plan. *Athletic Business*, pp. 48-52.

Farrell, P.V., & McCann, D.J. (1997). Computers, the internet, and marketing college athletics. *Sport Marketing Quarterly, 6*(3), 12-14.

Gray, R.T. (December, 1995). Shaky declarations of independence. *Nation's Business*, pp. 26-28.

Gulick, L., & Urwick, L. (Editors) (1937). *Papers on the science of administration.* New York: Institute of Public Administration.

Jones, E. (October 1, 1996). 'Code words" cloud issue of discrimination at work. *USA Today,* pp. 1-B, 2-B.

Katz, R. (1955, January-February). Skills of an effective administrator. *Harvard Business Review, 33*(1), 34-35.

Mackay, H. (1988). *Swim with the sharks without being eaten alive*. Ivy Books, New York: Ballantine Books.

McKenzie, B. (1988, August). Mastering the art of fundraising. *Athletic Business, 12*(8), 54-58.

Palmisano, M. (1984, May). Fundraising's first rule: Get organized. *Athletic Business, 8*(5) pp. 20-23.

Palmisano, M. (1988, October). Michigan raises funds for new swimming facility. *Athletic Administrator*, pp. AA15-AA17.

Stier, W.F., Jr. (1986, Spring). Athletic administrators expect qualities, competencies in coaches. *Interscholastic Athletic Administration*, pp. 7-9.

Stier, W.F., Jr. (1992). Understanding fundraising in sport: The conceptual approach. *Sport Marketing Quarterly, I*(1), 41-46.

Stier, W.F., Jr. (1994). *Successful support fund-raising*. Madison, Wisconsin: WCB Brown & Benchmark.

Stier, W.F., Jr. (1996a). An Overview of Administering Competitive Sport Programs Through Effective Marketing, Fundraising and Promotion. *Applied Research in Coaching and Athletic Annual, 11*, 116-128.

Stier, W.F., Jr. (1996b). Fundraising—Arts & Sciences 101. *Athletic Management, VIII*(3), 10.

Stier, W.F., Jr. (1998). *Coaching: Concepts and strategies* (2nd ed.). Boston, Massachusetts: American Press.

Stier, W.F., Jr. (1999). *Managing sport, recreation and fitness programs: Concepts and practices*. Boston, MA: Allyn & Bacon.

Stier, W.F., Jr. (2000, November 30). *Fund-Raising and Promotion Secrets for the Busy Athletic Administrator*. Presentation at the 19th National Athletic Business Conference, Orlando, Florida.

Stier, W.F., Jr. (2004). *Athletic administration — Successful decision making, risk taking and problem solving*. Boston, MA: American Press.

Stier, W.F., Jr. (2009). Fundraising projects for sport, recreation, leisure and fitness programs. Boston, MA: American Press. (3rd edition. Boston, MA: American Press.

Stier, W.F., Jr. (2010). Coaching: Becoming a successful athletic coach

Wong, G.M. (1996, October). Contract law. *Athletic Business, 20*(10), 10, 14.

DISCUSSION QUESTIONS

1. Explain why the taking reasonable risks is so important in the areas of fundraising and promotions. Also, provide examples of taking such risks both in fundraising efforts and promotional projects.

2. Explain which (and how) the resources, tools, and assets outlined in this chapter might help you the most in terms of fundraising for a sport or recreation entity that you might be engaged in as a profession.

3. Outline how you might develop and utilize conceptual skill in the performance of duties and responsibilities in terms of fundraising and promotions within a sport organization.

4. Why should professional administrators or coaches in a sport entity be concerned both with perceptions and reality of situations in which they find themselves?

5. Explain, with examples, how one can become a renaissance person both in terms of one's personal life and in terms of one's professional life.

3 | BOOSTER CLUBS AND SPORT SUPPORT GROUPS

Kids Sports Night can get the whole family involved

CHAPTER HIGHLIGHTS

This chapter will emphasize:

- The history of the booster club concept in the United States
- The role of *sport support groups* (SSGs) and *recreation support groups* (RSGs)
- Challenges to be faced when instituting changes in an organization
- Advantages and disadvantages of a single SSG and multiple SSGs within a college or university

- The seven steps in the establishment of a quality sport support group (SSG)
- Various pitfalls in the creation of a sport support group (SSG)
- The organizational structure of a sport support group (SSG)
- The contents of by-laws of a sport support group (SSG)
- Advantages for having both "continuity" and "new blood" in terms of membership within the board of directors and corps of officers of a SSG
- Differences between the two schools of thought regarding limiting the number of terms which individuals may *consecutively serve* on the board of directors or as officers
- Dangers of a "three o'clock booster wonder" within one's program
- Specific gifts that donors may accrue for their contributions to a sport or recreation program

Many leaders find that having an affiliated entity to help support their sport or recreation organization in its fundraising efforts is a decided advantage. These support organizations can go by different names but all have the same overall objective, that is, to aid the sport or leisure organization in raising much needed funds.

HISTORY OF AMERICAN SPORT BOOSTER CLUBS

PRINCIPLE #30: *Support groups are not a recent phenomenon*

Organizations (such as booster clubs) existing for the express purpose of supporting or boosting sports programs have a long history in the review of amateur sports in this country. Some organizations or clubs were originally created either through a cooperative effort between school administrators and civic-minded sports leaders for the purpose of meeting specific financial needs of an athletic program. Others were established through efforts of parents of athletes desiring to provide a more beneficial and safe learning experience for their youngsters. But not all schools have so-called sport support groups or booster clubs, for a variety of reasons. For example, the University of Notre Dame, an outstanding institution of higher education with an impeccable reputation for academics and possessing one of the premiere sports programs in this country, had no athletic booster clubs as such (May, 1990).

Just as sports programs have expanded and evolved throughout the years in this country, sport support groups or booster clubs have similarly grown in number, degree of sophistication, and impact. Today, sport support programs have been established and have evolved into rather sophisticated, effective, and efficient entities, throughout the country, and at all levels, from youth sports to the intercollegiate level. The result in many instances has been increased financial support for the sports programs and an enhanced positive image for both the sports programs and the sport support groups or booster clubs.

> **PRINCIPLE # 31:** *Support groups or booster clubs are not the exclusive domain of competitive sports programs or school athletic programs— recreation programs can also organize such support entities*

It should be remembered, however, that support groups or booster clubs are not the exclusive domain of amateur sport teams or school athletic programs. Many recreation entities, programs, and activities also have such support organizations to facilitate their efforts at carrying out their specific mission(s) for various constituencies.

Two of the challenges facing support groups or booster clubs in the years ahead involve the (1) maintaining of continuity in general membership, as well as in the officer corps, and the (2) consistent generation of essential resources on an annual basis, to insure that the vital elements (money, equipment, supplies, facilities, staff, etc.) are available for the sports programs.

Membership by both women and men within such support or booster-type organizations has continued to grow as these organizations themselves have expanded and matured in scope, significance and attractiveness to the general public. Officers of such groups have provided excellent leadership and guidance for the organizations themselves, as well as for the members therein. Officers have been trained through experiential means, as well as through formal educational programs. The end result is the availability of more qualified and highly sophisticated men and women who find themselves involved in either a leadership or "followship" role within the sports support group or booster club organization.

> **PRINCIPLE # 32:** *Ideally, support groups or booster clubs should provide for enhancement funding only—however, more and more support groups find themselves, through necessity, providing funding for essentials*

While these groups or organizations, in the past, have been involved in obtaining so-called "extras" for the sport or recreation programs, many of the support groups of today are getting involved more and more in generating *essential* support (money, goods and/or services) for the sport teams, programs, and individual athletes. Thus, the importance of such support organizations or booster clubs and the significance of their involvement and contributions have quadrupled within recent years (Stier, 2010). The end result is that the support entities (whatever name they go by) have become, in many respects, true essential elements within the sport or recreation scene in the early part of the 21st century.

It behooves every sport administrator, coach, booster, and fan to seriously examine the advantages of being involved with such a support organization. These advantages can take the form of providing both tangible and intangible (moral) support in the area of resources, as well as providing a sound foundation for an excellent public relations component so necessary for any sport program. A support group should be considered as another tool that may be utilized to help meet the needs, objectives, and goals of the total sport program.

If viewed in this manner, such organizations can indeed be an invaluable asset to the sport program and to the participants, the athletes, fans, etc. For, in the final analysis, the justification of sports or recreational activities is whether or not the participants actually benefit from the experience(s). The ultimate justification of sport support groups or booster clubs is whether or not these support organizations truly facilitate the sporting or recreational experience so that the participants can experience and enjoy these benefits.

JUSTIFICATION FOR THE EXISTENCE OF SUPPORT ORGANIZATIONS— SPORT SUPPORT GROUPS (BOOSTER CLUBS)

The number of sport and recreation programs (at all levels) having problems or challenges in securing sufficient funding for their existing or desired level of competition and variety of sport offerings is very high. There are many reasons why there is a real need for additional sources of financial support for sports programs, at all levels and in all types of sport or recreation organizations. Some of these reasons include, but are not limited, to the following factors.

Why Sport and Recreation Programs Need Additional Financial Support

1. General Inflation

The cost of doing business today, that is, to provide a meaningful learning experience for the participants, costs more than it did in the past and will undoubtedly cost more in the future. Such is life, as we know it.

During 1988 and 1989 the cost of operating major collegiate athletic programs with football programs rose some 13.5 percent. This outpaced earned income that saw an increase of 9 percent. There was a 35 percent increase during the three-year period 1985-86 through 1988-89. In fact, at the Division I college and university level, the median costs exceeded $9.75 million. The maximum and minimum costs during the 1988-89 academic year were $19.57 million and $4.24 million respectfully.

It should not be surprising to find that more and more universities are showing sizeable deficits in their athletic programs. In fact, the average deficit in 1988-89 was $112,000. In the CFA Financial Survey conducted by the College Football Association it was revealed that more than 75 percent of those responding cited low gate and post-season receipts, fewer cash gifts, and a decline in radio and television broadcast licensing fees as the major reasons for the decline of income for intercollegiate athletics (Operating Costs, 1990).

And, the same can be inferred in the area of recreational pursuits. Hence, it is necessary to plan for greater expenditures in almost every category associated with the administration of sports and recreation activities. For example, transportation, salaries, officials, maintenance and repairs, utilities, crowd control measures, medical costs, equipment, supplies, repairs, refurbishments, etc. The list goes on and on.

2. *Increase in the Cost of Liability Insurance*

Spiraling costs within the liability insurance industry is a well-known fact within our society. Sport and recreation programs are not immune from this plight. The alarming increase in successful lawsuits by sport consumers and participants, coupled with landmark cash settlements awarded plaintiffs, are legitimate causes of concern for the administrator charged with responsibility for the recreation or sport (athletic) program. In fact, increases in insurance costs have become one of the major challenges facing those responsible for financing sports at all levels. Some expenses associated with sport and recreation organizations must just be absorbed, period. Unfortunately, liability insurance is all too frequently just one such expense.

PRINCIPLE # 33: *Good safe practices reduce the likelihood of accidents, the potential for successful lawsuits and the cost of liability insurance*

---

3. *Increase in the Cost of Medical Insurance and Medical Services*

The entire area of health care continues to expand in terms of capabilities and in terms of cost to the consumer. The individual participant, especially in competitive sports, is better cared for today than at any time in the history of sports. But the cost of such protection, treatment and rehabilitation is high and must necessarily be passed onto either the participants or to the sponsoring organization itself. The end result is an even greater portion of many sports or recreation budgets being allocated to medical related expenditures.

With seemingly ever increasing annual premiums being charged to the sponsoring programs to provide adequate insurance coverage for their participants, more and more organizations are facing a financial crunch in their efforts to come up with the funds to cover such premiums. Some organizations, such as athletic departments at the college or university level, have chosen to eliminate their responsibility for securing and paying for medical insurance for their athletes entirely because of the seemingly ever-increasing cost of such insurance policies. In fact, in the late 1980s several institutions belonging to the State University of New York Athletic Conference (SUN-YAC), including SUNY Brockport, SUNY Cortland and the State University of New York at Binghamton, elected to eliminate athletic insurance coverage paid for by their respective athletic departments—and instead required individual athletes to provide and pay for the insurance themselves.

4. *Increase in the Cost of Obtaining, Training and Retaining Qualified Staff*

There has never been more emphasis on, and recognition of, the need for qualified, experienced and motivated staff associated with sport and recreation programs than at the present time. When such staff members are on salary or stipend, the cost of financing the staff's salaries can rapidly become a weighty burden on the already tight financial resources of the sport or recreation program. Even in those instances where the staff consists of volunteers (youth sport coaches, recreation workers, etc.), there is still the cost involved in their continual in-service training or education. It is inevitable that there be escalating expenses associated with the staffing of any sport or recreation program.

5. *More Opportunities for Participation by More People*

There are more participants involved in recreation and sport activities, at every level, than at any other time in our country's history. Programs in amateur and recreational sporting activities in this country have steadily increased since the beginning of the 20th century. This expansion is evident from the lower elementary levels through high school and extending into colleges and universities and continuing through later life as individuals continue to be engaged in recreational type pursuits as part of their leisure time experiences. There has also been a dramatic increase in the number of females participating in amateur athletics in recent years. And, in terms of school sponsored sporting activities, there has also been a corresponding increase in the number of sports being made available for both males and females, both on the secondary school and collegiate levels.

Title IX (1974) has certainly had a significant impact in the area of increased athletic participation by women, especially in schools. Likewise, the Civil Rights Restoration Act of 1987, passed by Congress on March 22, 1988, has served as a significant boost to the original intent of Title IX (Kramer et al., 1988). And, the surprising vote by the Supreme Court of this country, on February 26, 1992, really put the teeth back into the 1972 law. It was on that date that the court, with an unanimous 9-0 vote, decided in the Franklin v. Gwinnett County Public Schools case (Ga.) that Title IX plaintiffs of intentional sexual discrimination and bias under the statute in schools may sue for unlimited money damages instead of just pursuing a promise to end the bias or the discrimination (Mauro, 1992).

However, it must be noted that the increase in sports participation and availability of opportunities are not limited to only women. Greater participation by both males and females has been evident in the past and continues well into the 21st Century—and in a wider range of sports activities. Ditto in terms of people of all ages being more inclined to be active in sports and sport related activities. To put it plainly, more teams are being sponsored today by various youth sport organizations, junior high schools, and high schools. In high schools alone, during the 1987-88 school year, over 5 million (5,275,461) boys and girls were involved in sports, an increase of 75,023 from the previous year (Sunday Democrat and Chronicle, 1988).

The college and university level has not been immune to this ever-increasing participation by men and women. Even sports at the professional level has had increases in participation due to the fact that there are more professional teams, in every sport, than only a decade ago (Lipsey, 1992).

6. *Insufficient Gate Receipts*

There is only so much funding available from gate receipts. And gate receipts are dependent upon seating capacity, attractiveness and competitive level of the particular sport activity in competing for the consumers' time, interest and disposable or discretionary income dollars. Anything that reduces or limits the income from gate receipts can have a significant negative impact upon the financial support base of the athletic program. One such factor that has had a devastating effect upon the gate receipts of a sizeable number of sport programs and recreation activities is the proliferation of the number of options open to the viewing public having an interest in sports and recreational pursuits.

The seemingly never-ending growth, expansion, and availability of collegiate and professional sports programs are in constant competition for the consumer's discretionary dollar. Never before has the consumer had greater opportunities and more options available to spend his or her entertainment dollar and valuable time.

PRINCIPLE # 34: *It has long been recognized by sport administrators that reliance exclusively on gate receipts is not possible if the sport entity is to be fiscally solvent*

Additionally, the opportunity, almost on a 24-hour basis, to watch major college, as well as national and international sporting events on television (witness Sports channel WTBS and ESPN's efforts in this respect), tends to erode the income traditionally generated from gate receipts for many sport or recreation related programs. This phenomenon is pervasive and can have a debilitating effect at all levels of sports from youth sports to high school athletics to the college and university level and even extends to the professional ranks. The over-saturation of sporting "opportunities" for the consumer is already upon us. And, in a sizeable number of sport and recreation programs at all levels, this over-saturation is currently affecting gate receipts (income) in a negative fashion.

7. Decrease in Funding from Traditional Institutional Resources

It has been estimated that 50 percent of the students attending our nation's secondary schools are involved in competitive sports on an annual basis. With such a high percentage of participating students, it remains unfortunate indeed that the financial resources typically allocated to the sports programs by boards of education remains between 1 to 5 percent of the district's total fiscal budget (Olson.

In the summer of 1990 the Slayton High School (Oregon) board of education eliminated all competitive interscholastic sports. This was due to the failure of two property tax levies that went down to defeat. The consequence was that the board had

> **PRINCIPLE # 35:** *In school based sports programs there is a tendency for school authorities to cut back or remain stable in terms of institutional funding of sports programs leaving athletic administrators and supporters with the responsibility of generating needed financial resources*

to cancel the school paper, band concerts, as well as the school play in addition to the high school sports program (Oregon High School, 1990). Many schools are having to look at other sources of income to support school sports.

School athletic programs, in general, are getting a smaller piece of the institutional financial pie, at both the secondary and the collegiate levels. More and more, such programs are being expected to assume a greater responsibility for their own financial well-being. With a lessening of financial support from central administrative budgets, it falls upon the administrators and coaches of these programs to examine and pursue other avenues for replacing lost revenue, as well as generating new sources of income for enhancement purposes.

In light of the seven factors cited above, it becomes obvious that there is a real need for assistance in the generation of much needed financial resources for sport and recreation type programs. This assistance can be realized through a well-organized and administered support group or booster club. An organization that has a clear overall goal, excellent leadership, specific organizational guidelines, and a receptive atmosphere in which to work for specific objectives for the betterment of the participants is what is needed in many cases.

The rationale for the existence of such a support group or athletic booster-type organization essentially centers around one major question. The question is simply this: Is the support organization able and willing to facilitate the realization of specific objectives and general goals that might have been beyond the reach of the athletic or recreational program without the existence and work of the support group? If the support group can actually help the sport or recreation program, in a real and material fashion, *without getting in the way of or interfering with the operation of the program or activities*, there may indeed be real, tangible advantages to establishing such a support organization for the sport or recreation program.

SUPPORT GROUPS FOR SPORT AND RECREATION ORGANIZATIONS

One of the first things that come to mind when one considers obtaining outside assistance for the sport or recreation program is the viability of so-called sport booster clubs or recreation support groups. Generally speaking, booster type support groups (organizations) have the potential to assist sport *and* recreation programs by providing fiscal support and moral backing as well as assistance in communicating a positive message about the program and activities to the various constituencies.

> *PRINCIPLE # 36:* **When considering sport support groups there are two questions to consider: (1) should there even be a support organization and (2) if so, should there be only one or several?**

Sport support groups (SSGs) at the collegiate level, especially among those athletic programs that provide athletic scholarships, more and more find themselves engaged in significant fundraising efforts. As early as the early 1990s the support groups at the University of Iowa (13,000 members) reportedly generated over $4.5 million while The Ohio State University support group (1,600 members) raised almost $3.3 million. Even NCAA Division II and III institutions have become very active in raising money through support groups. Robinson (1999, p. 40) revealed that almost half of the NCAA II Division schools were successful in the mid-1990s in raising over $100,000 on an annual basis.

Certainly there are differing opinions as to the advantages and disadvantages of such support groups or organizations. In school based athletic programs, one position is represented by the athletic director who, when asked why there was not a booster club or sport support group (SSG) associated with the school's athletic program, reportedly indicated: "Why would I want to organize my own lynch mob?"

However, the opposite position is reflected by the statement made by the then athletic director (Dr. William F. Stier, Jr.) at the State University of New York, Brockport, who was quoted as saying:

> The support group (Friends of Brockport Athletics–FOBA) at this University has played a major role in rejuvenating the intercollegiate athletic program—especially

in terms of generating moral support, fan interest, and in providing thousands and thousands of dollars in much needed fiscal assistance. Without the meaningful support of the Friends of Brockport Athletics our total athletic program, involving some 27 teams, would not be the quality, successful program that it is today. (Stier, 1990)

A Single Support Organization or Multiple Support Organizations?

A major factor when it comes to considering the organizational structure and purpose of potential support or booster type organizations is whether there should be one single booster club or support group for the entire athletic program or multiple support (booster) groups organized around different sports. For example, in a high school or college situation, should the football program have its own football booster organization (Touchdown Club)? Should there exist a Tip Off Club supporting the basketball program? Should there be a separate booster club for women's sports and another for men's sports?

Each of these questions must be answered in light of individual circumstances and the specific situation in which the administrator or manager finds oneself. *There is no single "right answer" to the above questions.* It depends upon the individual situation and any number of variables. To the question of whether or not a booster club or support group should even be organized, there is no single answer. Likewise, to the question of whether there should be a single booster club or multiple support groups, there is also no single answer.

The answers to both questions above depend, to a great extent, upon the individual circumstances in which the staff and supporters find themselves. The answers depend upon (1) the tradition and history of support and financial assistance with that particular sport program, (2) the background and experiences of the people involved, (3) the prejudices, opinions, expectations, and power of administrators, athletic staff, and potential boosters, (4) the level of financial and other forms of support needed or desired for various segments of the sport program, (5) the philosophy and persuasiveness of the administration and staff; and, (6) the political and economical climate in which all of the planning, discussing, questioning, and consulting takes place.

PRINCIPLE # 37: *Be cautious before instituting major changes quickly within an organization—especially when such changes are in conflict with well-established policies, procedures and practices*

Challenges to be Faced when Instituting Changes

People tend to resist change. This is especially true when they have worked in or been associated with an organization for a period of time. In such a situation, individuals are more resistant to significant changes, especially when a person new to the position or to the organization is proposing the changes. As a result, sport or recreation administrators and promoters need to be cognizant of this tendency to react to proposed changes with hesitancy and reluctance—if not downright resistance.

> **PRINCIPLE # 38:** *People tend to resist change when they have grown accustomed to the "way things have been"*

A good rule of thumb to follow is not to make any major changes for at least 2-3 months after assuming a new administrative position unless absolutely necessary. The rationale behind this tactic is threefold. *First*, it frequently takes that long to learn about the organization and its inner workings and its personnel. *Second*, there is a tendency for a new administrator to any organization, office or position to be bombarded with information and input from any number of individuals, all attempting to influence the decision-making ability of the new manager or administrator.

Unless one is very careful, the decisions that the new administrator makes may not be those of the administrator, but of those who were able to influence the new person. It is best to wait until one is familiar with the organization, its staff and its operation prior to rushing off making major decisions.

The *third* reason why some time should elapse, before significant changes are made by a new administrator, is to lessen the possibility of bruised feelings among those individuals who still remain on staff and who feel that the previous way of conducting business was just fine and dandy. And, of course, there might also still be some people on staff who had had a role in instituting the present policies, procedures and practices and who might very well still be in positions to serve as obstructionists if not handled in a diplomatic fashion.

> **PRINCIPLE # 39:** *It is the responsibility of the sport or recreation administrator to adequately deal with, guide and control the support organization and the members therein*

CREATING A WHOLESOME, PRODUCTIVE ATMOSPHERE WITHIN SPORT SUPPORT GROUPS (SSGs) AND BOOSTER CLUBS

The failure, in some situations, to control sport support groups (SSGs) or booster groups from excesses is well-known and frequently publicized, especially at the collegiate level of big-time competitive athletics. There are numerous examples of where sport support groups have run amuck at big-time athletic programs and, as a result, had gotten sport programs in hot water with the NCAA. For example, the boosters at Syracuse University (New York) played a roll in the basketball team receiving a one-year probation during the 1993-1994 season. Additionally, several Texas A&M University football players were either suspended or dismissed form the squad because of what was termed unethical practices by the Aggie boosters (Bradley, 1993, p. 15)

However, the failure of the few should not dictate to the vast majority whether or not such support organizations should be created and utilized. The failure of sport administrators, central administrators, and members of support groups or booster clubs to appropriately take advantage of the inherent strengths that such organizations offer is tragic. This failure, however, is often the result of a lack of planning; a lack of foresight; a lack of organization; a lack of safeguards, policies and procedures; coupled with the administration's inability to be decisive in critical situations.

The ultimate purpose of booster clubs or similar sport support groups (SSGs) is to serve in the role of a facilitator and supporter of the sport or recreation program—not to dictate policy, not to manipulate the decision-making process and not to be involved in day-to-day operations of the sport or recreation program. The words "to facilitate" best describe the role of the booster club (or SSG) and its members. The support organization exists and the members belong so that there might be significant assistance (in a variety of ways) provided to the program, the activities, both paid and volunteer staff, to spectators and to the actual participants. The support entity should indeed facilitate the overall operation. When it fails to assume this role, the justification for its very existence ceases to exist.

The existence of sport support groups means that money raised by community members through this vehicle must be considered as part of the overall fiscal support that is provided both male and female sport squads. In other words, the funds that are raised through the booster club must be factored in the Title IX equation. In brief, the money that is raised by sport support groups (SSGs) at schools (high schools and colleges) must be appropriately shared with the male and female athletes. Recent court decisions have ruled that monies generated through the efforts of sport support groups do indeed count in the Title IX equation. Today, it is simply not appropriate (nor is it legal) for a SSG to exist that supports one sex better than the other (Berry, 2001).

> **PRINCIPLE # 40:** *The sport support group exists to* **provide assistance** *to the organization, its programs, its activities, its staff and the participants*

Many supporters and parents have to realize that when money is raised through the efforts of the sport support group for a particular team, a boy's basketball squad, for example, then the administrators of the total athletic program are faced with the task to see that the girls' basketball program has appropriate (equitable) resources to the boys' program—*even if there is no sport support group out there raising funds for the girls.*

CREATING AND ORGANIZING A SPORT SUPPORT GROUP (SSG) OR RECREATION SUPPORT GROUP (RSG)

Support groups for sport and recreation organizations, whether they are called booster clubs or are identified by some other designation; do not come into being by themselves. It takes a great deal of work to plan and organize a sound, effective and efficient sport support group. Nor, once such an organization has come into existence, does its mere presence automatically guarantee that the organization will have any positive, long-term impact in terms of the financial or other types of support of the sport or recreation program. It takes work to make such an organization a workable force in providing meaningful and consistent support.

Craft shows can generate big money and tremendous exposure

A Single Support Group or Multiple Groups—An Important Consideration

As stated earlier in this chapter, one of the key questions is whether there should be a single all-encompassing support or booster organization or should there be more than one. In school athletic programs, there are many examples of multiple support or booster clubs, different clubs for different sports. And, there are examples of other schools having only a single such entity supporting all of the school's sports. There are justifications on both sides of the issue.

> **PRINCIPLE #41:** *There are both advantages and disadvantages of having a single support group as well as having multiple support groups, each supporting a specific sport*

Those supporting a single support (booster) organization cite the advantages of have a dedicated single entity working for a common goal—rather than many splinter groups, each with their own specific agendas and own loyalties (Robinson, 1999; Stier, 1999). On the other hand, having multiple support or booster clubs working to support different sports within a school takes advantage of the enthusiasm and the loyalties that individuals have for a specific sport and may result in greater generation of financial support for some teams. Let's face it, some fans and boosters are only interested in supporting and contributing to a single team. And if they know that their efforts will be benefiting their favorite team they are more likely to get behind the booster club's activities and help that support group work for the betterment of their favorite team.

> **PRINCIPLE # 42:** *One must be extremely careful in moving from a multiple support group situation to a single group—it is far easier to move from a single support group to having many such groups*

Of course, it is always easier to switch from a single support group to have multiple supports groups rather than vise versa. People (supporters, donors) infrequently willingly give up something that they have enjoyed in the past. Thus, if supporters and donors have a tradition of belonging to and financially supporting their own favorite sport by belonging to a sport specific club or organization, it is hard to give up that practice in exchange to making contributions to all of the sports via means of a single umbrella-type support group providing assistance to numerous sports.

Regardless of whether there are multiple support groups or a single entity, the key to creating a successful support group rests in adequate advanced planning coupled with skilled leadership—external and internal leadership. When it comes right down to it, the success of such an organization is dependent upon the quality of those individuals who make up the organization.

Chapter 3: Booster Clubs and Support Groups 61

SEVEN STEPS IN THE ESTABLISHMENT OF A QUALITY SUPPORT GROUP

1. *Recognition of the need for such an organization*

   It is important that the awareness of the need for such a support group be shared with a large number of individuals, groups, or constituencies. If the only person who believes that the organization should exist is the director of the program, the likelihood that the support group will come to fruition and fulfill its mission is extremely limited.

2. *Communication with appropriate officials associated with the sport or recreation organization*

   In terms of a school situation, the appropriate school administrators and staff must understand the purposes of such an organization. Similarly, they should become familiar with the administrative structure of the entity and its objectives and goals. Ditto if the situation involves a recreation program or department. Appropriate administrators and staff affiliated with the organization must be cognizant of the need and advantages of such an entity. This might involve those elected or appointed officials having oversight for the recreation program or activities that will be affected by the creation of such a support group.

3. *Consultation with representatives of various internal and external constituencies*

   Various segments of the community or representatives of the numerous publics should be consulted in terms of the feasibility and advisability of such an organization, in light of the existing circumstances in which the sport or recreation program finds itself. Similarly, in the case of a school athletic program, input should be sought from within the school and/or athletic program, from coaches, from teachers, from staff, etc.

4. *Establishment of general principles and guidelines of the support group*

   There is a need to delineate the purposes and goals of the organization in clear, concise language so that all will readily understand the function and purpose of the sport support group. There should be absolutely no ambiguity in terms of the purpose (mission) of the support organization.

   The personal interaction between the administrator and the members and potential members of the support group is all-important. How one communicates to this constituency and what one communicates can be instrumental in building a sound foundation on which to build a trusting and long lasting relationship (Hessert, 1999).

PRINCIPLE # 43:   *Competent Administrators Anticipate Challenges, Problems, and Pitfalls and Take Appropriate Proactive Steps*

5. *Recognition of potential pitfalls that should be avoided*

   Being cognizant of the problems and pitfalls that one should avoid is half of the battle for many sport and recreation managers. Some of these potential challenges or pitfalls are listed below.

   A. Dealing with the potential challenges of overzealous or super eager boosters or supporters, who may want to exert inappropriate or undue influence over the sport or recreation program
   B. Selecting the proper method of accounting for all fiscal transactions
   C. Establishing priorities in terms of activities of the support group
   D. Determining the appropriateness of special projects sponsored, supported or endorsed by the organization
   E. Establishing the proper relationship between the booster and support group(s) and the sport or recreation program
   F. Planning for continuity in members, officers, and board members of the support organization while also insuring opportunities for "new blood" in terms of membership within the support entity
   G. Creating the proper relationships between the members of the support group and the coaching and administrative/managerial staff

   There are numerous additional potential challenges, no doubt, that might be addressed in the planning stage of the establishment of such an organization as a sport support group (SSG) or a recreation support groups (RSG). How these challenges will be addressed will depend upon the circumstances surrounding the athletic program and the quality of the personnel involved—paid and volunteer. The objective remains essentially the same. That is, to establish appropriate guidelines to enable the support group to fulfill its mission, i.e., to help the sport or recreation program, the staff and the participants.

6. *Dissemination of information about the organization and its purpose(s)*

   One of the first and most important steps to take, once a support group has been established, is to extensively publicize both its existence and the reason(s) for its existence to all appropriate constituencies. The creation of such a group might call for a special "kick-off" activity (luncheon, dinner, breakfast, wine & cheese gathering, etc.). This presents an opportunity for past, present and potential supporters, contributors, and members to gather together to talk and learn about the athletic program and the newly organized booster group. Such a situation also provides an excellent opportunity for fans and the general public to actually make a commitment to support the sport or recreation program via the support organization.

7. Determination of the organizational structure of the group

The specific organizational structure (the constitution and/or by-laws) of the support group needs to be clearly established and well-defined. The organizational structure will provide the framework for all future activities of the club or group and, hence, one way to help insure that such an organization assumes its proper (facilitating, supporting) role is to have the structure of the club or support group properly organized with an appropriate set of by-laws. This governing document is a key ingredient for insuring that the support group or club fulfills its appropriate mission. See appendix A.

By-laws provide the framework as to how the organization is to be organized and run by addressing each of the following issues: (1) organization structure, (2) purposes, (3) membership, (4) officer and board member elections, (5) duties of officers, (6) executive committee, (7) responsibilities of the executive board, (8) meetings, (9) standing and special committees, (10) property rights, (11) constitutional amendments, (12) dues structure, and, (13) relationships with the chief school administrator and the athletic department (in the case of a school) and relationships with members of the appointed governing board and city council (in the case of a city recreation department).

> **PRINCIPLE # 44:** *By-laws should be carefully scrutinized prior to being officially adopted as they serve as the framework (foundation) for all subsequent activities by the support group*

ORGANIZATIONAL STRUCTURE OF SUPPORT GROUPS

Although the exact organizational structure of sport support groups or recreation support clubs may vary, there are many common elements that are applicable for any such support group. Some of the major components of the organizational structure of such an organization include:

1. Officers of the support group or organization
   A. President
   B. Vice president (or president-elect)
   C. Treasurer
   D. Secretary
   E. Board members

2. Make-up of the membership of the board of directors
   A. "Inside" versus "Outside" members
   B. Ad hoc members of the board (sport or recreation administrator)

3. Orientation and training sessions for new officers and board members
4. Limitations or specific ratio of members, officers, and board members, in terms of:
   A. School personnel or staff of the recreation entity
   B. Athletic or sport personnel
   C. Community personnel
   D. Staggered terms of board members
   E. Right to succeed oneself
5. Establishment of minimum expectations of officers and board members
   A. Provision of recall of officers
   B. Provision of recall of board members
6. Committees
   A. Standing committees
   B. Ad hoc committees
7. Newsletters and other forms of communication to keep general membership informed
8. Membership criteria and membership levels
9. Number of meetings each year and the determination of the annual business meeting where elections take place
10. Determination as to whom the booster club is answerable to in the final analysis
    A. To whom or what body is the annual report presented? To itself? To the athletic director (school) or recreation administrator (recreation program or department)? To a particular administrator?
    B. Creation of an organizational chart coupled with a job description of all officers and board members

---

PRINCIPLE # 45: *There must be a balance between "continuity" and "new blood" in terms of leadership and membership within both the Board of Directors and the Officers of the support group*

MEMBERSHIP TERMS OF THE BOARD OF DIRECTORS AND THE CORPS OF OFFICERS

One of the challenges facing any organization, and especially support groups, is keeping a balance between insuring continuity in staff positions, as well as board membership, *and* insuring that there is sufficient so-called "new blood" for the good of the organization.

There are two schools of thought regarding limiting the number of terms which individuals may consecutively serve on the board of directors or as officers. One viewpoint holds that board members (or officers) should be limited to one or two such terms (whatever the regular term of office might be). The rationale behind this line of thinking is two-fold. *First*, an individual board member should not monopolize a slot on the board or become such a so-called permanent fixture that the individual becomes so powerful a force (so influential) within the organization that the overall effectiveness and efficiency of the overall board is diminished.

The *second* justification for mandating such a limit on board members' and officers' length of membership beyond a specified number of years is that there really is a need for new blood from the various constituencies that the support organization serves. Without vacancies periodically occurring, the likelihood of new members being able to join the organization at the board level or as officers is remote, if not non-existent.

There are others, however, who recommend that there should be no limit on consecutive membership as a board member or as an officer. These advocates hold that it is advisable, if not necessary, to have significant longevity in leadership at the board level as well as in terms of the officers. Besides, term limits always exist in the form of voting incumbents out.

Those who prefer no term limits believe that members of boards and officers function better when board members and/or officers have had significant experience in their respective posts. Thus, there is no such need to "reinvent the wheel," goes this argument, when there is extensive experience on the board or within the group of officers.

> **PRINCIPLE # 46:** *One should be alert to the potential problems that may occur when individuals gain undue influence over the organization (its direction and activities) merely because of their longevity as a board member or as an officer*

The basic concept remains. One must constantly be on the lookout for those with self-serving interests becoming permanent fixtures on self-perpetuating boards or as officers. Stipulations within the by-laws, as to length of consecutive terms and the inclusion of staggered terms of office for both officers and board members, can alleviate many potential problems in this respect.

Additionally, in terms of officers, the by-laws might call for a position of President-Elect to exist. An individual elected to this position would become President when the term of President-Elect expires. This concept can also work with other officers such as the position of Secretary-Elect and the post of Treasurer-Elect. The advantage of organizing the officer corps in this manner is the time that is available for an understudy to learn the "ropes" for the position that the person will assume when the term of office is rotated.

It is essential, for continuity purposes, as well as for effectiveness and efficiency of the organization, to provide orientation sessions and training sessions for both officers and board members of the support group. This is an effort to:

1. Create awareness and appreciation of past, current, and future activities, programs, goals, procedures, policies, and practices of the support group, the sport or recreation program and activities, and the school or sponsoring organization itself

2. Instill insight into the support role of the support entity insofar as the sport or recreation program is concerned

3. Contribute ideas for current and future activities of the organization

4. Actively play a role in the planning and implementation of activities sponsored by the organization, the program and the paid/volunteer staff

5. Motivate others within the support group and under the umbrella of the sport or recreation organization to work in support of the sport or recreation programs and activities

FINANCIAL CONSIDERATIONS OF SUPPORT GROUPS

The establishment of a support organization or club and the ongoing activities of such an entity involve work not only in the raising of funds but in the proper management of the monies gathered. Thus, there are several key financial considerations that should be thoroughly understood by those involved with the raising of funds for sports and recreation purposes. These are:

1. To determine whether or not the support group should elect to incorporate as a non-profit organization and operate as a tax-exempt organization (under the eyes of the Internal Revenue Service)

2. To secure an attorney or other qualified individual to prepare and oversee incorporation process, if incorporation is desired, and to complete required annual reports

3. To establish procedures, if the group is not incorporated, whereby all contributions are made directly to the institution's tax deductible entity (alumni office, development office, foundation, etc.), thus retaining the tax deductibility of contributions

4. To secure an outside auditor to conduct the annual audit of all financial records (all transactions and records must be available for inspection and be beyond reproach)

PRINCIPLE # 47: **When dealing with financial transactions—all actions should be beyond reproach both in reality and in terms of perceptions by others**

WHETHER TO INCORPORATE OR NOT— THAT IS THE $64,000 QUESTION

There are both advantages and disadvantages of incorporating as a support group or club. Being an unincorporated association or entity only necessitates a simple set of by-laws that defines membership, provides for the election of officers, the holding of meetings, and includes a statement of purposes. Usually it is not even necessary to file any documents in a public office.

A recognized (by the Internal Revenue Service, IRS) non-profit corporation may make it possible for the organizers to secure a tax-exempt status for the organization. While being a non-profit corporation has specific advantages relating to possible tax deductibility of contributions, there are rather strict tax laws, both federal and state, that must be complied with in an exacting manner. In this instance, the organization's documents, by-laws, and constitution must clearly stipulate that it exists for a non-profit and charitable purpose, i.e., is established to promote educational and sport activities, as well as meet other stringent requirements as set forth in the tax codes.

It should be noted, however, that it is not necessary for the support organization to be incorporated as a non-profit entity in order for the organization to play an integral and significant role in generating tax-deductible contributions for the school's athletic program or for a city or municipal recreation department. This may be accomplished by having such contributions and donations *made directly* to the school's development or alumni office or to the foundation or development office within the recreation department of the city or town—where such contributions might, in some instances, qualify the contributions as tax deductible (assuming that the respective development, alumni, or foundation office has successfully obtain tax exempt status on the basis of being a not-for-profit entity). Of course, in the final analysis, it is appropriate, for one's peace of mind, to confirm the actual interpretation of the federal and state laws with an accountant, attorney or a representative of the Internal Revenue Service.

PRINCIPLE # 48: *Never assume that contributions to sport or recreation organizations are tax exempt—always obtain an official interpretation from one's accountant, attorney or from the IRS itself*

BENEFITS TO THE MEMBERS OF THE SPORT SUPPORT GROUP

Why do people belong to sport support groups? There is no single answer to this question. Many people like to be associated with sports, with sport activities, with athletes, and with staff members who make up the sports scene. Others like to have a role in making significant contributions to a worthy cause. Parents of current, future, or former athletes join because of their children. Some individuals desire to pay back to the sporting "world" some of the benefits that they or their family received as athletes. And still others do it for the pure enjoyment they receive through such association and efforts. Whatever the reasons, and they are both numerous and varied, there are both tangible and intangible benefits that booster club and support group members enjoy.

Students at a Western Illinois basketball game celebrate winning a pizza during a Papa John's promotion for being the loudest fans in Western Hall

In terms of why any individual would want to join a SSG, "each booster has a different need or motivation for becoming involved" (Robinson, 1999, p. 42). In many situations, people who join or sustain their membership in support organizations often qualify to receive any number of tangible benefits. Frequently, there is a sliding scale of benefits accruing to those members who join the booster organization at varying levels or within specific categories. This is especially true at the larger colleges and universities, although it need not be the exclusive property of such programs.

SPECIFIC GIFTS ACCRUING TO DONORS CONTRIBUTING TO THE SPORT OR RECREATION PROGRAM AND THE SUPPORT ORGANIZATION

Generally speaking, the range of benefits or gifts that are provided to donors may include, but not be limited, to the list provided below. The larger the program, naturally the more options there are in terms of benefits that might be made available to contributors to the sport or recreation program *and* to the support group organization. The range of benefits that the sports promoter might provide for contributors include: (Briggs & Duffy, 1987; Bronzan, 1986; Jiannakis & Branstein, 1983).

1. Preferred parking
2. Complimentary or reduced price tickets
3. Special events ticket priority
4. Dinner and banquet seating priority
5. Plaque or other gift items (premiums) to recognize donor
6. Invitation to social events
7. VIP lounge privilege membership card
8. Periodic newsletters

9. Press guide(s) and other publications
10. Ticket and seating priority (purchase)—various sports
11. Mention and recognition in game programs
12. Away game ticket priority
13. Travel with specific teams
14. Access to press box or other special areas for special teams and/or events
15. Specific apparel to identify donors and contributors
16. Private booth for home contests
17. Auto decal(s)
18. Free golf at university course
19. Free or reduced membership in college health/wellness center
20. Scholarship named after donor
21. Building named after donor
22. Dinner to honor donor
23. Perpetual award given in donor's name
24. Others . . .

One such membership plan initiated some years ago at the College at Brockport (State University of New York) a NCAA Division III athletic program, provided corresponding tangible benefits accruing to members of its sport support group (SSG) at varying membership levels. This plan has numerous levels of memberships (including one for corporate sponsorship) with each level possessing different benefits that accrue to the purchaser of the membership in the support group. See appendix B.

Other educational institutions have initiated similar programs. Slippery Rock University, a Division II institution, is one such school. Another is Temple University, a major NCAA Division I basketball power located in Philadelphia. Its Temple Owl Club provided various membership/donor levels and corresponding benefits as part of its effort to attract donors and boosters). And, St. Bonaventure University, a small Catholic school with a NCAA Division I basketball program, was able to raise $750,000 in less than a year and a half through the use of a similar effort as part of an annual giving campaign—rather than as a booster club membership program (Diles, 1996). Just like the College at Brockport effort, that the plans of Temple University, Slippery Rock University, and St. Bonaventure utilized different "giving levels" with each level providing donors with different benefits—the greater the donation, the greater the benefit.

CONTROLLING POTENTIAL NEGATIVE "OUTSIDE" INFLUENCES

The fear of the potential abuse of power and the concern over the balance between positive and negative influences that booster, support groups or influential individual donors might wield are the principle arguments generally expressed in opposition to such sport organizations. This abuse of power and exertion of negative influence is exemplified in the situation in which donors to a high school or collegiate athletic program feel that they have an automatic right, or even an obligation, to exert extreme pressure in terms of how the athletic department is managed or administered in terms of programmatic areas, finances and personnel, just to mention a few areas of concern.

A case in point can be found in the *Sports Illustrated* article by Dohrmann (2001) that described how "a bullying North Dakota alumnus built the school a $100 million rink but tore its campus asunder" (p. 45). The article describes how a wealthy donor came to exert what many felt to be undue influence over the decisions that rightly belonged to the institution because of significant promises of donations. This article illustrates the potential dangers that can exist for a sport program as well as for an educational institution when the "tail" (a potential influential donor) "wags the dog" (the sport program or organization). Inappropriate influence over decisions belonging to the sport organization should not be tolerated by either the sport administration or by the administration of the sponsoring organization—regardless of the potential loss of donations from individuals and/or groups.

Dr. William F. Stier, Jr., former junior high, high school, and university athletic director, and currently Distinguished Service Professor and Director of the Athletic Administration Graduate Program at the College at Brockport (State University of New York), was quoted as saying:

> The only reason for booster clubs is to raise money and give support for the various programs at the school. Once a club raises money, its job is finished. It should have no say in how the money is spent. It should all go through the athletic director. Coaches should not be able to go to the club and pitch various fundraising projects. When that happens, the club is out of control. Whoever determines how the money is spent has all the control (Bradley, 1993, pp. 17, 18)

At the University of Massachusetts, John Nitardy, then Executive Director of Athletic Development and Marketing, was instrumental in totally revamping its booster club program. The result was an umbrella organization that controlled the use of all funds generated. Boosters could still donate money to a specific team but the athletic administration and the coach would determine how the funds would be used. Another change was that the funds generated by supporters were to enhance the athletic program (teams), not support or fundamentally fund the program or a specific team. Nitardy's efforts resulted in a situation in which *donors were given the flexibility to support the team(s) that they favored without being in a position to decide the priorities of the athletic department or program* (Bradley, 1993).

Chapter 3: Booster Clubs and Support Groups 71

While solicitation of outside input is healthy and often advisable, when such input hinders the normal operation of the sport or recreation program, it becomes interference rather than meaningful assistance. On the other hand, a tax-paying citizen should not lose rights just because an individual elects to become a member of a support group, such as a booster club. One of the solutions to this potential problem is to have a very clear delineation as to what is acceptable and unacceptable behavior of the booster club itself, as well as its members. With the proper organizational document coupled with skilled and dedicated leadership, the so-called booster organization or support entity can become an invaluable ally to the total sport or recreation program, the staff, and the organization itself.

> ***PRINCIPLE # 49:*** *Sport and recreation managers must be constantly vigilant for any abuse of power and exertion of negative influence by support groups*

HANDLING THE "THREE O'CLOCK BOOSTER WONDERS"

Another real concern to sport managers and administrators is the so-called "three o'clock booster wonder." It is imperative that the administrators in charge of the fundraising and promotional efforts be aware of this category of would-be helpers and be able to identify and deal with them.

These "three o'clock wonders" are those individuals who *talk* about doing great things but rarely, if ever, actually produce. They are similar to the high school athletes who do great and show much promise during the 3 o'clock practice but, when times comes for the actual athletic contest, when production really count, these would-be performer fall flat on their faces. Often, these individuals are honest, well-meaning persons who would like to be able to do what they say they want to do—the problem is that they cannot or will not perform or produce. *They are talkers and not doers.* No coach would want to be saddled with a "three o'clock wonder athlete" who talks a great "game" during the three o'clock, weekday practice sessions, but, when it comes time to actually produce during the 8 p.m. game on Friday night, the result is utter failure. Similarly, no person responsible for a fundraising wants to have to rely upon and count on the services of someone who is all talk but who cannot or will not perform up to expectations.

> ***PRINCIPLE # 50:*** *Beware the "three o'clock booster wonder" who is all bluster and little action*

The "three o'clock booster wonder" frequently takes a significant toll in terms of motivation from others within the group, steals the time and drains the energy from those who are, or could be, the true producers. They end up taking far more in terms of time, effort and resources than they contribute to the sport or recreation program. The best course of action in terms of handling these "three o'clock booster wonders" is to isolate them in such a fashion that they cannot do any real harm to the efforts of the organization, without (if possible) alienating them completely.

REFERENCES

Berry, L. (2001). Balancing booster budgets. *Athletic Management, XIII*(2), 31-33, 35-36.

Briggs, J., Jr. & Duffy, J. (1987). *The official soccer fundraiser's guide.* North Palm Beach, Florida: Soccer Industry Council of America.

Bradley, M. (1993, October/November). Controlling the fanfare: A booster club can provide much needed support—As long as it is kept under reins. *Athletic Management, V*(6), 15, 17-21.

Bronzan, R.T. (1986). *Public Relations, promotions, and Fund-raising for Athletic and Physical Education Programs.* Daphne, Alabama: United States Sports Academy Publishing House. Copyright 1977, by John Wiley & Sons, Inc.

Diles, D.L. (1996). Turning on the revenue stream. *Athletic Management, VIII*(11), 51-52, 54.

Dohrmann, G. (2001, October 8). Face off. *Sports Illustrated, 95*(14), 44-49.

Hessert, K. (1999, August/September). Courting your boosters. *Athletic Management, XI*(5), 9, 10.

Kramer, W.D., et al. (1988). *Guide to Title IX & intercollegiate Athletics.* Squire, Sanders & Dempsey and the National Collegiate Athletic Association. Mission, Kansas.

Lipsey, Richard A. (1992). *Sports market place.* New Jersey: Princeton.

Mauro, T. (1992, February 27). Sex bias law applied to schools. *USA Today*, p. 1-A.

May, M. (1990). A booster club can work miracles. *Athletic Director, 7*(4), 24.

Operating costs for athletics continue to climb. (1990, October). *Athletic Director, 7*(10), 10.

Oregon high school cancels athletic program. (1990, October). *Athletic Director, 7*(10), 15.

Robinson, M.J. (1999). Booster club blues? *Athletic Management, X*(X), 40-42.

Stier, W.F., Jr. (1990, January 3). *Fund raising tactics and promotional practices for intercollegiate athletic programs.* Presentation made at the National Convention of the National Collegiate Athletic Association (NCAA)—Professional Development Seminar, Dallas, Texas.

Stier, W.F., Jr. (1999, summer). A fundraising and promotion primer for sport: Part One. *Applied Research in Coaching and Athletics Annual 1999, 14*, 219-242.

Stier, W.R., Jr. (2010). *Coaching: Becoming a successful athletic coach.* (3rd edition). Boston, MA: American Press

Sunday Democrat and Chronicle, (1988, August 21). Rochester, New York, p. 3-C.

DISCUSSION QUESTIONS

1. Summarize the history of booster clubs and explain implications in today's society, if any. Be specific in providing details.

2. Explain the rationale behind the statement that "ideally, support groups or booster clubs should provide for enhancement funding only" in contrast to the belief that "such clubs should provide for essentials."

3. What should administrators be aware of when contemplating the making of changes within the organization relative to fundraising and provide suggestions as to what to do and not do when faced with making such changes.

4. What are the advantages of having a single support group versus multiple groups and explain the challenges of establishing either as well as making a change from one type to another. What are the advantages of having multiple groups over a single support group?

5. Provide a summary of the advantages and disadvantages of having various terms of office for both officers and board members as well as having/not having term limits for each.

4 | THE IMPORTANCE OF PLANNING IN FUNDRAISING ACTIVITIES

Breaking ground after a successful capital campaign

CHAPTER HIGHLIGHTS

This chapter will emphasize:

- The importance of planning
- The proper cultivation and use of centers of influence
- Liability considerations in fundraising
- Insurance considerations when fundraising
- The essence of *strategic planning* in terms of fundraising
- The *ten commandments* of fundraising
- The *rifle approach* to fundraising
- The *shotgun approach* to fundraising
- The *program evaluation review technique*
- The value of *soft* and *hard* data
- The need to follow federal and state tax laws

THE IMPORTANCE OF PLANNING

Without the establishment of agreed upon or recognized objectives and goals, there is little possibility of meaningful or purposeful activity in the future. Planning is an essential ingredient in the establishment of objectives or goals of any fundraising or promotional effort. However, in the planning process it is imperative that one does not lose sight of what has been attempted, successfully as well as unsuccessfully, in the past. The success of fundraising strategies and promotional activities revolve around seven essential components. Refer to figure 4.1.

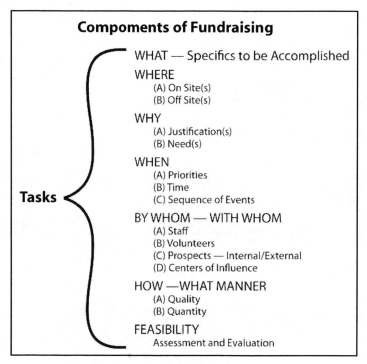

Figure 4.1 Components of Fundraisisng

PRINCIPLE # 51: *Learn from others—build upon prior experiences, one's own and those of others*

One learns from prior successes, as well as prior failures, our own and those of others. The important thing is to *learn*—period. Taking stock of what has been successful in prior times, in similar and dissimilar situations, is important. It enables one to assess, evaluate, and eliminate errors and time wasters. It enables one to replace ineffective, inefficient efforts with

Chapter 4: The Importance of Planning in Fundraising Activities 77

tactics that are effective, efficient, and successful in reaching objectives and goals. This is because recognizing the critical factors that determine success and/or failure enables one to identify those principles that might be applicable in circumstances that currently exist. Thus, we learn from the mistakes as well as the correct decisions and actions of others. One doesn't have to reinvent the wheel when planning and implementing fundraising programs or promotional activities. One should not be too proud to borrow, beg, and adopt ideas and successful techniques, tactics, and activities relating to public relations strategies, promotional activities and fundraising efforts.

The principle is clear, *one must be willing to learn from others*, in terms of (1) the setting of reasonable objectives and goals, (2) the selection of appropriate tactics and strategies, (3) the actual implementation process of those programs, activities, and projects designed to meet the then established objectives and goals, and (4) the assessment of one's activities insofar as their effectiveness and efficiency in getting the task(s) successfully completed.

> **PRINCIPLE # 52:** *Strategic planning is necessary for the successful generation of resources for sport causes*

APPROPRIATE STRATEGIC PLANNING

Just as real estate has the aphorism of location, location and location, the maxim of fundraising is planning, planning, and even more planning. Only with sufficient, timely and advance planning will fundraising efforts reach their maximum potential in terms of generating financial resources, positive public relations and effective publicity.

Fundraisers, as strategists or tacticians, must be able to decide on a specific master plan of attack. They must agree upon a strategy involving tactics, resources and timing designed to raise money within the confines or limitations of available resources, established priorities, and within a specific timetable. The use of an appropriate strategy enables knowledgeable decisions to be made. Proper planning also involves the setting of priorities coupled with realistic timetables, the elimination of conflicts, the securing of sufficient lead-time to allow for proper preparation, and the involvement of adequate staff in the project.

Essentials of Planning

When thinking about conducting any fundraising project there are literally hundreds of ideas (and questions) that may pop into one's mind. The challenge is where to begin, both for the neophyte and the experienced fundraiser. A successful fundraising project necessitates that a plan, a strategy, be established before one actually commits to a specific fundraising project; and, certainly before actually beginning to implement any part of the fundraising effort. Yet, this is not always what happens, to the regret of those would-be fundraisers who start off on their trek to generate additional resources without considering every aspect of a fundraising effort. The result, not surprisingly, is failure.

THE PLAN—WHAT IT IS AND WHAT IT IS NOT

The so-called plan is really a blueprint that directs the organizers along a series of steps that eventually leads to the successful conclusion of a meaningful, enjoyable and financially rewarding fundraising project. The plan needs to be complete, usually in great detail, in terms of what to do, who is to do to what, and when. The ultimate goal is to end up with a plan for a fundraising project that is both is feasible and financially successful.

A plan is certainly not a guarantee that the proposed project will succeed. Nevertheless the development of a plan provides the organizers with a glimpse into the possible future, both positive and negative. It is up to the organizers and planers to then make decisions that will most likely reduce (if not eliminate) the negative aspects of the project and enhance the likelihood of eventual success. Planning is step # 1.

PIA—PLANNING IN ADVANCE

Towards this end it is necessary to make some early decisions in terms of priorities and specific objectives in light of one's particular situation and circumstances. And, in order to arrive at these decisions it is necessary to look at several factors relating to one's existing situation and the special circumstances that might exist presently or in the immediate future. To do this it is imperative that one engages in PIA—*planning in advance*.

PRINCIPLE # 53: *Know in advance how you are going to spend the monies generated through your fundraising efforts*

Planning is the essential element in the fundraising process. Without it the sponsors are merely flying by the seats of their pants. Success of any project, without careful advance planning, is as much a factor of luck as it is of competency. Planning helps reduce or eliminate the reliance on luck and substitutes one's skills and knowledge into the fundraising equation. As a result there is a far greater likelihood of any given fundraising project to be successful with adequate planning and accurate foresight

INITIAL STEPS

In the initial stages of (PLANNING) fundraising, there are really three very important steps that must be completed. The *first* is the determination of the need to raise money. That

Chapter 4: The Importance of Planning in Fundraising Activities 79

is, can the fundraising efforts be justified? The *second* is the decision making process itself—deciding on what exactly will be done and how. That is, deciding upon tactics or strategies. The *third* is the approval process—the gaining of endorsement, of permission for the actual implementation of the plan from all appropriate parties, prior to the initiation of the activities.

BEFORE ONE STARTS—IMPORTANT EARLY DECISIONS TO MAKE

There are several key decisions that must be made prior to the actual initiation of any specific attempt to raise funds. These decisions will help forge the direction in which the fundraising activity will take in the future and will define the parameters of the fundraising efforts. These decisions will also help gain the approval of the appropriate higher administrators by revealing that a sound examination has been made of all aspects of the proposed project(s). These decisions revolve around the following:

1. Realization that promotion and fundraising starts at home. Just as the ripples expand outward when a pebble is thrown into a pond, so, too, should efforts to promote and raise funds start at the very center of the sport program—that is, with the participants, the staff, and members of the athletic entity. If those close to the sport program will not participate and significantly contribute, how can outside constituencies be expected to do so?

2. Determination of whether the fundraising activity is to be considered a *one-shot effort* or as a *repeat* activity or as an *annual event*. This reaches to the basic philosophy of the organization itself and the purpose for which the fundraising activity is being established. If the activity is an annual event, during the second year the homework time is reduced by 80-90%, the planning or meeting time could be reduced by 50-60%, while the project development time may be reduced by as much as 40-50%.

3. Determination of the *number* of fundraising activities that will be undertaken within a specified period of time. In terms of major fundraising efforts, it is generally conceded that the mastery of a single successful fundraising project, in a professional fashion, should be achieved before a second or a new fundraising activity is undertaken. Spreading oneself or an organization too thin prevents organizers from doing justice to any one single activity. This is a common fault and should be guarded against. When a major fundraising activity has proven to be successful and when the multitude of tasks involved with the project have been mastered, then it might be appropriate to think about planning for another major project.

> **PRINCIPLE # 54:** *The major difference between the* **shotgun** *and the* **rifle** *approach in fundraising involves whether prospects are "qualified" or not*

4. Determination of whether the *shotgun* or the *rifle* approach should be used in dealing with prospective contributors. The shotgun approach involves attempting to blanket a wide range of potential prospects, for example, sending out a mailing containing a request for contributions to everyone in the community. Contrast this approach with the rifle technique that involves zooming in on a select but smaller target population. For example, mailing the same request as cited above, but only to parents who have had children who were involved in sports at the school.

5. Determination of the worst case scenario in an effort to determine what could possibly go wrong at the worst possible time—then planning for that eventuality. Be aware of Murphy's Law that states that *anything that can go wrong will go wrong at the worse possible point in time*.

6. Determination of the criteria by which the fundraising activity will either be continued or terminated. At some point in time during every fundraising effort, there comes a time when a decision has to be made whether or not to continue the effort or activities to their ultimate conclusion. However, the criteria underlying this decision must be made prior to the actual start of the fundraising efforts.

Planning by Means of the Program Evaluation Review Technique

The *Program Evaluation Review Technique* (PERT) is a system or method of planning and controlling any project. The PERT system assists one to identify and prioritize all key components, steps or activities that must be completed in order to accomplish a given project or to successfully reach a specific goal. The PERT principle can be used to greatly facilitate the successful planning and implementation of any sophisticated fundraising or promotional project.

> **PRINCIPLE # 55:** *Use a variation of the program evaluation review technique (PERT) to plan the timing of appropriate steps in the fundraising and promotional process*

A simplified version of the PERT system involves the identification of all individual activities or steps that must ultimately be completed in order for the fundraising project to be successful. This listing of each and every major task or step is paramount for the successful utilization of the PERT principle. Essentially, once a complete and detailed list of such tasks and steps involved with the project is completed, the fundraiser then constructs a flow chart involving a *time line* or *critical path*, figure 4.2. On this flow chart the fundraiser can then categorize the major tasks according to priorities and place each task, step or component along the time line or critical path.

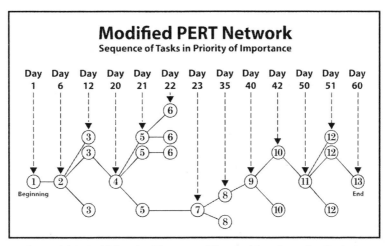

Figure 4.2 Prioritizing the Elements of Fundraising through a Variation of the Program Evaluation Review Technique [PERT]

This flow chart can also include the (1) amount of time, (2) the kinds of resources needed, and (3) specific human performance that will be required to accomplish each task. When viewing the modified PERT flow chart the fundraiser should be able to easily determine which task or job must be completed at any given point in time as well as which components or resources that must be in place prior to tackling a specific activity or task.

Kraus and Curtis (1977) suggest utilizing a "network" of essential activities established and plotted on a chart in a logical time sequence. The start as well as completion times for each component or activity should be shown to create a pictorial description of the time relationships of all of the steps, the activities or the components involved in the complete project.

> **PRINCIPLE # 56:** *The PERT network helps in prioritizing one's actions*

The major advantage for the PERT-type analysis is to keep the planners and administrators abreast of the progress toward the ultimate task or project at hand. The identification of each component or activity necessary to be completed prior to the realization of the ultimate goal is essential. So too, is the allocation of the amount of time necessary for the completion of each component or activity. Thus, the planners are able to better understand not only what must be accomplished prior to reaching the ultimate objective but are able to monitor the progress of the attempt to do so throughout the time spent on task(s).

The Ten Commandments of Fundraising

Those involved in fundraising would do well to subscribe to following *Ten Commandments* for planning any fundraising project or event that are presented below. These rules help the organizer(s) to insure that appropriate strategies and timely decisions are made so that the fundraising effort will be efficient and effective, resulting in receipt of financial resources as well as quality public relations and positive publicity (Stier, 1998).

1. Develop an overall fundraising plan—a plan for the present and a plan for the future
2. Anticipate the worst case scenario and plan accordingly
3. Select the easiest and most feasible fundraising project in light of one's particular situation and circumstances—keep things simple
4. Don't compete unnecessarily with other groups, organizations or with oneself
5. Select efforts and projects that are appropriate (both in content and in timeliness) for your situation and the existing circumstances
6. Adequately and appropriately publicize and promote the sponsor's efforts and the fundraising project itself
7. Evaluate your fundraising efforts on a continuous basis
8. Be sure and follow all laws, regulations and rules as they affect your fundraising efforts
9. Work closely with volunteers, educate, train and motivate them
10. After the fundraising effort, assess what went well and what might be improved should the event be repeated in the future and always express your appreciation and thanks to those who have helped you with the fundraising project

NASPE's Position Paper—"Implementing Fundraising Project in Public Schools When State Funding is Cut or Nonexistent"

Brent Steurwald, then athletic director at New York's Shenendehowa High School, and a former chairperson of the *National Association for Sport and Physical Education's Coaches Council,* wrote the following position paper (involving ten statements) for **NASPE** that dealt with "fundraising on the high school level for those districts faced with budget cuts or inadequate funding" (Cohen, 1991, pp. 30-31). These statements are appropriate today as well as when they were penned.

1. When faced with budget shortfalls, do not fragment the existing program by eliminating sports or cutting specific individual programs. Be proactive, not reactive. Programs lost are virtually impossible to recover.
2. Establish well-defined, ethical guidelines for control of fundraising events
3. Do not engage in small, nickel-and-dime fundraising schemes
4. Do not use individual athletes in any fundraising scheme
5. Never adopt a pay-to-play program. However, you may have to take a position of accepting donations from participating families
6. Engage in high-yield, low-energy fundraising tactics
7. Do not tie coaching salaries or supplements to fundraising efforts
8. Once funding is accomplished, the funds must be subject to acceptable auditing procedures, under the supervision of the school district
9. Outside support is limited only to fundraising. Administration of programs will remain in the hands of the school authorities who normally conduct these activities.
10. Continue to lobby legislatures, school board members and the general pubic, and educate them that athletics are currently in place because of a definite need, within the total educational package.

Gambling/tests of skills are always exciting contests

ATTEMPTING TO INFLUENCE OPINIONS OF OTHERS—
USE OF CENTERS OF INFLUENCE

Those who are associated in fundraising and promotional activities are, for the most part, involved in changing or reinforcing opinions of others and getting people to act in a specific fashion—that is, to contribute money or some other commodity of value. In attempting to approach potential donors, it is often wise to obtain the assistance of an intermediary (*center of influence*) to introduce you, etc.

> **PRINCIPLE #57:** Centers of Influence *can open doors and can provide instant credibility for fundraisers*

A center of influence is an individual who has influence with the prospect. This is especially important if the potential donor is a stranger and/or someone who travels in a different social or business circle. Obtaining a mutual friend to serve as that all-important "bridge" via an introduction can be a significant boost in building one's credibility. In addition to the use of centers of influence in an attempt to influence opinions of others, there are six other tactics commonly utilized in attempting to exert an influence on the decision-making ability of others.

These include the (1) use of authority figures, (2) use of respected individuals, (3) use of popular idols, (4) use of persuasive arguments, (5) use of emotional statements, and the (6) use of needs satisfaction. Naturally, use of any of the above tactics depends upon the circumstances one finds oneself in, as well as the status of the prospective donor.

DETERMINATION OF NEEDS

> **PRINCIPLE # 58:** *Develop a strong case for your needs (justification for support and assistance)*

There must be a good reason to be involved in fundraising. Don't become involved merely because others do it or because fundraising is perceived as glamorous or big time. The best position to be in for school personnel, such as an athletic director or coach, is to have the school or organization take the posture that there will be adequate funds available for the sport and leisure program via the regular budget process of the school, etc.

This means that there might not be a need to raise funds. While this is undoubtedly true in some situations, in the vast majority of sport organizations and schools this is far from the case. In the majority of schools, colleges, and other sport and recreation programs there is a real need to raise supplemental funds for the enrichment (if not for the bare essentials) of the sport and leisure experience for the participants.

Of course, even in those rare situations in which outside funding is not required there will still be a need to promote and publicize the athletic program. And, there still exists a need to implement a positive public relations program.

When one hears the phrase *fundraising* one immediately thinks of attempts to raise money by going outside of one's own organization to individuals, groups and organizations with a request for contributions or, perhaps, attempts to sell merchandise to members of the general public. And, one should not neglect two other avenues through which much needed support may be generated. Specifically, sport or recreation leaders should be aware that conceptually there are actually three sources ways of gaining much needed support, i.e., three sources of monies, for the sports program, figure 4.3.

The *first* so-called source of money lies in the general athletic operation itself. For every dollar that is saved through wise and efficient fiscal management within the sport organization—there is a corresponding reduction in the need to go "outside" to raise that dollar. In other words, one can raise money by saving money.

The *second* source of money is through the sponsoring organization itself. The organization (whether it is a recreation department, sports federation, high school, college or a youth sport organization) should be targeted for additional financial request(s) prior to attempting to go "outside" for funding. Being able to justify to the sponsoring organization the need for a greater share of the financial pie and to actually receive such monies reduces the amount of outside fundraising needed.

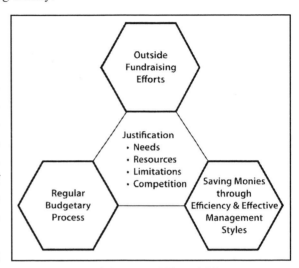

Figure 4.3 Sources of Financial Support

The *third* source of obtaining funding involves fundraising outside of the organization, the school, sport or recreation program itself. The objective, of course, is to raise sufficient funds and/or support that will enable the sport program to meet the specific needs of the participants and the various constituencies. Tapping a combination of sources as outlined above enables the sport administrators to take full advantage of every means possible to generate sufficient funds to support the various segments of their program.

However, regardless of how the financial resources are obtained, the money generated must be put to productive use by purchasing such items as uniforms, new lights for the field, team trophies, upgrade in terms of facilities, additional staff, etc., for the greater good of the program and the participants. The important point to remember is that these specific objectives (trophies, facilities, lights, vehicles, uniforms, etc.) are merely means to an end, merely tools to enable the program to achieve a higher, more important, and essential goal, that of meeting the needs of the participants so that the sport or recreation experience is indeed a wholesome and safe one.

REALIZATION OF GOALS AND OBJECTIVES

The realization of goals and objectives is a multifaceted challenge for those involved in promotional and fundraising efforts. The tasks involved in reaching any specific goal, whether that goal is an increase in generated revenue, additional spectators at a contest, increased public exposure, or an improved positive image of the program or specific event, are frequently affected by a wide variety of activities. These activities can be carried out under the auspices of (1) publicity, (2) marketing, (3) advertising, (4) sales, (5) promotions, (6) public relations, (7) fundraising, (8) positive opinions/attitudes and (9) accurate perceptions of reality, figure 4.4.

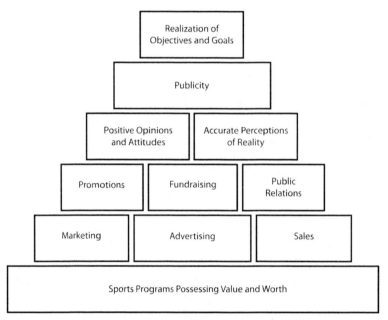

Figure 4.4 Realization of Goals

LIABILITY CONSIDERATIONS—
FUNDRAISING AND PROMOTIONAL ACTIVITIES

Promoters and sport fundraisers must be constantly aware of the potential for litigation as a result of the activities they sponsor. And litigation is increasing each year. In fact, we have become almost a society of litigants (Stier, 2010).

> **PRINCIPLE # 59:** *In terms of legal liability—one is judged by what a similarly educated, trained, experienced professional would have done in similar circumstances*

Negligence is the failure to act as a *reasonable* and *prudent* professional would have acted in a similar situation, assuming the person possessed similar educational credentials, practical experiences, training, and expertise. In short, we are judged by the standards set by our peers in similar circumstances when it comes to legal liability. And, the determination of what is reasonable care is directly affected by the age, sex, health, skill, maturity and reputation of the individuals involved in the activity or program. Naturally, greater care and closer supervision must be shown when dealing with youngsters in grade school than with 21-year-old college students or other adults.

Generally speaking, there are *five factors* that must be present to be guilty of negligence. *First*, there must be a duty or obligation that an individual has for the person who becomes injured. That is, a person must have responsibility for another person. One must have an obligation for caring or protecting another individual. *Second*, was that duty breached? Did the person fail to perform the assigned duty, either by an act of omission or through commission of an unsafe act? *Third*, was the act of omission (*not doing what one should do*) or commission (*doing something one should not have done*) the result, the proximate cause of the injury? *Fourth*, was the injury avoidable or unavoidable? Or, was the person injured partly at fault or was there a third party/person who shares the blame for the injury? *Fifth*, and lastly, did the plaintiff actually receive an injury, physical, emotional, or psychological?

The Purple and Gold fundraiser complete with a silent and live auction along with dinner, to raise money for Western Illilnois University Intercollegiate Athletics

In defending against the charge of negligence, one attempts to prove that one or more of the five factors listed above are not applicable. Other possible defenses against being found negligent are:

1. Assumption of risk—the person involved in the activity recognizes and assumes that there are specific risks associated in the activity
2. Contributory negligence—the injured person was at fault (more difficult to prove when the person is a youngster)
3. Comparative negligence—the person who is injured is only partially deemed negligent. There is an apportionment of guilt or fault between the plaintiff and the defendant. As a result, there is a weighing or sharing of responsibility of negligence.
4. Act of God—an unforeseen and unpreventable act or event took resulting in injury

---

PRINCIPLE #60: *Practice foresight ("ounce of prevention") when it comes to preventing accidents—prevent, don't merely react*

Administrators and managers need to be reminded that the majority of litigation areas in sports revolve around seven specific areas. Hence, it is advisable for the fundraiser, in the planning of the sponsored activities, to take into consideration the need to insure that proper safety procedures are followed in terms of:

1. Supervision of the specific event by qualified and trained adult supervisors
2. Use of safe equipment and supplies
3. Use of appropriate and safe facilities, inspected prior to use
4. Proper instruction of those being asked to perform specific tasks
5. Use of appropriate vehicles driven by qualified adults
6. Warning of the dangers and perils which might be inherent in the activity
7. Provision of first aid and emergency care in the event of an injury

RISK MANAGEMENT FOR PREVENTING EXPOSURE TO NEGLIGENCE CHARGES

Risk management are popular "buzz words" in legal circles today (Maloy & Vivian, 1992). Risk management implies evaluating the risk(s) involved in any activity and planning for the worst case scenario. It is a matter of asking "what if" and then planning to prevent accidents from taking place. Essentially, risk management involves three major factors (Figone, 1989). *First*, the study of the hazards that might or do exist. *Second*, the planning as to how to eliminate such hazards or potential for injuries. And, *third*, the planning on what course of action to take in case of accidents that might occur in spite of one's best efforts.

PRINCIPLE # 61: *Risk management involves evaluating potential risks and asking "what if"—then taking appropriate action to prevent potential disasters*

Factors that are taken into consideration in determining whether or not one is negligent in the conduct of a fundraising activity include (Nygaard & Boone, 1985):

1. Who sponsored the activity (school or booster club)?
2. What is the age of the individual injured in fundraising?
3. What is the type and extent of training provided?
4. Were directions obeyed or not?
5. Was adequate supervision and warning provided by appropriate persons?
6. Were hazardous conditions and specific dangers inherent in the activity or product?

7. What was the extent of product liability for those products sold by the sports program (Dennison, 1985)?
8. Did the injury occur on school property? Were there witnesses?
9. Was the accident/injury foreseeable? Was it preventable?
10. What was the approximate cause of the accident/injury?
11. Who was responsible for the accident/injury?
12. Was a so-called standard liability release obtained from the participants if the event or activity could be considered inherently risky, i.e., 10-K race, a marathon, etc?

Some fundraising projects have resulted in tragic results. For example, in 1997 (Teenager dies) a youngster died in a fundraiser that involved a boxing match. The young man, age 17, died when he fell to the mat of a makeshift boxing ring that was part of a fundraising project. Another example of a tragic consequence following a promotional activity associated with a football game occurred in 1996 when a woman was accidentally killed after being landed on by a parachutist who was part of a half-time promotional event at a high school in Spearman, Texas (Brewington, 1996).

Of course, sport entities can get sued for just about anything. Dr. Pepper was sued in an Austin (Texas) court, as a result of a football contest ("Pepper Punt Payoff") the company promoted. It seems that a woman, who won the opportunity to attempt to catch 3 footballs that were launched from a machine that simulated punts, claimed that all 3 balls were uncatchable. Had the contestant caught one ball the prize would have been $50,000; if two balls had been caught she would have taken home $250,000; and, if all three attempts were successful she would have won a million dollars. The suit was for the million dollars that the women said she was denied winning (Dr. Pepper Sued, 1999).

INSURANCE CONSIDERATIONS— FUNDRAISING AND PROMOTIONAL ACTIVITIES

Check with the school's ore recreational department's attorney and with the insurance company to determine liability insurance coverage for activities in which the booster club or sport support group (SSG) is engaged, both on the organization's grounds and away from the site. Similarly, booster clubs need to be concerned about securing adequate insurance in their own right if they cannot be covered under the school's umbrella policy.

PRINCIPLE # 62: *Sport and recreation entities must be insured, either through self-insurance or second party insurance*

Naturally, all activities and all actions by individuals associated with the sport support group (SSG) and the sport fundraising activities should be beyond approach. Everyone associated with the fundraising effort must exercise extreme caution in his or her daily actions in order to reduce the likelihood of improper action (negligence through omission or commission) that could result in a legal wrong to another person or person's property. The goal is to adhere to the necessary standards of performance, supervision, and safe and prudent conduct by *all* personnel, paid and volunteer, associated with the sport fundraising efforts.

APPLICABLE FEDERAL AND STATE TAX LAWS — FUNDRAISING AND PROMOTIONAL ACTIVITIES

The process of incorporation in most states is not a complicated one. The laws governing businesses and the creation of corporations vary from state to state. Some states do not mandate that an attorney must file the necessary incorporation papers. However, it is wise to consult with a lawyer conversant with corporation law prior to making a final decision whether or not to incorporate. To obtain definitive information regarding the laws in one's own state, one has only to contact the Secretary of State in the state in which the organization exists to obtain up-to-date facts relative to incorporating the fundraising entity as a not-for-profit organization.

> **PRINCIPLE # 63:** *Examine carefully the advantages and challenges associated with incorporating the fundraising organization*

The Internal Revenue Service (IRS) has specific tax laws governing organizations that are organized for profit, as well for those organizations that have been organized (and meet the requirements of the laws) for charitable, education, and religious purposes. There are three categories recognized by the IRS under which organizations might be categorized as not-for-profit. These include (1) charitable, education, and religious agencies, (2) social welfare organization and civic leagues, and (3) social recreational clubs. In this respect, it is highly advisable to contact the Internal Revenue Service and/or a knowledgeable accountant or attorney to examine the benefits, limitations, and requirements that are applicable for the so-called profit and not-for-profit businesses and corporations.

PERMITS, LICENSES AND PERMISSION

We tend to live in a very regulated and regimented society today. Sport and recreation managers should remain cognizant of this fact since many of the activities associated with public relations, publicity, fundraising, selling, promoting, etc., may fall under jurisdiction of a particular rule, regulation or law at a local, state and/or national level.

Some municipalities require a special permit and insurance for skydivers to jump into a sport stadium. It is frequently necessary to obtain city, township, county or state permission (via permits) to conduct gambling-type activities or games of chance. Ditto with alcohol, wine and spirits. Today, almost every community has rules and regulations governing the preparation and serving (sale) of food and drink items.

> *PRINCIPLE # 64:   We live in a society with many rules, regulations and laws governing our actions, both personally and professionally—being aware of such edicts prevents problems and difficulties*

When concession or food operations are involved in any fundraising project it is essential that all health department regulations be followed in terms of food storage, preparation, and sale. Also, the promoters must be responsible for securing all appropriate permits and licenses that regulate food and concession operations. Typically, such permits may be secured from the municipal offices or the office of the town clerk.

Restrictions on Selling and Distributing

Some fundraising activities involve the door-to-door, hawking or peddling of items to sell or the distribution of (free) printed materials. These items can be tickets, candy, chances, printed flyers or announcements—or almost anything. In some communities it may be necessary to obtain a specific license or permit to do this type of activity.

More and more communities are passing ordinances that prohibit, restrict, or regulate efforts to hawk, peddle or solicit potential customers on a so-called door-to-door basis within the confines of the community. Similarly, many communities even regulate the distribution of (free) materials on a door-to-door basis. Towards this end many cities, towns and villages have instituted specific requirements that must be met by individuals and organizations seeking to peddle, hawk, sell, or distribute within the geographical limits of the community.

Licensing Transient Retail Merchants

Other related ordinances have been implemented by some towns or communities in terms of restricting the activities of so-called transient retail merchants. A transient retail business is frequently defined as a business being conducted for a period of less than six or eight months and can take place within a building, a motor vehicle, a tent, in the street, on the sidewalk or in front of a building. Typically, the transient retail merchant ordinance is aimed at restricting or regulating village, town or city flower vendors, furniture salespersons, car washers, and art merchants displaying their merchandise and services at street intersections or in parking lots.

Exemptions from Licenses and Permits

Licensing or permit exemptions commonly exist for numerous worthwhile organizations such as bona fide charitable organizations, groups from the area school district or college(s), recreation departments, city sponsored organizations and nationally recognized service organizations or clubs. *However, not all communities provide for such blanket exemptions.* Thus, it behooves the promoters of a proposed fundraising project to check with the local municipal office (town clerk) having responsibility for issuing the permits or licenses to see what, if anything, must be obtained prior to actually initiating a fundraising effort that might fall under the local hawking, peddling and soliciting ordinance.

PRINCIPLE # 65: *It is far better to be safe than sorry when it comes to securing permission to engage in a particular fundraising, promotion, publicity or public relations activity*

In summary, it is always best to check with local, county, and state authorities to insure that the proposed promotional and fundraising activity meets all *legal* requirements. It is indeed embarrassing and counter-productive to find out after the fact that a law or regulation was violated out of either ignorance or negligence. Or, that a required permit or license was not obtained or a mandated report not appropriately filed in a timely fashion. When these mistakes and oversights take place it reveals that the fundraising organizers and managers were not operating at an acceptable level of competency. The result is a potentially embarrassing and damaging situation in terms of public relations and publicity—a fact that can quickly erode confidence in the competency levels of those involved in the fiasco, as viewed by others.

Alcoholic Beverages and Fundraising Projects

In order to serve alcoholic beverages at a fundraising event, you must first secure the necessary state and/or local liquor licenses or permit. The type of permits required varies among locales. Some jurisdictions require specific permits for hard liquor (scotch, whiskey, vodka, gin, etc.); another for light spirits (beer, wine, and champagne). Other areas require a specific license if alcohol will be served with food and not purchased separately. Still another permit may be issued when a cash bar will be provided, and another when alcohol will be dispensed on a free basis. You must secure the appropriate permits for your individual community. Of course, the sponsoring organization may have other restrictions or prohibitions against serving alcohol, so check ahead of time to see what is permitted and what is prohibited.

Chapter 4: The Importance of Planning in Fundraising Activities 93

> **PRINCIPLE # 66:** *When serving alcohol, pay particular attention to prevent patrons leaving the sporting or recreational event while under the influence*

Organizers of a promotional and/or fundraising event where alcoholic beverages are served must also be alert to a situation in which a patron is becoming intoxicated. The negative consequences of such an event are significant not only for the patron but also for the sponsoring organization and the person who served the alcohol. Sponsors and planners of an event where a person consumes an excessive amount of alcohol are increasingly being held responsible by the courts for that person's actions. No sport or recreation group wants to be involved in scandal, so those responsible for planning and implementing an event involving alcohol must take assertive action to prevent both underage drinking and overindulgence by those who do drink. In addition, organizers should:

1. Post signs indicating that patrons will be asked for appropriate identification, and then carefully scrutinize the IDs
2. Make arrangements with a local cab company to drive home those who have overindulged in drink, or provide designated drivers among the volunteers of the sponsoring group
3. Encourage people attending the event to team up with friends who are willing to be designated drivers

These steps will help prevent negative consequences of excessive consumption and driving under the influence. These efforts will also enhance the image of the sponsoring organization as being sensible, caring, and proactive.

RESULTS ORIENTATION

Deciding upon a specific publicity campaign, fundraising strategy or promotional project is often easier said than done. As anyone who has ever been involved in sport knows all too well, talk is cheap. What counts are results. Nowhere is this truer than in the areas of fundraising, publicity and promotional activities. Although there are a 1001± different promotional tactics, fundraising activities and publicity plans that could be attempted—not every school, sport group or recreation organization can utilize such projects in an identical fashion without some customizing and adapting of the activities to fit the specific circumstances, resources, and parameters that affect one's own unique program.

Going through all of the motions of attempting to raise monies, doing all sorts of work and spending inordinate amounts of time attempting to raise funds are meaningless unless the results, i.e., the actual resources sought, are realized. The same can be said of public relations efforts and promotional activities. Results do count!

> **PRINCIPLE # 67:** *Mere practice and effort do not produce results*—**quality** practice *and* **quality** effort *produce results*

In the greater scheme of things, it is not necessarily how hard one works or how long one works, although these might be important ancillary considerations. Rather, it is how effective one is in doing those things that end in the desired *results*. We are living in an age of accountability. We work in a results-oriented society. Rightly or wrongly, we are judged by results—not how long or how hard one seemingly works at the job. This is especially true in terms of the publicity, fundraising and promotional arenas.

Individuals involved in the area of recreation or sport promotions, public relations and fundraising must be *goal oriented* and *success driven*. While effort expended and good intentions are important, it is far more important to have concrete results. Of course, that is easier to say than to accomplish. Many would-be or wannabe fundraisers and/or promoters exist. The number of successful, effective, and efficient fundraisers and promoters are far fewer in number.

How does one measure success? What criteria are used? Are anecdotal stories sufficient? Are mere feelings adequate? Or, is there a real need for hard, concrete data—information that stands up to the scrutiny of close examination? Although managers believe that results are important, it is obvious that it is easier to measure results in some areas than in others. All too frequently, and sometimes most unfortunately, especially in the world of amateur sports and recreational activities, anecdotal information and gut feelings form the foundation for many of the decisions made relating to fundraising, promotions, publicity and public relations.

It is, therefore, of the utmost importance to attempt to obtain objective, measurable data and figures, whenever possible. Doing so prevents projecting an image of a hit and miss operation. Doing one's homework by planning and conducting *feasibility research* (such as a pilot study), and assessing prior activities, is indicative of a professional approach. Such action helps to establish confidence and provides much needed experience to those involved in such work as fundraising, promotions and public relations. In fact, Mark Eisengrein, director of athletics at Valdosta State University, indicated that " . . . the most single important tool for any fundraiser is a reliable database and functional support software" (1994, p. 8).

> **PRINCIPLE # 68:** *It is very important to obtain reliable, objective, measurable data and figures to aid in the decision making process*

Administrators must be able to make timely and appropriate decisions within the realm of fundraising, promotions and public relations. These decisions result from one's experiences, level of competency, personality, education, training, and knowledge as well as from factual information in the form of soft or hard data. Ultimately, decisions are made upon one's interpretation of information and it is this information that the sport and recreation leader must have if informative, intelligent and correct decisions are to be the result.

COLLECTING AND STORING DATA FOR DECISION MAKING

Hard Data Collection

Some examples of measured results and data that can easily be collected include such information as the amount of money raised, the number of tickets sold, the number of people within a community, the number of specific organizations in the community, the number and type of other sport organizations within a geographical area, the demographic snapshot of the community, the number of prospective contributors within a specific area, the number of prospects contacted, the number of phone calls made, the number of individuals attending an event, the number of people contributing specific sums of money, and the number of programs printed and sold. The above may be referred to as *hard data* collection. A variety of decisions can be made on the basis of such information. And, it is possible to compare such information with other concrete data in a comparative analysis so that appropriate decisions can be made.

The local chamber of commerce, local newspapers, area libraries, schools, and even the community city hall are key sources of hard data about the community in which the sport program finds itself. Also, one's own records and files may well contain valuable information (data) that can aid in future fundraising, promotional, publicity and public relations efforts. This is why record keeping is so vital. The ultimate objective is to be able to find, collect, collate, and present, in a meaningful and understandable format, information that will prove to be helpful in making sound and defensible decisions relative to one's own efforts. In other words, decisions are able to be made based upon some type of reasonable rationale rather than mere anecdotal information or stories.

Research can be relatively inexpensive (Cohen, 1993). If you are working within a school, perhaps your own students could provide "working hands" as interns or as volunteers to collect, store and organize data. Or, if you are involved in a non-school organization, visit your local college or university and inquire of the sport management department or the business department and see if there might be students desiring to undertake such a data collection (manipulation) effort as part of a class project.

Soft Data Collection

There is another type of data collection and assessment that is often helpful when dealing with sports fundraising, promotions and public relations. This second type of data is called *soft data*. An example of soft data is commonly referred to as opinion research. Although more difficult and challenging to obtain, the data and results dealing with the opinions of individuals, the acceptance of ideas by others, the perceptions held by others, and reasons people act as they do, can be of great help in the decision making process for the sport and recreation manager. This type of data can be obtained through the use of surveys, as well as informal input gathered via conversations with others.

It is important to note that opinions of individuals are generally determined more by actual deeds and events than by mere words. Also, opinions are essentially determined and shaped by self-interests and tend to diminish without acute reinforcement by words or actual happenings. And, individuals tend to form more opinions, more easily, regarding specific goals and objectives than about the means and methods to reach these same goals and objectives.

Conducting opinion research involves three distinct but related activities. *First*, to assess the current situation. That is, what do people currently think about the sports program and why? *Second*, to determine how public opinion operates in the community in which one operates by attempting to identify the various forces that help shape public opinion. Every community has a different power structure that helps to formulate public opinion. *Third*, to utilize

---

PRINCIPLE # 69: *Opinion research is very important in helping decision makers arrive at appropriate choices*

---

testing before and after a specific period of time during which one's fundraising and/or promotional efforts will take place. For example, one might test a certain segment of the population for opinions and attitudes before and after a season of a specific sport **or** before and after a specific promotional project or change in personnel—in an effort to determine the extent of change, if any, that took place among the people involved during the interim.

It is clear that those involved in such activities as fundraising and promotions need to build upon a database of knowledge, information, and facts so that *accurate* and *timely decisions* can be made. A partial list of such information includes: (1) names of donors [past, current, potential], (2) past ticket sales [regular, special event, seasonal]; (3) mailing lists of representatives of news media [print, television, radio, web sites (blogs), etc], (4) identification of current and potential centers of influence, (5) summaries of past fundraising and promotional activities [successes and failures], (6) updated list of various publics and constituencies, (7) needs assessments of various constituencies, (8) membership list of the sport or recreation support organizations, (9) mailing addresses of parents and constituents, (10) mailing addresses of businesses and corporations, (11) activities of other sports related organizations, (12) listing of dates on which other sports activities are being held, and (13) amounts of money previously raised, etc.

> **PRINCIPLE # 70:** Sport fundraisers and promoters are in the business of determining the publics' needs and then meeting these same needs

There is a real advantage to ascertaining what people think about specific topics, particularly in terms of their actual or perceived needs, desires and preferences. With this knowledge, sport fundraisers and promoters can plan an appropriate course of action to meet the needs of the public(s) and to take advantage of people's perceptions. There is even an urgency to keep up-to-date as to what manner (whether positive, neutral or negative) various constituencies and segments of the general public hold one's sports program. In short, it becomes profitable to know the actual, as well as the perceived, needs of individuals and groups within the community.

Sport fundraisers, promoters and publicists are constantly involved in determining the needs (real or perceived) on behalf of the consumers, constituencies, or publics (or even creating the needs themselves, in some instances). Then it behooves the sport personnel to do whatever it takes to satisfy these same needs. Unless one is cognizant of the feelings and opinions of the potential donors, contributors, supporters, and consumers and unless the sport promoter recognizes the so-called needs of these same individuals and groups, how can the sport program(s) be publicized and promoted in an effective and efficient fashion?

Simply stated, there should be a match between the real and perceived needs of the various constituencies or segments of the public, and the offerings of the sport program. Without such a match many of these needs cannot be adequately satisfied.

REFERENCES

Brewington, P. (1996, October 7). Parachutist's mishap kills woman on ground. *USA Today*, p. 15-C.

Cohen, A. (1991). Money comes into play. *Athletic Business, 15*(2), 25-28, 30-31.

Cohen, A. (1993). Research for tomorrow. *Athletic Business, 17*(1), 16.

Dennison, M. (1985). Product liability: A legal dilemma. In H. Appenzeller. (ed.). *Sports and law, contemporary issues.* Charlottesville, VA: The Michie Co.

Dr. Pepper sued for football contest. (1999, December 12). *Democrat and Chronicle*, p. 2-D.

Eisengrein, M. (1994, December). Fund raising in a non-division I environment. *Athletic Administration, 29*(12), 9.

Figone, A. (1989). Seven major legal duties of a coach. *Journal of Physical Education, Recreation and Dance, 60*(7), 71-75.

Kraus, R., & Curtis, J. (1977). *Creative administration in recreation and parks* (2nd edition). St. Louis: The C. V. Mosby Company.

Maloy, B.P., & Vivian, J. (1992, May). Risky business. *Athletic Business, 15*(5), 43-46.

Nygaard, G., & Boone, T. (1985). *Coach's guide to sports law*. Champaign, Il: Human Kinetics.

Stier, W.F., Jr., (1998). It's All in the Planning. *Athletic Management, X*(6), 26, 28.

Stier, W.F., Jr., (2010). *Coaching: Becoming a successful athletic coach* (3rd edition). Boston, MA: American Press.

Teen-ager dies in boxing fund-raiser. (1997, May 26). *Democrat and Chronicle*, p. 2-D.

DISCUSSION QUESTIONS

1. Explain the role(s) of an effective center-of-influence and how one might secure the services of such an individual. Finally, provide some specific examples of how such a person can actually help the sport or recreation entity in terms of fundraising and promotions.

2. What are some sound steps that one should take relative to preventing situations in which you (your group) might be successfully sued because of negligence surrounding a fundraising event or promotional effort.

3. Describe realistic examples of both *rifle* and *shotgun* approaches to fundraising projects.

4. Outline a realistic example of an extended fundraising project by utilizing the *program evaluation review technique* including appropriate dates.

5. Describe the advantages of *soft data* and *hard data,* provide examples of each, and specify how each can be used to facilitate your fundraising and promotional efforts.

5 | THE WHO, WHAT AND WHY OF FUNDRAISING

Selling hot dogs and soft drinks in front of a box store

CHAPTER HIGHLIGHTS

This chapter will emphasize:

- Why philanthropic activity is big business in the United States
- Potential problems with would-be charitable requests
- The "Guilt and Glitter" syndrome
- The importance of the timing of specific fundraising activities
- The different categories or vehicles of giving
- The importance of keeping fundraising expenses to a minimum
- Mistakes that some organizations have made in respect to fundraising
- The categories or vehicles of giving

- Several types of donations
- Sources of charitable contributions
- The value of endowments
- The importance of record keeping
- The major reasons why fundraising efforts fail

PHILANTHROPIC ACTIVITIES

Fundraising is a **big time business** in the United States today for charitable, philanthropic, and non-profit programs. Philanthropic contributions have continued to increase within the United States in recent years. Contributions to charitable causes come from individuals, from foundations, and from the business world.

Even some twenty years ago it was estimated that total contributions toward charitable causes approached $230 billion dollars (Fund-a-thon, May 3, 1991). Total gifts from individuals, corporations, foundations and other sources rose some 5.1% per year during the decades of the 1980s and 6% during the 1990s. In the past two decades it has been estimated that donations from all sources has risen in the neighborhood of 3.3% to 3.5% annually (Stier, 2009).

> **PRINCIPLE # 71:** *Fundraising on behalf of non-profit organizations continues to be a big time business*

Problems with Would-Be Charitable Requests

Unfortunately, there are some individuals and organizations that purport to represent legitimate charities and attempt to raise money on the pretense of charitable causes—but, they do not. Rather, these efforts represent nothing more than deceitful efforts at best and outright fraud at worse, attempting to confuse would-be donors and contributors into thinking that their gifts or contributions would be going to legitimate non-profit causes.

There are numerous fraudulent efforts every year by unscrupulous individuals and organizations that seek to solicit resources from would-be donors and contributors on false pretenses, that is, they represent worthy not-for-profit entities. Instead, they represent just the opposite, a selfish attempt to line the pockets of selfish individuals while preying upon the unsuspecting and unknowing. Some would-be charities deliberately use sound-alike names in an effort to confuse would-be contributors. Such efforts sometime hinder the conscientious efforts of real non-profit fundraising attempts in that the general public, those who would otherwise tend to be contributors often become hesitant to give to another possible charity, lest the money not be routed to a worthy cause.

Even traditionally well-respected charitable organizations can come under fire for seemingly unacceptable, shady or deceptive business practices when it comes to handling money donated for specific charitable causes. Witness the infamous September 11, 2001 terrorists' attack on the World Trade Buildings. The American Red Cross announced, shortly after this tragic attack on America, that it was establishing a separate fund [Liberty Fund] to accept donations and contributions to specifically benefit the victims of this attack. **However, in reality, the American Red Cross was forced to admit some weeks later** *that it was not going to spend all of the money donated,* **estimated to be $550 million at the time,** *for those victims of the September 11th attack.*

Instead, the ARC announced that less than half of the money raised on behalf of the victims was to be spent for the victims—their families or rescue workers. The rest was going to be spent for an upgrade of its own organization as well as for other needy causes involving other disasters elsewhere in the country. However, "donors expected their money to be helping now" (Tyrangiel, 2001, p. 77).

> *PRINCIPLE # 72:* **Organizations involved in fundraising should do what they publicly say that they intend to do or run the risk of losing credibility and future contributions**

The result was an outcry and severe criticism from a wide range of constituencies, from individuals as well as the news media throughout the country. Special outrage was expressed by those individuals who had donated money to this special fund only to find out that their donations were not being used for the purpose promised by the Red Cross. Radio shows criticized the ARC for the fact that the organization had initially promised that **all of the money** in this special fund [Liberty Fund] would benefit the victims of September 11th while in reality what the ARC actually did was take a significant amount of the money donated for this purpose and spend it for other purposes, some charitable (elsewhere, not for victims of the World Trade disaster) and some for a computer system upgrade for the organization itself.

In an editorial appearing in the *Chicago Tribune* on October 31, 2001 (Red Cross squanders goodwill) the following quote succinctly summed up the controversy.

> "Besieged by the controversy, the Red Cross announced Tuesday that it had stopped seeking donations for the Liberty Fund and that the money in the fund will be directed to victims of the Sept. 11 and future victims of terrorism. This is what is known as damage control. The Red Cross has some real work to do to restore its reputation. It can start by establishing a very simple idea as rule number one: Don't mislead your donors. . . . The fiasco at the Red Cross carries a reminder for everyone involved in philanthropy. Credibility is everything" (p. 14).

The eventual fallout included the resignation of the president of the American Red Cross. And, on November 13, 2001, it was announced over national television that the ARC did an abrupt turnaround and had indicated that contrary to its earlier position, it would indeed spend 100% of the money ($543 million) that had been donated for the victims (Liberty Fund) of the September 11th attack to the victims and their families (Nasser, 2001; Roy, 2001).

Determining the Percentage of Money Raised Which Actually Goes to the Worthy Cause

Another factor sometimes related to misinterpretation or misunderstanding associated with fundraising is the amount of money raised that actually goes to the worthy cause for which the fundraising effort is being conducted (McMillen, 1990a; Miller, 1999). Another way of looking at this situation is to determine the *cost of raising* the money. For example, in a particular fundraising project, of every dollar raised what percentage goes to pay for expenses (including salaries, fees, consulting costs, merchandise, products, etc.)? And what percentage actually finds its way to the worthy cause for which the project was originally undertaken (team uniforms, trophies, awards, equipment, supplies, construction costs of a new facility, etc.)?

No one likes to contribute money and see a high percentage of the contribution go to pay for the actual cost of raising the money. People contribute to see their money go for truly worthy causes—to help the sport program, to meet the needs of the participants, etc. One tactic that has been used to counteract this potential problem is to have two separate income accounts. One of the accounts is structured in such a fashion that 100% of all donations placed in that account are actually used for the actual benefits of the sports program. All overhead expenses are to be taken from the second account.

In this situation, the prospective donor who expresses concern about what percentage of the contribution will actually go to the sports program can be assured that 100% of the funds contributed to the first account will be funneled to meet the actual needs of the program, with none of those funds being diverted for overhead costs. Money for the second account can be solicited from those contributors who either do not express a concern about exactly where their money goes or from those contributors who understand that in almost any fundraising effort, there are necessary and ordinary expenses which must be taken care of and are customarily covered from the gross proceeds of the contributions collected.

A study of 51 colleges revealed that it costs the institutions' development offices an average of only 16 cents to raise each dollar in their general fundraising effort. This 525-percent return on investment included all directly related fundraising expenses (McMillen, 1990b). In general, it is recommended that *at least* 60% of funds generated for charitable causes via fundraising efforts be funneled to the charitable causes for which the money was raised—and, in many instances, this percentage is significantly higher. The National Charities Information Bureau supports this recommendation (Harbaugh group, 2000). Charities and would-be charities that provide a smaller percentage than this to the charitable causes for which they obtain donations are suspect at best. Naturally, the greater the percentage that goes to the worthy cause the better. It is difficult to generate significant monies if a large percentage of money raised goes to pay for the cost of generating the money (not counting the cost of goods that are sold as part of the fundraising project).

An example of the problems that might arise when a relatively small percentage of money raised for a charitable cause actually finds its way to the charity can be seen in the charity that former San Diego Chargers quarterback James Harbaugh established. It was reported in June of 2000 (Harbaugh group) edition of *USA Today* that a mere 21 cents of every dollar raised between 1995 and 1998 by means of the charity (The Harbaugh Foundation) actually found its way to the charity. The rest of the money (79 cents of every dollar raised) went to expenses, included salaries and an annual golf outing. In actual dollars, some $528,000 was raised during this time period but a mere $113,000 was provided to charity. Some $249,000 was spent on the expenses, travel and, of course, the golf outing. Also, some $166,000 was invested.

> **PRINCIPLE # 73:** *Emphasize the small percentage of the money raised that will go toward the cost of generating the funds (exclusive of the cost of goods that are sold as part of the fundraising effort)*

The problem arises with some so-called national as well as more local non-profit fundraising efforts of individuals and/or organizations that sometimes spend as much as 75% to 85% of the money raised to cover expenses involved in the fundraising effort, including paying the organizers and leaders of the project hefty salaries or consulting contracts.

Corporate Giving

From 1975 to 1985, corporate annual giving increased from around $700 million dollars to approximately $4.3 billion. In 1990 corporate America gave a record $5.9 billion to charity and other non-profit organizations. Estimates for 1991 ranged in the neighborhood of $6.2 billion (Corporations find, August 1991). At the turn of the century, estimates for 2001 and 2002 ranged in excess of $7 billion a year. Corporate contributions are seen as being good for business. Such contributions help the community while permitting the company to take tax deductions as well as to attract new customers. In reality, contributing is seen as good marketing and advertising tools for businesses in this country.

Although on the surface it might seem that the majority of contributions (in terms of dollars contributed) would be forthcoming from the world of big business (corporations, industries, etc.) or from foundations, in reality, this is not the case. In this country, it has been individuals who have contributed the greatest amount in terms of actual dollars to charitable causes, much more than either foundations or the business sector.

> **PRINCIPLE # 74:** *Making contributions is viewed as good advertising and marketing tools for businesses in the United States*

Sources of Charitable Contributions

Over 100-billion dollars were donated to all types of charities, non-profit organizations and programs in the United States by philanthropic organizations annually to all non-profit causes from individuals, foundations, bequests, and estates In examining all charitable contributions made, categorized according to the source of donations, it is evident that the vast majority of philanthropic contributions were from living individuals (in contrast to individual donations made via wills). In fact, more money has traditionally been contributed by individuals than from all other sources combined. Of all charitable contributions made in this country the trend is that individual contributions represented the vast majority of all contributions to non-profit causes followed by bequests (wills) and foundations in third place.

Contributions to Educational Institutions

In terms of contributions to educational institutions, United States corporations donate billions and billions to schools. Today, there are some 26,000 foundations headquartered in the United States. Of these, there are nearly 400 large general purpose foundations that control about 2/3 of the total foundation assets in this country. These 400 super large foundations also distribute approximately two-thirds of the grants in terms of dollar amounts. While one might think that grants from foundations and other sources involve so-called "big dollars"—50% of all grants are under $1,000 and 80% of grants awarded for charitable purposes are under $5,000.

Using Grants as a Funding Source

Recreation administrators would do well to search out potential grants for funding or supplemental funding of recreation departments and programs. Grants from local, state and federal sources are certainly possible and readily available—for those willing to spend the time and energies searching for and screening potential donors. Federal grants may be searched for on " . . . the searchable database of the Catalog of Federal Domestic Assistance (www.gsa.gov/fdac). Hard copies are available at most public libraries"

Chapter 5: The Who, What and Why of Fundraising

> **PRINCIPLE # 75:** *Grant writing requires one to have a clear goal enabling a match between intended activities and sources willing and able to fund such activities*

If there is a secret of grant writing it is having a clear idea of your goal so that you can match your intended activities with a source willing to financially support such activities. Finding the appropriate (right) funding source is the objective so that an appropriate proposal can be prepared in light of the requirements of the funding entity. Michael Stewart provides a good summary of what the fundraiser might want to share with a prospective contributor (providing grant money) when he said:

"Look, I understand that you're willing to give away funds to support specific objectives that are part of your philanthropic agenda. Your foundation, your department, your company wants to accomplish some specific goals. Can you please share with me what those are so I can discuss with you how I think we can help you, the donor, carry out your agenda?" (Cohen, 1996, p. 18).

Car shows attract families and car enthusiasts alike

Some high schools, such as Dobbs Ferry (New York) school district, are involved in grant writing in a big way. In fact, Dobbs Ferry actually went out in 1996 and hired a full time fundraiser for the district, an individual who was able to generate $269,000 in his very first year on the job. Most of the money he raised came from writing grants. In the 21st century the process of raising money for worthy causes is far more sophisticated that in years past. The actual process of attempting to solicit resources has become more sophisticated, more complicated and more competitive. And today, companies and organizations making contributions have become more sophisticated, more proficient, and savvier, in their evaluation of the wealth of prospective recipients (Cohen, 1996).

TYPES OF DONATIONS

What exactly can be donated? What should one seek as contributions? The answer is simple: **everything and anything of value**. This includes m*oney, product(s) services, as well as ideas*. For example, (1) cash or negotiable instruments, (2) real and personal property, (3) equipment and supplies, (4) stocks, (5) bonds, (6) life insurance policies (proceeds to beneficiaries), (7) time (donated), (8) expertise (donated), (9) advice, and (10) donated services.

> **PRINCIPLE # 76:** *The solicitation of donations should not be restricted merely to cash*

TIMING OF FUNDRAISING EFFORTS

Generally speaking, fundraising activities can be thought of in three ways in terms of the time or frequency in which such efforts take place. The three classifications are: (1) one-shot or one-time events or activities, (2) events or efforts that can be repeated a second time at some point in the future, and (3) those events which are annual or continual in nature.

One-Time Events

Some fundraising and promotional activities, by their very nature, are best thought of as *one-time events*. An example of such a one-time activity might be a wine & cheese reception for initial (charter) memberships within the new sport support group (SSG) or recreation support group (RSG). Once this event takes place, it is over and cannot be repeated since there can only be one initial charter membership kick-off drive. There are numerous examples of such activities that really are one-time projects.

Repeatable Activities

> **PRINCIPLE # 77:** *Some fundraising projects can be repeated in subsequent years but are not appropriate as annual events*

A *repeatable fundraising and promotional activity* is one that can be utilized more than once but which is not of such a nature that lends itself to being an (automatic) annual event or a continuous activity. An example is a typical car wash as a fundraiser. Although this event can be repeated, and often is, this event does not lend itself in terms of importance or significance to become something of a real tradition, to be something of an annual event within a sports program. Perhaps the car wash might be repeated but it nevertheless lacks that certain something that would be necessary to become a tradition, an annual promotional and fundraising activity.

The Annual Event

The *annual* or *continual promotional and fundraising event* is such that, by its very nature, the activity lends itself to being repeated year after year, on an annual basis. For example, the typical Annual Hall of Fame Induction Ceremony for a school, held each fall during homecoming weekend, is an ideal annual promotional and fundraising activity. Such an event can be conducted each and every year and is expected to be held by specific internal and external constituencies. Such an event becomes, after a number of years, part of the sports tradition of the organization. In fact, if such an event would not take place one year, it would be solely missed.

CATEGORIES OR VEHICLES OF GIVING

In the world of fundraising today, donors are frequently asked to contribute or make commitments for future contributions in response to a variety of different programs or vehicles designed to generate monies for the sport program. Fifteen of these so-called vehicles are:

1. Major donors programs—solicitation of large contributions from individuals and/or organizations

2. Capital campaigns—providing for capital funding, new construction, renovation of existing structures, purchase and/or gifts of land, buildings, and equipment (Diles, 1996)

3. Annual scholarship appeals—providing money for student scholarships (in the form of room, board, tuition, etc.)

4. Charitable remainder trust—referred to as a *life income trust*, this gift creates a life income [fixed income or variable annuity] for the person making the donation (**or** for someone else the donor designates). Upon the death of the person receiving the life income, the portion of the money remaining is given to the beneficiary.

5. Annual giving campaigns for a total program—providing for ongoing needs of the sport program supplementing the regular sources of income. Between major fund drives, the annual giving programs receive a high priority.

6. Annual special event or projects—contributions generated from such activities as dance productions, sport medicine seminars, hall of fame ceremonies, social functions, etc.

7. Annual giving campaigns *for specific purpose*—designated giving to support a specific sport or cause

8. Annual giving campaigns *on an unrestricted basis*—donations that are not specifically designated for a special purpose. This permits significant flexibility in the support programs.

9. Deferred/planned giving programs—take place over an extended time period and involves estate planning, assignment of life insurance annuities, securities, as well as real (estate) and personal property (Blum, 1994)

10. Memorial giving programs—gifts made in memory of deceased individuals

11. Honor gifts—gifts given in honor of a living individual or to commemorate a special occasion

12. Charitable gift annuity—a gift that guarantees the beneficiary a fixed income, an amount that is determined by the age of the beneficiary at the time the gift is made (Helping NAGWS, 1993)

13. Gifts in kind for the total sport program or specific teams—contributions in other form than money, i.e., products, advertising, services, expertise, etc.

14. Gifts made by will—a bequest (that can take the form of cash, property or securities) from an individual that will take effect upon that person's death

15. General endowment programs (scholarship, coaching stipend, facility upkeep, etc.)—establishing athletic or coaching *chairs*, research programs, and student scholarships. Such programs can provide operating funds from the interest generated from the endowment monies.

Endowments Provide for Long-Term Support

> **PRINCIPLE # 78:** There is a trend for endowments to be established by big-time athletic departments to help provide perpetual financial assistance for their sport programs

The purpose of endowment programs is to provide for long-term support over a number of years, in perpetuity (Cole, 2000; King, 2001). Endowments are created when the original gifts consisting of money and/or stock, etc., accrue interest indefinitely. Some of the annual proceeds (profits) from the endowment provide available monies throughout time to provide financial support for the program, while leaving the original money intact. And, part of the profits from the endowment also is plowed back into the endowment fund to increase future annual profits due to anticipated increases in costs in the future due to inflation. Thus, there is the potential for continued benefits accruing to the sport or recreation program, generated from the interest earned, as well as from profits from wise investments made with the original gift(s). These benefits may be enjoyed in perpetuity as long as interest and/or profit is generated from the use of the original resources contributed.

Cornell University received $1.5 million in 1999 from a former athlete, Rick Booth, to endow a baseball coaching position. This was the sixth coaching endowment for the Ivy League school. The gift of money was invested in the school's long-term investment pool and a portion of the interest generated each year will be allocated in perpetuity to the athletic budget to provide general support for the varsity baseball program (Booth endows, 1999).

In 1991 the largest athletic endowment at the college/university level was at Stanford University. That year the school's endowment account stood at what was considered a very significant $46 million. The endowment has increased each since then and in 1999 the athletic department was able to add some $17 million to the endowment total. The athletic endowment fund reached $210 million as of September 1, 2000. This sum in 2000 provided the intercollegiate athletic department an annual income of somewhere between $10 million and $13 million to spend for the 33 men's and women's sports at the prestigious west coast higher education institution (Weiner, 2000; King, 2001). Today it is considerably higher and growing.

It would be a mistake to assume that endowments are the exclusive property of large colleges and universities. Not so. The strategy of establishing endowments for the benefit of a wide range of worthy causes can include all levels of athletic programs including youth sports and secondary schools. All that is needed is the outline of a plan and the successful solicitation of potential donors.

PRINCIPLE # 79:   *Endowments provide for perpetual income to an organization*

There are numerous types of endowments. *One* type is the scholarship endowment trust. In this instance there is a permanent scholarship fund established by the contributor who may be allowed to name a scholarship as well as to designate the sport for which the scholarship money may be used. As in any endowment, the interest generated each year on the money originally donated is used towards tuition, etc.

A *second* type of endowment might provide for payment of an annual coaching stipend or salary. On the college level, this might be termed an Endowed Chair for Coaching, similar to an Endowed Chair for Physics—although paying for the salary of a specific coach rather than the physics professor. A similar situation could exist on the high school level where the salary of the coach would be paid for with the interest generated from the monies placed in an interest bearing bank account.

A *third* variation of the endowment strategy calls for the interest (profit or proceeds) earned from the principle (contributions) to be paid for the maintenance on the facilities. Since there will always be costs associated with maintaining sport facilities it is wise to plan for a steady source of income to help offset this perpetual expense that will invariably increase each year due to inflation as well as normal wear and tear.

> **PRINCIPLE # 80:** *Deferred giving programs involve taking the long view toward raising money*

Deferred/Planned Giving Programs

Rather than concentrate on what is called by many as the *trinket mentality*, that is, soliciting annual giving and gifts in exchange for tickets, parking passes, sports apparel, etc., the tactic of *deferred/planned giving programs* involves taking the longer view, over many years. Deferred/planned giving involves the promise, in the future, that some asset will be funneled to the sport or recreation organization or program. Of course, planned (deferred) giving is just that, deferred to the future. It might very well take many years for the fruits of the gift to be realized by the recipient of the gift. Additionally, it may take a long time to cultivate prospective donors and to motivate them to actually act in terms of making the deferred contribution of a sizeable amount. Normally, more significant amounts (value) of money are involved in a deferred, planned giving situation (Blum, 1994).

Deferred/Planned Giving Programs—Proceeds from Life Insurance

A growing emphasis is being placed on what is called the *Living Life Insurance Trust*, which is a type of a deferred, planned giving program. In this instance, the premium is paid by the contributor as a donation to the sport program. The sport organization in turn makes the premium payment on a life insurance policy that provides coverage for the contributor. The beneficiary of the policy is the sport or recreation organization. When the policy reaches maturity, its value will be placed in the Endowment Trust (for whatever purpose the endowment has been established) in honor of the designated donor. Upon the death of the donor (the insured) the proceeds of the life insurance flow to the endowment of the sport organization.

WHO CONTRIBUTES

Earlier it was pointed out that individuals, businesses, corporations, and foundations are all potential donors to charitable and other worthwhile causes, such as educational and sport organizations. Since we have already seen that the vast majority of charitable dollars come from individuals, as well as from businesses, it is only natural to concentrate on these sources of monies. "The key to successful fund-raising is to identify those reasons and design an approach that will motivate people to contribute" (Cole, 2000, p. 30).

Chapter 5: The Who, What and Why of Fundraising

Identifying and cultivating potential donors for one's own program is very, very important. The donor is the key element to a successful development program. Naturally, the more sources (individual donors and organizations) of revenue you have, the more stable your fundraising program will be and the greater the likelihood for substantial and continual success.

> **PRINCIPLE # 81:** *Contributors like to give for tangible purposes and to successful programs*

It is far easier to obtain contributions for tangible purposes, buildings, facilities, equipment, awards, etc., than intangible purposes such as utilities or postage. Similarly, donors are more likely to contribute when their gift(s) can have a long lasting impact upon the program. Obtaining money for uniforms, lasting 4-6 years, is usually easier than attempting to gather funds to pay for the current year's phone bill. This is the reason buildings have names of the donors on the side of the structures. It is more difficult to locate a plaque crediting "Mr. Smith" for a contribution that paid for the electric bill for the athletic program in a certain year.

Facts to be Considered in Soliciting Support

When considering the potential for receiving assistance (money, time, goods, services, volunteering, etc.) from individuals and organizations, it is useful to note the following information regarding people who tend to contribute to sport programs (Yiannakis and Braunstein, 1983; Cole, 2000).

1. Contributors tend to *follow certain patterns*. Approximately one-half tend to match their previous donations; about 20% will give less, while 20% tend to make a larger contribution. New or reactivated donors will be the remaining 10%.

2. The *more individuals have given in the past*, the more likely they will increase subsequent donations

3. Those who *have* or *have had a family member* associated with the program are more likely to contribute, help or volunteer

4. Those who *attend the sport activities* or *related activities* tend to be more receptive to assisting and contributing

> **PRINCIPLE # 82:** *It is important for those involved in fundraising to be aware of the motives of people who contribute to worthy causes*

5. Those who *have an interest in sport activities or related activities* (fans) are more prone to give of themselves
6. Those with an *interest in the goals and objectives* of the organization and its activities are potential supporters
7. Others who are prime candidates to become contributors include:
    A. Those who are *members and/or employees* of the sport organization
    B. Representatives of *other sport businesses*
    C. *Vendors* associated with one's sport organization
    D. *Area business owners and managers*
    E. *Alumni* (athletes, coaches, administrators) of athletic organizations and programs
8. People *tend to contribute in round numbers*—therefore provide such opportunities in the areas of donations, as well as in the pricing of items for sale
9. Individuals and organizations favorably disposed (for whatever reasons) to such worthy sport causes tend to contribute more

> **PRINCIPLE # 83:** *There are known characteristics of donors*

KNOWN CHARACTERISTICS OF GIVERS (BRIGGS, 1984; COLE 2000)

1. *Age*—historically those 30 and over tend to be more responsive to appeals for funds because of their financial situation and experience
2. *Sex*—males still tend to be more responsive to contributing to sport causes than females. However, this may be changing with the emerging women who are involved in sports and who are financially independent.
3. *Social Class*—middle and working class people are excellent sources for fundraising for sports and sports related programs. Those in the lower social/economic class, due to their economically deprived position, are often incapable of sizeable donations. However, there continues to be a growth potential of middle class contributors. At the other end of the spectrum, those who might be considered to be the so-called higher social class are often difficult to reach for the typical sport fundraiser. The one exception might be if these potential donors are approached by *centers of influence* who are of equal or higher social/economic standing.

4. *Income*—when sizing up potential donors it is important to look at total family income rather than focusing only on the primary income earner. From experience, it is safe to assume that the probability of contributing decreases as the amount of discretionary income decreases. Extremely wealthy people give the most. An experienced fundraiser once revealed that contributions of $5,000 and above account for almost 70% of total gifts to education at the national level.

5. *Proximity to the cause or program*—it seems logical that the closer the prospect is to the cause (such as an alumnus or alumna), the more likely the person is to contribute. Also, those closer to the cause or sport program are more susceptible to emotional appeals. Thus, those individuals who are farther removed from the cause of the campaign should be approached for contributions through more of an intellectual rationale.

6. *Residential proximity to school*—in a school setting those who live close to the facility are prime candidates to become donors

7. *Property owners*—individuals owning property in the general geographical area are more likely to contribute than renters

8. *Area of residence*—solicitation seems to be more productive in rural areas than suburban.

9. *Marital Status*—married persons with children are more likely to contribute to sport causes than those without children

10. *Economy*—individuals tend to contribute more in sound economic times. Corporations give more when profits are up and they also tend to give more to sport organizations within close geographical proximity.

In summary, contributors to sport related entities tend to be older, middle, or working class members of society, with a combined family income of more than $30,000. They tend to be male rather than female; married rather than single; and are likely to have children residing in close proximity to the school. Further, those who contribute have a tendency to have given previously, are graduates of colleges and universities, are often teachers or former teachers, have or had children in the same or similar school or organization, and/or are close to someone who participates in the program. Further, contributors to school athletic programs tend to be alumni, students, general activity consumers, owners of related businesses, owners of community dependent businesses, and community property owners (Yiannakis & Braunstein, 1983, p. 23-25).

Those who contribute to sport and recreation related organizations tend to be older, middle, or working class members of society, with a combined family income of over $45,000. They also tend to be male, married, to have children and to own a home close to the school or leisure facility.

Those who contribute tend to have donated previously, and often, to be graduates of colleges and universities, to have or have had children in the same or similar school or organization and/or are close to someone who participates in the program or organization. In addition contributors to school athletic programs tend to be alumni, students, consumers (fans), owners of related businesses, owners or community dependent businesses, and community property owners.

When examining the question of **who** contributes to worthy causes one should be aware of a general rule of thumb that commonly is referred to as the *80-20 rule*. This implies that, generally speaking, 80% of the monies generated in any given fundraising effort come from only 20% of the donors. Conversely, 20% of the money comes from contributions comprising the remaining 80% of the donors.

> *PRINCIPLE # 84:* **The majority of money is contributed by a minority of donors in major fundraising projects (80-20 rule)**

This principle is derived from the *Pareto Principle*, one of the most flexible, powerful management tools available. This Principle (commonly referred to as the *80/20 Rule*) states that a large percentage of problems are the results of a small percentage of causes. The fundamental tool of Pareto analysis is what is referred to as a "Pareto Chart," which is a simple bar chart that presents a ranking of problems (or some other activity) in descending order, "usually based on the events' frequency of occurrence" (p. 69). The Pareto Principle is named after an Italian economist, Vilfredo Pareto, who came up with the theory around the turn of the 19th century to help explain wealth distribution as well as other economic phenomena (Henricks, 1996, p. 69).

> *PRINCIPLE # 85:* **The one-third rule—in terms of direct contributions**

Another axiom in fundraising, in terms of *direct contributions* made to charitable causes, is the *one-third rule*. This so-called rule states that one-third of the monies raised usually come from the top ten contributors, the second one-third of contributions (in terms of money raised) are generally derived from the next 100 contributors, and the final one-third of contributions are attributable to all other contributors and donors combined (however many that happens to be).

In light of the above two so-called rules or principles, the initial step in planning for direct (major) contributions is to accurately identify the top ten probable contributors and then pinpointing the next 100 or so likeliest prospects. Fundraisers need to identify and prioritize those who could very well be actual contributors and those who will probably not be contributors or significant contributors—and then concentrate on the prime prospects. Potential contributors, once they are identified, become the prime targets of solicitors as they have the potential for producing the most on behalf of the fundraising effort.

> **PRINCIPLE # 86:** *People support deserving causes, successful individuals and meaningful programs*

WHY PEOPLE CONTRIBUTE

Advantages to Advertisers, Contributors, Supporters, and Sponsors

When attempting to plan and organize a fundraising effort there are two basic questions that should be asked. These are:

1. Why would or should someone contribute to the effort?
2. What are the real appeal factors of the fundraising activity to potential donors?

Bobblehead promotions have existed for years

The answers to these two questions may very well reveal whether or not the proposed fundraising activity is a success or failure. However, there are two more factors that the fundraiser needs to be cognizant of in seeking support. Namely, that there is a need to show that the sports program or activity is of value and that the present management is currently doing a good job with what resources are currently available. People do indeed support what they perceive to be deserving causes, successful people and significant programs.

In real life, individuals contribute for all sorts of reasons, as illustrated above. Some reasons are logical. Others are emotional. And still others defy reason. In real life there are almost as many reasons for contributing as there are benefactors. It is important to remember that there are indeed real benefits that can accrue to individuals, as well as businesses, contributing to worthy sport causes. It is up to the fundraiser and promoter, to match would-be contributors with benefits that they desire or need.

In addition to the satisfaction that is gained from knowing that a meaningful contribution had been made for a good cause there are other intangible *and* tangible consequences of such generosity. Some give because of a genuine and generous desire to assist or contribute to worthy and/or charitable causes. Others contribute their money, goods, time and skills because there are tangible and intangible benefits which may accrue to the giver. A partial list of the reasons why benefactors contribute to sports programs is provided below (Briggs, 1984; Cole, 2000; Lopiano, 1983; McDermott-Griggs & Card, 1992; Robinson, 1997; Yiannakis & Braunstein, 1983).

1. Need to belong
2. Desire to change something
3. Loyalty
4. Need to exercise power, influence
5. Results orientated (motivated by possibility of seeing their contributions resulting in something positive)
6. Commitment motivation (allegiance to the sport or sport program)
7. Pride (personal, community, and school)
8. Desire for some benefit—tickets, name in publications, gifts, premiums, social involvement or recognition
9. Need for recognition
10. Tax advantages
11. Curiosity (interest in the sport program)
12. Membership benefits
13. Involvement motivation (wish to be associated, involved)
14. Guilt elimination
15. Personal satisfaction (feeling good)
16. Opportunities for input and influence
17. Religious beliefs
18. Need to achieve
19. Indebtedness (gratitude) and obligation
20. Ego satisfaction
21. Permanent remembrance—facility named after oneself
22. Identification through children or youth
23. Desire to help others
24. Publicity and public relations
25. Group pressure (internal and external)
26. Personal recognition
27. Elimination of fear
28. Desire for association with an organization (achievement of respectability by association)
29. Vote casting privileges and opportunities
30. Identification with an image or a cause
31. Self perpetuation (to be remembered in some fashion in the future)

"Guilt and Glitter" Syndrome

> **PRINCIPLE # 87:** *Some people donate because of "guilt" and "glitter"*

Lopiano (1983) cites the "guilt and glitter" syndrome as being a significant motivating factor in people's tendency to contribute to sports program. In this respect, people tend to contribute because of the desire to be associated with the so-called "glitter" of the sport world. There is something exciting about sport teams regardless of the level at which they compete. Whether one is talking about youth teams, high school sports or collegiate/university athletic programs, there is an excitement, a thrill, and a unique experience that attracts people and motivates them to become involved. That they become associated with the sports program through their contributions speaks towards the "glitter" aspects of motivation.

The second part of the syndrome as expressed by Lopiano refers to "guilt." That is, individuals are sometimes motivated to contribute because of the guilt or uneasiness they tend to feel in having more resources and advantages than the average person in society. Being able to share with the less fortunate is a worthy motivational idea and one that has resulted in numerous contributions to a wide range of worthy causes, including those under the sport umbrella. Acting upon these twin motivating factors, "guilt and glitter," as well as any of the others listed above, can significantly increase the fundraising efficiency and effectiveness of any sport organization.

TEAM CONCEPT FOR DIRECT CONTRIBUTIONS— ONE TYPE OF IMPLEMENTATION OF THE FUNDRAISING EFFORT

> **PRINCIPLE # 88:** *The team concept of fundraising is essential in today's society*

Use the team concept of fundraising. Employ the spirit of competition among individuals involved. Each team has its owner, coaches, and players. Prizes and awards are given to owners, coaches, and individuals. Have a kickoff dinner or luncheon, a midway progress lunch, and a final victory banquet meeting.

One of the more successful organizational techniques for soliciting donations is the *squad concept* (Briggs, 1984). This concept calls for the formation of squads structured within a league in an effort to generate motivation and to stimulate production. Each squad has an elected captain chosen on the basis of proven leadership. Using names from one of the national sports leagues, the squads or teams compete for group and personal prizes on the basis of sales production.

After the top 100 or 200 top donor prospects are identified, they are allocated among the various squads. There is a 24-hour trading period during which target donors are traded. Upon receiving the final prospect list, a squad may assign one of the members to contact each potential donor without fear of competition from another squad or member until, after a specific predetermined amount of time passes, the so-called commissioner declares that particular prospect as a free agent.

Free agency may occur during the last week of the campaign when it is apparent that a prospect had not been approached or not been effectively approached or had resisted all appeal attempts. In this event, the individual deserves to be considered fair game for any solicitor with the ability to persuade the prospect to action.

This technique can also be used in other activities, such as ticket and product sales and using geographic zones instead of prospect lists. The concept itself, however, is sound.

> **PRINCIPLE # 89:** *Establish prior to the start of the fundraising effort the exact point of no return or determine in advance when to "cut one's losses"*

The essential factor in any major fundraising project is simply this. Before ever beginning a fundraising activity, a decision should be reached as to whether or not there are criteria that must be met or satisfied in order for the fundraising activity to continue. Knowing when to call it quits and to cut one's losses is as important in fundraising as it is in gambling.

Far too often sport organizers become enthralled with the "hunt" and with their own efforts and time expenditures in working toward a goal. The end result is a poor decision made in the heat of battle, based upon one's emotions, rather than with cool logic. One should never change the "rules of the game," i.e., the guidelines as to whether or not to continue the fundraising activity, merely because one is emotionally involved and excited about the project and/or with one's efforts expended up to that date. Throwing "good" money after "bad" is foolish. Throwing good effort after unproductive effort is foolish. Knowing when to stop the downside risk and to call a halt to the activity takes great courage. But, it must be done.

For example, let's examine the scenario in which a booster organization decides (on December 1st) to kick off the sale of 600 raffle tickets ($50 each for $30,000 in gross sales) for a brand new automobile on March 15th. The scheduled date for the actual raffle is set for May 1st. The car will cost $20,000 with the anticipated maximum net proceeds of some $10,000 remaining with the booster organization. The club must make the final commitment to the dealer no later than April 15th.

When April 14th rolls around, only 300 of the 600 tickets have been sold, generating only $15,000 of the $20,000 needed to *even pay for the cost of the car,* much less make any profit. The officers of the club need to decide whether to call off the raffle or to continue, and hope that the remaining number of tickets can be sold so that there would be at least sufficient money to pay for the cost of the car that is to be raffled.

However, this decision should have been made back on December 1st, when the officers of the booster organization were in a *calm, cool, and collected frame of mind*. The thinking and the decision making process should be unaffected by the emotions attending the fundraising activities and excitement on April 14th. Far too often, decisions are made in the heat of the moment and are made with emotions rather than logic, much to the detriment of the image of the organization and the fundraising activity.

Of course, if new information becomes available prior to April 14th that would shed a different light on the prospect of successfully meeting the ultimate goal, then by all means, a re-examination of the earlier decision (to cancel the activity if less than 400 tickets were sold by April 14) might be certainly warranted.

Many promotional and fundraising projects involve the use of student-athletes in a variety of different roles. While there is nothing inherently troublesome in involving student-athletes, it is important to remain up-to-date in terms of the various eligibility rules and regulations promulgated by various conferences as well as state and national governing bodies.

The NCAA has placed certain restrictions in regards to the use of student-athletes for promotional activities. Years ago a basketball star, Steve Alford, on the Indiana University men's team took part in a promotional effort that involved pictures being taken of the athlete and used as part of a fundraising calendar. The athlete received no direct or indirect benefit by posing for the photographer. In fact, the calendar was sponsored by one of the University's sororities and the proceeds from the sale of the calendar were earmarked for a non-profit, worthy organization. Nevertheless, when the NCAA found out about this situation, the basketball player was punished by being declared ineligible for one basketball game. Since that time the NCAA has instituted a less stringent policy regarding such involvement. At the present time there are several pages [*Institutional, Charitable, Educational or Non-Profit Promotions*] dealing with this type of situation within the current NCAA Manual that are applicable in this type of situation.

High school athletic associations or conferences may also have eligibility rules restricting the role that athletes may play in terms of promotions and fundraising. Competent sport administrators and promoters should anticipate potential problems. Thus, before embarking on any scheme involving the direct participation by athletes in promotional or fundraising activities one should double check with the appropriate governing organization.

Another general topic that must be addressed when dealing with promotion and fundraising activities is that of the legal ramifications, i.e., risk management. Under this category are four general areas that deserve the close attention of competent fundraisers or promoters and will be discussed in the following pages. These areas are (1) legal liability, (2) insurance considerations, (3) applicable federal and state laws, and (4) licenses and permits.

Successful Record Keeping

> **PRINCIPLE # 90:** When dealing with money the two key words are **accountability** *and* **security**

Implementing successful fundraising and promotional projects is not possible without accurate and timely record keeping. Everyone involved must keep some kind of records: the organizers and planners of the fundraising projects, the young people and other volunteers, and even the booster clubs or sport support groups. Some of the documentation that is often retained includes records of prospects, past donors, customers, alumni, inventory, vendors, budgets, income, expenses, pledges, items purchased for later sale, insurance, taxes, permits and licenses, minutes or summaries of meetings, copies of letters received and sent, and evaluations of past fundraising projects.

One area of concern to all fundraisers is money. Two key words where money is concerned are *accountability* and *security*. Many schools and recreation departments require that all income from fundraising efforts be deposited in a special activity account. They also require that periodic reports of expenses and income (reconciliations and audits) be made to appropriate parties. Additionally, all checks issued on such accounts usually require at least two (and sometimes three) signatures. Organizers need to pay special attention to financial record keeping; nothing can tarnish the reputation of a fundraising organization more effectively than mistakes or scandals associated with the handling of money.

CRITERIA FOR A SUCCESSFUL SPORT FUNDRAISING ACTIVITY OR PROMOTIONAL PROJECT

> **PRINCIPLE # 91:** *To determine how successful a project is examine the cost effectiveness in terms of time spent, effort expended and resources utilized*

In the evaluation of fundraising and promotional efforts, a key determinant is how cost effective the project or activity becomes in terms of *time spent, effort expended,* and *resources utilized*. Additionally, there are three characteristics that are exhibited by most successful sport promoters and fundraisers—at every level. These attributes or characteristics, in terms of a person's actions, are (1) quality of work, (2) consistency in performance and (3) systematic continuity of effort. Refer to figure 5.1.

There is a need for *quality* in everything one does. Quality in terms of time spent, quality in terms of one's efforts, and quality in terms of one's accomplishments. It is the quality of what an individual accomplishes rather than the quantity of one's work that garners respect for one's efforts and places value upon one's contributions.

In addition to quality, there is a need for *consistency* in one's actions. Anyone can be successful once, a flash in the pan, so to speak. A mark of a truly competent fundraiser, promoter or publicist is one who can consistently, over a period of time, produce positive, quality results (measurable) that can be directly attributed to the planned, systematic, and well-coordinated activities.

Finally, there is a need for systematic *continuity* in one's efforts. That which is accomplished should have some long term, positive, residual effects so that further efforts will be able to be built upon what has been achieved before.

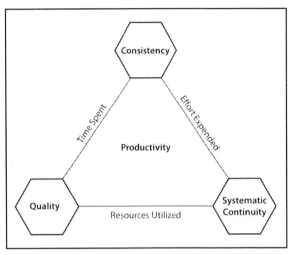

Figure 5.1 Productivity of Fundraising Efforts

PRINCIPLE # 92:   Use hindsight as a tool to assess one's work

Hindsight is indeed a wonderful teacher. Too often, however, we fail to learn from the past, ours as well as others. One does not have to reinvent the wheel in terms of what has been tried before. This is an important principle to follow throughout one's involvement in sport fundraising, promotion and publicity.

A helpful tactic in assessing the effectiveness and efficiency of such activities is to take the time to periodically review what has already taken place. This is especially useful once the task has been completed. It is then that the staff can sit down with the added value of hindsight in a calm, cool, and collected atmosphere and review what could or might have been done differently, as well as what should be repeated to improve the project and enhance the likelihood of greater success, should the task or activity be attempted in the future. Learning from one's successes and failures, as well as those of others, only enhances the likelihood of success in the future.

> **PRINCIPLE # 93:** *Be cool, calm and collected when making important decisions*

An administrator of a large new sports facility once had a challenge one day when during the day of the big home opener the toilets were flushed by the hundreds of fans in attendance during a break in the action on the field. It seemed that no one had the foresight to test the water pressure of the facility's sewer system and there was some overflowing in the restrooms. Years later when that same administrator was in charge of another brand spanking new sports facility, this individual learned from the previous embarrassing situation by bringing in scouts from all over the community for two purposes. *First*, to give these youngsters a glimpse of the wonderful facility before opening day and, *second*, to have all of the scouts, on a prearranged signal, flush all of the toilets at the same time in an effort to test the water pressure and the capacity of the facility's sewer system hookup. In this example, one's prior experiences certainly predetermined how this sport administrator subsequently acted when faced with a similar situation.

The above story is also an example of people learning from the mistakes of others. Once this earlier disaster with the facility's toilets became public knowledge, facility managers quickly followed suit and insisted that the sewer systems of new facilities were adequately tested prior to opening day. Again, the principle is simple; none of us live long enough to learn from all of our own mistakes. Rather, it is vital that we learn from the mistakes (and the successes) of others—as well as our own.

> **PRINCIPLE # 94:** *Scrutinize one's own past activities and the previous efforts of others in order to be able to make timely, appropriate and intelligent decisions in the future*

Many experienced administrators follow the practice of sitting down at the end of each day and deliberately reflecting upon the activities of that day. They scrutinize what went well that day, what they did that worked out just fine, what didn't work out so well, what went wrong, and what would they do differently if they were to relive that day knowing all that they now know about the day's activities, the people involved and challenges that faced them. From this type of reflection upon the immediate past, astute managers are able to better learn from their experiences (both positive and negative) and are in a better position to plan appropriate future activities, priorities, strategies and tactics.

Conducting an Audit of Public Relations, Promotional, and Fundraising Activities

Globally speaking, continually appraising one's efforts by conducting periodic public relations, promotional and fundraising *audits* is beneficial. An ongoing process of error detection and correction is mandatory (Hardekopf, 1989). The highest priority should periodically be given to assessing the effectiveness and efficiency of one's decisions, actions and the activities conducted. A desire to maintain a high level of quality in all that is done within the promotional, public relations, and fundraising arena is essential and an important aspect of this maintenance of quality is dependent upon an audit. However, an audit is useful only if one is willing to ask oneself searching, pertinent questions and be able to provide honest responses. Doing so provides much needed insight into one's performance level and the need, if any, for change in behavior or priorities.

> ***PRINCIPLE # 95**: Conduct a periodic "audit" of one's fundraising and promotion efforts*

Discovering what various constituencies feel about an organization or program, what they know about its accomplishments, goals, and objectives and its needs, will help direct future fundraising and promotional activities. In short, there needs to be an honest, continuous, comprehensive effort to not only determine what people feel about one's program, activity or organization but also to assess the effectiveness and efficiency of the public relations, promotional, and fundraising efforts. Without knowing where one is at, it is awfully difficult to plot, with any accuracy, what one needs to do or what path to choose to follow to reach the ultimate goal.

STEPS IN ASSESSING PROMOTIONAL AND FUNDRAISING ACTIVITIES

Once the campaign or project is over, there is still much work to be done. One of the first things that should be done is to adequately thank all those who played a role in the success of the campaign or activity. *This is an absolute must.* The more professional and visible this expression of appreciation can be made, the better.

Additionally, there is a need to review the activities and the accomplishments during and immediately after the conclusion of the event, while things are still fresh in one's mind. This is the time to review the written reactions and suggestions that had been made throughout the campaign. In this way, it is possible to have ready reference to ideas and suggestions that, if implemented, might improve and enhance the operation in the future. Thus, maintaining detailed records of what takes place in any promotional project or fundraising activity is an important requirement. Such record keeping (hard data as well as soft data) is the first step in establishing a meaningful and complete evaluation of the activities.

There should also be a checklist of things that had to be accomplished and an indication whether they were accomplished in a timely and acceptable manner. There will need to be a recommendation sought as to whether or not the project should be repeated in the future, and if so, what changes should be implemented to improve the campaign. This is where the value of hindsight comes into play. However, one must work at using hindsight by keeping explicit records and seeking input and recommendations *immediately* after such a project has been completed. Waiting several months will impede the ability of those who worked with the project to remember details and will dilute the quality of the information provided.

WHY FUNDRAISING AND PROMOTIONAL EFFORTS FAIL

There are numerous reasons why promotional and fundraising tactics fail. There are almost as many reasons for failure as there are different projects. However, a few of the reasons stand out above the rest and deserve mention here. *One* reason is that individuals try to copy exactly what another program has done without taking into consideration the different circumstances, limitations, and resources that exist in their own particular situation.

> **PRINCIPLE # 96:** *Being cognizant of the reasons why other organizations' efforts typically fail will enable one to avoid such pitfalls in planning, organizing and implementing one's own project*

A *second* reason is the expectation of immediate gratification. That is, there is an expectation that the so-called successful fundraising project or promotional activity will take place almost immediately, without adequate, advanced and sustained planning. Finally, a *third* reason for failure of fundraising activities is the attempt to substitute quantity for quality in terms of both individual and group activity. It is still better to do a few things correctly than attempting to spread oneself so thin that the result is less than a quality effort, and ends up being an inferior product or service.

Naturally, a lack of any of the essential ingredients necessary for a successful fundraising effort will significantly hinder the attempt to generate funds. The absence of proper leadership, as well as "followship," the absence of periodic assessment of efforts, the lack of necessary resources, inadequate allocation of resources, lack of priorities, poor timing, outside competition, misunderstanding of the needs of the publics, absence of a marketable or promotable product or service, absence of a good cause, poor or adverse publicity and/or public relations, failure to emphasize the urgency of the fundraising opportunity, tasks that are too complicated, campaigns or activities that last too long, a lack of motivation to act (lack of urgency), as well as poor implementation tactics can hinder or even doom the fundraising project.

REFERENCES

Blum, D.E. (1994). Athletics departments turn to planned giving. *The Chronicle of Higher Education, XLI*(13), A-36.

Briggs, J., Jr. (1984). *The official football fundraiser's guide.* North Palm Beach, Florida: Boosters Clubs of America.

Booth endows Cornell coaching position. (1999, September 2). *Brockport Post*, p. 10-A.

Cohen, A. (1996). Raking it in. *Athletic Business, 20*(8), 16-18.

Cole, S. L. (2000). A cash crop. *Training & Conditioning, X*(2), 30, 32-35.

Corporations find giving pays in hard times. (1991, August, 29). *USA Today.* p. B-1.

Diles, D. L. (1996,). Turning on the revenue stream. *Athletic Management, VIII*(10), 51-52, 54.

Fund-a-thon season hits full stride. (1991, May 3). *USA Today*, p. D-1.

Harbaugh group bought more golf than charity. (2000, June 2). *USA Today*, p. 19-C.

Hardekopf, B. (1989, January). Developing the campaign. *College Athletic Management (CAM), I*(1), 36.

Helping NAGWS. (1994, Winter). *GWS News, 20*(2), 1.

Henricks, M. (1996, April). 80/20 vision. *Entrepreneur,* pp. 68-69, 71-72.

King, B. (2001, June 11-17). Big, hairy, audacious goals. *Street & Smith's Sportbusiness Journal,* pp. 3. 31.

Lopiano, D. A., (1983). How to raise funds for non-revenue sports. *Athletic Purchasing & Facilities, 7*(11), 32-37.

McDermott-Griggs, S., & Card, J. (1992, January). Creating a successful fundraising letter. *Journal of Physical Education, Recreation and Dance, 63*(1), 57-58.

McMillen, L. (1990a). Philanthropic Contributions. *The Chronicle of Higher Education, XXXVI*(39), A-1, A-23.

McMillen, L. (1990b). A study to determine the cost of raising a dollar finds that average college spends just 16 cents. *The Chronicle of Higher Education, XXXVII*(1), A31.

Miller, L. (1999). Charity begins on line. *USA Today*, p. 6-D.

Nasser, H. E. (2001, November 15). Sept. 11 Victims will receive all of Liberty Fund, *USA Today,* p. 5-A.

Red Cross squanders goodwill. (2001, October 31). *Chicago Tribune*, p. 14.

Robinson, M. (1997). The motivation behind the money. *Athletic Management, IX*(2), 45-48.

Roy, Y. (2001, November 15). Red Cross now says all monies to go to victims of 9-11 attacks, *Democrat and Chronicle*, p. 6-A.

Stier, W.F., Jr., (2009). *Fundraising projects for sport, recreation, leisure and fitness programs.* Boston, MA: American Press.

Weiner, R. (2000, September 19). AD puts Stanford on a winning track. *USA Today*, p. 1-C, 2-C.

Yiannakis, A., & Braunstein, S. (1983). *The complete guide to successful fundraising.* North Palm Beach, Florida: American Sports Education Institute.

DISCUSSION QUESTIONS

1. Provide some examples of difficulties that some fundraising entities have experienced in their efforts to raise funds and how these difficulties might have been prevented.

2. Outline the major sources of funds being raised with current examples.

3. Explain how different fundraising efforts might be appropriate for different time frames in terms of one-time event, annual events and repeatable events. Provide examples of such efforts for each such category.

4. How do endowments work and what is the history of endowment creation for sports?

5. Explain the *Guilt and Glitter* syndrome and provide examples how this concept might work for a college athletic program. Provide examples.

6 | STRATEGIES AND TACTICS OF RAISING MONEY

Take advantage of homing festivities as a opportunity to generate exposure and support

CHAPTER HIGHLIGHTS

This chapter will emphasize:

- The *supermarket approach* or the *business revenue approach* to raising money
- The *KISS philosophy* in fundraising
- The need to create a sense of urgency in the eyes of the potential donor when raising funds
- How to determine whether or not a specific proposed activity is worthwhile in terms of expenditure of money, time and effort.
- Why sound fiscal management in the current operation of the sport program is a prerequisite for successful fundraising

- Justification for soliciting money internally, from one's own staff, before initiating funds from outsiders
- The necessity for obtaining permission from superiors prior to beginning a fundraising project
- Potential pitfalls of initiating a fundraising effort that competes with another fundraising activity already planned by one's own organization
- The necessity to have fundraising and promotional efforts compatible with community and institutional standards
- The restrictions placed by an organization (through a clearinghouse office) on any effort to generate resources by its personnel
- Various State laws and regulations that govern fundraising by educational institutions
- Why repeat fundraisers are easier to conduct and are more successful the second time around
- Several businesses that participate in the national *matching gift program*
- The rationale for the initiation of a *feasibility study* prior to embarking upon a full blown fundraising effort
- The quiet phase of major fundraising
- The rationale as to why organizers should know where a majority of funds are coming from prior to announcing a general fund drive
- The use of appropriately stationed "ringers" to motivate prospective donors to action

DEVELOPING A CONCEPTUAL APPROACH

To be successful in generating additional resources requires a thorough understanding of all of the separate elements or components associated with fundraising, promotion and public relations. The knowledge base that accompanies the mastery of the principles outlines in this book will go a long way to help the reader become an effective and efficient fundraiser. Figure 6.1 depicts the wide range of activities and elements that successful fundraisers and promoters can engage in within their respective job descriptions.

Chapter 6: Strategies and Tactics of Raising Money

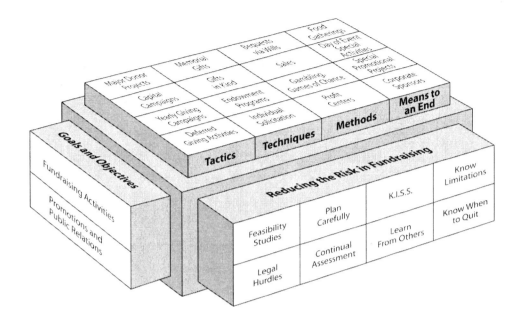

Figure 6.1 A Conceptual Approach to Fundraising and Promotions

TWO APPROACHES TO THE RAISING OF MONIES

The raising of money (resources) can be accomplished through two approaches, *first*, via the so-called **supermarket** or **merchandising model**. The *second* method is through the formal **solicitation model**.

> **PRINCIPLE # 97:** *The generation of money can be conceptually viewed as involving two distinct models*

In the **supermarket** or **merchandising model** there is an actual sale or transfer of items or services. Items such as pennants, ashtrays, t-shirts, publications, car washes or coupon redemption plans with various kinds of retail establishments can all be sold. Additionally, other things that can be marketed include drawings of one kind or another (with prizes going to the winners) and various gambling activities.

Others have also called this model the **business revenue approach**, highlighting the value of the product or service to the customer/donor. The buyer purchases and/or donates monies, products or services in exchange for an expectation of something of value (a benefit) in exchange. In this situation, the motivating factor underlying the purchase of the so-called benefit is the benefit itself while the worthiness of the sport program itself frequently plays a secondary role in the motivation scheme (Bronzan, 1984). A national telephone survey conducted in 2001 of 1,000 adults (men and women) revealed that 74 percent had recently purchased something from a school or youth group that was involved in fundraising for a worthwhile project (http://www.efundraising.com).

The **solicitation** or **appeal model** involves the solicitation or asking of money, services and/or products from prospective contributors. The motivational force behind the donation, on behalf of the donor lies in the charitable, intangible, or worthy cause aspect or facet. That is, the donor gives primarily because of the worthiness of the cause and only secondarily (if at all) because of any real or tangible benefit reverting to the donor.

Donating versus Buying "Something"

> *PRINCIPLE # 98:* **Donations generate more net monies for charitable causes than sales of products or services**

When comparing the *charitable industry* (securing donations based on solicitation) with the so-called *product fundraising industry* (securing monies based on selling a product or service) one finds that people *contribute* (simply give or donate) far more to charitable causes than they *spend* (for goods and services) in an effort to help charitable causes. A recent national study confirmed this when it was revealed that the giving donations to charities is a $135 billion annual enterprise while purchasing products and services in an effort to support or help charities is a mere $7 billion annual enterprise. What this means is that people who help charitable causes do so via the donation process 18 more times than they do by buying a service or product.

> *PRINCIPLE # 99:* **Develop a sense of urgency to act when discussing or presenting needs to prospects**

There should be a full understanding on behalf of the prospective donor of the *urgency to act* as well as the *worth, value,* and the *importance* of the sport program. Finally, there must be an appreciation of how the actual contribution will lead to the realization of specific goals of the program that are of value and worth supporting.

It is the responsibility of the fundraiser to insure that each potential donor is made aware of these facts. Donors must be motivated to act. Unless there is a real urgency, in reality, why should the prospective donor make the contribution now rather than at some time in the future? It just becomes too easy to procrastinate and to put off the act of actually making the donation until a future time unless there is a real need (an urgency) for the act to be consummated at the present time. This urgency or need to act can be further facilitated by the presence of excitement and enthusiasm (which is contagious) derived from the association with the sport or recreation program and the fundraising activities.

To successfully raise funds it is not necessary for the staff or support group to always cite an emergency situation with potentially dire consequences if monies are not forthcoming. Sometimes additional resources are needed to provide for enhancements of a sport program. Without these additional resources, however, the program and related activities will not wither, die, and blow away in the sunset. There are other justifications for soliciting support than citing potential catastrophes. In fact, if one always solicits contributions on the basis of averting some calamity (the "Chicken Little syndrome") it does not take too long for the prospective donors to grow tired and wary of such thinly veiled threats or predictions. No one wants to repeatedly give to a perpetually sinking sport program.

THE FEASIBILITY OF RAISING FUNDS

The answers to the following questions will go a long way to determine whether or not a specific proposed activity is worthwhile in terms of expenditure of money, time, effort, etc.

1. Does the fundraising activity meet the needs of the sport program?
2. Is there really a need?
3. Is this the only way, or the best way, of meeting this need?
4. Is the program itself worthy of support?
5. Is there adequate and competent leadership available?
6. Is the necessary "followship" available? Are there sufficient volunteers?
7. Is there an athletic support infrastructure capable of achieving the successful conclusion of the fundraising effort?
8. Is there is a support organization or booster club in existence?
9. Is this organization recognized as the official representative of the sport program in terms of fundraising?
10. Is there a positive image of the support organization in the eyes of the various constituencies?
11. How much will it "cost" to raise the desired amount in terms of time consumed, money spent, effort expended and services used?
12. What are the downside risks? Is the effort cost effective in terms of money, time and effort, personnel, and other resources?
13. Are the necessary resources available in terms of budgeting, publicity, office management, etc.?

14. What are the requirements in terms of time to reach the objective(s)? Can the objective(s) be reached in that time?
15. Are legal matters taken care of (incorporation, taxes, special permits, etc.)?
16. Is the image of the total sport program a positive one as viewed by various constituencies?
17. Are the financial and political climates conducive to success?

When soliciting contributions, one should be willing and able to fully discuss with potential donors the needs and strengths of the organization, the activities, the program, as well as how the money will benefit the program and the participants with the prospect(s). Donors like to know how their contributions will be used to facilitate or improve the program. People like to see results, tangible results, of their efforts.

> **PRINCIPLE # 100:** *Don't bad mouth the organization or program when attempting to raise money*

Although this seems like an overly obvious statement, this principle is violated repeatedly. Citing a problem or deficiency with the support received from the central administration, as the reason that additional funds are needed, creates as many problems as may be solved. A sport program may be in need of additional monies or services without having to place *blame* on any one individual, group or organization. It isn't necessary or appropriate to criticize or to cast a negative light upon others to raise money for one's program. An upbeat, positive approach is far more productive, both in terms of internal and external public relations and in terms of actual dollars raised. No one likes to hear individuals speak ill of others. And, that is just what fundraisers do if they cite the lack of support by the organization or by higher administrators as the justification as to why they "have" to raise *outside* funds for the sport program (Stier, 1997).

Too frequently school based fundraisers attempt to garner funds by stating, either outright or through implication, that the school or the athletic program is unwilling or unable to adequately support the athletic or sport activity in the manner in which it should be supported. And, as a result, the present fundraising effort has to be implemented. Naturally, the impression left is one of negativism towards the school and/or the athletic program, not to mention the staff and administrators within the school and athletic program. Such an approach is needless and counter-productive. The end result will often be ill will and the creation of an adversarial relationship.

It is all in the way the fundraising activity is approached. If approached in a positive vein, from a perspective that the sport program will be *enhanced* with additional financial resources, etc., the end result will more likely be positive in terms of both financial contributions and in terms of positive public relations. It is important to remember that athletic fundraising efforts will have an important impact upon the public image and upon the public relations perception of the total sport program, as well as upon the total organization. If approached from the positive aspect, everyone can win.

If approached from the negative aspect, and the justification for the fundraising causes the overall organization or sport program to look like it is not fulfilling its responsibilities, the fundraising effort will have certainly failed in terms of creating a positive public relations image. In fact, just the opposite would have taken place, i.e., the creation of a negative image.

> *PRINCIPLE # 101: Never pay (full price) for anything you can get for a reduced cost or for free*

It is important to never pay for anything, whether a product or a service, that can be obtained for free via a contribution. Not spending money for tangible resources or services that can be obtained for free or on a reduced cost basis is an important goal of any sport program. Doing so is the same as generating real cash, for it allows the sport organization to free up the cash, that would have had to be spent for the acquiring of these resources, for other purposes.

If resources cannot be obtained via discounts or through donations, attempts should be made to barter or trade for needed resources. Exchanges or trade-outs of *athletic resources* such as tickets, appearances by members of coaching staff, provision of advertising space, etc., can be exchanged for such *needed assets* as cash, advertising space, services, supplies, equipment, etc. The object is clear. The sport program is in need of resources. These resources can be obtained either via contributions or via an exchange of assets (which may or may not be discounted) with individuals or organizations. The possibilities and opportunities are endless and yet the principle is simple.

Another wrinkle in this whole area of utilization of resources obtained through charitable contributions or through exchanges of assets revolves around what is actually done with the resources or assets once they are on hand. For example, merchandise, services or products, once obtained can be utilized in the *general operation of the sport or recreation program* or can be used *as a resource that can generate additional resources*. For example, a side of prime beef that was donated to or exchanged for something of value with an athletic department can become (1) steaks for the athletes at their training table or (2) can be used to generate actual cash via an auction held in conjunction with a formal fundraising event.

Sport people interested in increasing the financial base for their athletic or recreation program should make known to potential contributors that the internal fiscal management of their athletic program is conducted on sound principles. This includes the assurances that the day-to-day management operation is sound and that the fiscal or accounting procedures meet all generally accepted criteria. It is vital that the current fiscal management of the sport operation be viewed as being responsibly managed. That is, that the dollars that are available to the sport program within the budget are well spent. It becomes increasingly difficult, if not almost impossible, to generate additional funding from outside sources when the fiscal management of the resources that are available leaves much to be desired.

> **PRINCIPLE # 102:** *It is easier to raise money when one can show sound fiscal management in the current operation of the sport program*

A generally accepted assumption in fundraising is that if the cause is just and worthwhile, the organization's internal staff personnel should be willing to provide substantial support, in a material fashion, to the fundraising effort by significantly contributing to the effort themselves. If the organization cannot convince its own people to contribute to its cause, why would a so-called outsider feel a compulsion to make a contribution? That is why it is important to have the data as to what percentage of one's own internal staff contributes to the program. Having this information available, combined with the knowledge of the average contribution of the organization's internal constituencies, can go a long way to convince outside individuals and organizations that those individuals closest to the sport or recreation organization hold the program in high esteem. The end result is a greater likelihood of contributions from outside donors.

SOURCES FOR GENERATING NEEDED RESOURCES

> **PRINCIPLE # 103:** *Exhaust internal avenues of generating support prior to instituting external fundraising projects*

Prior to attempting to institute a full-blown external fundraising campaign or major project one should examine other sources of income, particularly those sources of money internal to the sports organization. It is suggested that only after the internal sources of funding are exhausted should one focus on outside fundraising efforts.

Generally speaking, there are four ways to be able to increase the athletic program's purchasing power, figure 6.2. These four avenues are listed below in terms of priority, that is, in the order of importance within the sports program.

The *first* method of increasing the program's fiscal resources is through the justification of additional funding from the sponsoring organization. The principle is the same when dealing with non-school sport entities or recreation departments. The ability to convince the "powers to be" of the need for such additional funds can greatly reduce the need for outside fundraising activities.

A *second* method or tactic that can be pursued in terms of obtaining additional fiscal resources (money, goods, and services) revolves around the wise fiscal management of resources that are currently available to the sport or recreation program. Every dollar saved, in reality, is a dollar earned. This is no trite statement. It is a significant fact. One must be frugal in one's management of resources and in one's purchasing practices. For every dollar saved through whatever methods are utilized there is a corresponding reduction in the need to raise money. In other words, one can raise money by saving money.

The *third* tactic revolves around the internal fundraising through profit centers that are organized and managed by the sports staff. To the extent that these profit centers (tickets, concessions, parking, etc.) are successful in generating significant amounts of money for the athletic program, there is a corresponding reduction in the need to raise additional funds outside the school or athletic arena.

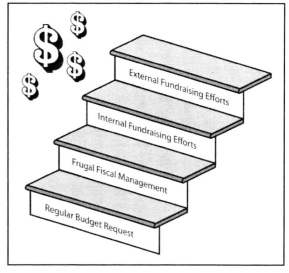

Figure 6.2 Sources of Financial Resources

However, there are times when there is a demonstrated need for additional monies *in spite of* effective and efficient fiscal management in the day-to-day operation of the sports program. And, in some instances money is needed *in addition to* the financial support provided through the sponsoring organization. Even internal fundraising efforts that might have been instituted are not sufficient to meet all of the program's needs. When all of the above methods fail to generate needed funds, then the *fourth* and final avenue for generating sufficient fiscal support for an athletic program, the so-called **formal, external fundraising effort** is not only warranted but also required.

Securing Permission to Engage in Fundraising Activities

> **PRINCIPLE # 104:** *Obtain input and approval prior to initiating promotional and fundraising activities—"spread the blame/responsibility"*

The administrative principle of seeking counsel and prior approval for fundraising activities is important for two very pragmatic reasons: (1) to gather potentially helpful ideas and suggestions and, (2) should anything go wrong, to distribute the fallout or negative consequences. This is sometimes referred to as the *spreading the blame/responsibility syndrome*.

Far too often, would-be fundraisers are in too great a hurry to carry out their plan of attack. The result is that they find themselves out on a limb, all alone. Those in authority, who should be passing ultimate judgment on the suitability of such activities and who are held to be ultimately responsible, are not consulted. This lack of consultation, this lack of securing approval can become a major stumbling block for the fundraiser.

> *PRINCIPLE # 105:* **Don't interfere with overall fundraising efforts of the central organization or administration—recognize the pecking order of one's own group or entity**

It is important not to have one's fundraising activities interfere (or be perceived to interfere) with the overall fundraising efforts of the central organization or administration. This is especially relevant in schools. Most school systems and many colleges or universities have policies that restrict fundraising efforts to those activities that have been approved by and are coordinated through a designated administrative office (McIntyre & Anderson, 1987).

There does exist a pecking order within any organization in terms of who will be encouraged or allowed to be involved in specific fundraising activities. Recognizing this pecking order or hierarchy eliminates many headaches for the athletic fundraising practitioner. The pecking order in terms of fundraising importance within schools might include fundraising efforts on behalf of or by the school board, the superintendent or the principal, various department chairpersons, the band, various music groups, numerous athletic teams, the school newspaper, the year book, numerous organizations, special class trips, etc. The list could go on and on.

There must be an established procedure or system for requesting permission to engage in fundraising and promotional activity. There should be set criteria against which all requests to raise funds may be judged. Additionally, there must be priorities established that guide the approval process. Finally, there must be a clear understanding of exactly who will be the individual (or individuals) who will have the power to actually authorize the "go-ahead" of any specific fundraising proposal.

Of course, great care must be taken to insure that there are provisions for equal treatment and protection of all sports in terms of compliance with both the letter and intent of Title IX, if applicable. Towards this end, it is advisable to involve members of the central administrative staff. In high schools those individuals might be the vice principal, principal and perhaps the superintendent. In colleges and universities the athletic director, the dean, the Vice President, and even the President, might be involved in reviewing and approving the establishment of the criteria and procedures to be used to determine what type of projects are appropriate, etc.

> **PRINCIPLE # 106:** *Many organizations have some type of internal clearinghouse (office) though which requests to fundraise must be passed and approved*

Frequently, such criteria and procedures are included within the *Athletic Handbook of Policies, Procedures, Practices, Priorities and Philosophy(ies) [5-Ps]*. One educational institution has the policy that stipulates that requests for sport fundraising activities be first submitted in writing to the athletic director for review and possible approval. The information included within the formal request to engage in raising monies includes:

1. How the money would be generated—details of the methods to be used
2. How much money is needed
3. The time involved
4. Who will be contacted in the quest for money
5. The method for accounting of the funds generated
6. For what purpose(s) the money will be used

Following approval at the departmental level, the request is channeled "upstairs" to the next appropriate administrative level for review and approval or rejection at that level. However, the final approval is reserved for the chief executive officer or designee who will decide whether or not the specific request has merit and can be permitted to be implemented.

At each of the levels of review, the appropriate administrator or staff member may provide written statements relating to the reasons why the request is rejected or written statements which stipulate under what circumstances the fundraising project can be initiated. There are two significant advantages of such a review process. *First*, the coaches or boosters who desire to engage in fundraising activities have valuable input and guidance from other administrators, some of whom are experienced fundraisers within the institution. *Second*, the central administrators are aware of the specifics of the request to raise funds and are able to pass judgment on its merits, taking care that such activity would not interfere with the *big fundraising picture* of the total institution or organization.

An example of such a request form that is utilized by coaches to receive permission from the central administration of a university is provided within **Appendix C**. This form was created to be used in the review process so that a number of central administrators, athletic and non-athletic, will be able to review each request and to render a decision as to its suitability for the institution.

> **PRINCIPLE # 107:** *Fundraising and promotional efforts must be compatible with community and institutional standards*

One of the first questions that should be raised in any consideration of a fundraising project or promotional activity is whether such activity would meet the standards for the community in which the event(s) will be held. For example, in some communities gambling activities might be not only frowned upon by the various constituencies (on religious or moral grounds) but might also have legal limitations. The importance of considering the educational, ethical, traditional, religious, and social code should not be minimized in evaluating the suitability and acceptability of any proposed activity or event.

Of course, the determination of what is appropriate and what is not appropriate will vary in light of what type of sport or recreation program is involved. It may also vary in different sections of the country and from community to community within the same state. What may be suitable, in terms of raising monies or promotional events for a university located in New York City might be totally inappropriate for a midget football program in a small farming community located in the south.

Some examples will suffice. The question of accepting tobacco (cigarettes, cigars and chewing tobacco) advertisement for the sport program or for inclusion on sport schedule cards is very controversial in some parts of the country and at different levels of competition. On the one hand, athletic programs in schools are attempting (or so they say) to educate students-athletes as to the evils of stimulants and depressants (misuse, abuse, and use of drugs). On the other hand, many of these same sport programs are accepting advertisements from companies that produce, advertise, market and sell cigarettes, cigars and/or chewing tobacco.

The same scenario can be drawn in respect to alcohol. Is it appropriate on one hand to take money, services, and products from these corporations and businesses, while on the other hand discouraging the use of these products of these businesses among the athletes? This is another area of controversy that must be decided on an individual basis.

Food sales by Booster Clubs are always helpful in generating money and support

Various individual institutions as well as national organizations, including the NCAA, had initiated a dialogue over two decades ago concerning the appropriateness of accepting advertisements for alcohol as well as tobacco products in various tournament publications (Advertising, 1989). Similarly, there are ever increasing concerns being expressed in athletic circles in terms of any type of advertisements for sporting events from the alcohol and/or cigarette industries. The final word has not been heard on this continuing controversial subject even in the 21st century.

What is evident, however, is that should such advertisements become *persona non grata*, it will be more difficult to generate monies to replace these lost revenues. This is because advertisement monies and contributions towards sports at many levels from the alcohol and tobacco industries have been significant in terms of total dollars, services and goods provided. Should these dollars disappear, the challenge for the sport fundraisers will be to replace these contributions (in terms of actual dollars, goods and services) with similar support from other sources. It has become very easy, almost too easy, for administrators to supplement their sports budgets by tapping the almost bottomless pot of gold held out by the tobacco and alcohol corporations.

And, of course, there can always be found examples of poor taste and inappropriate promotions (some of which involve efforts to increase funding). The Charleston RiverDogs had such a promotion when it planned and implemented a special Father's Day promotion for the class A baseball team. The *Father's Day vasectomy promotion* met with less than obvious enthusiasm among the general public—for obvious reasons. Shortly after the team's management announced the Father's Day vasectomy promotion, team officials backtracked and withdrew the offer (Charleston RiverDogs, 2000).

RESTRICTIVE PHILOSOPHIES

> *PRINCIPLE # 108: Always be cognizant of any restrictions pertaining to fundraising activities*

Fundraisers must remain cognizant of *any restrictive philosophies or policies* existing *within their organization or school* that might have an effect upon their plans. These restraints may take the form of *internal* or *external restrictions*.

State Laws and Department of Education Rules Restricting Fundraising at Schools

There are many regulations that exist in various states that affect fundraising efforts, especially at schools as well as for other non-profit as well as for-profit entities. These regulations can be state, county or municipality laws or department of education department's rules and/or guidelines that pertain to fundraising efforts. These restrictive directives must be followed and adhered to by the sport as well as the recreation administrator who engage in fundraising efforts.

The State Department of Regents in New York, for example, has very specific guidelines and rules regulating fundraising within educational institutions (K-12) within the Empire State. For example, there is a prohibition in terms of direct solicitation of charitable donations from public school students on school property *during school hours* (this includes during home room periods, lunch periods and during extracurricular activities). Although student organizations and school related organizations are allowed to engage in fundraising activities, the activities *may not take place at school during school hours, period* (NYSAHPERD Link, 1999).

Clearinghouse for Fundraising Activities

In some schools and sport related organizations, there are restrictions on the number of fundraising projects that are allowed to be implemented during a specific time period of the school year. In some communities, there is an unwritten agreement or understanding between the school and the local Merchants Association that individual merchants will not be "hit" with repeated requests for money by numerous groups from the school. For example, band boosters, individual coaches, athletic boosters, representatives from student government, or from the school paper, or from the school radio or television station, or from individual student organizations within the school. Rather, these schools and organizations attempt to coordinate or regulate all such fundraising efforts so that the individual merchants will have only a few *official* requests from representatives of the school. Such an arrangement goes a long way towards creating a positive, professional image on behalf of the school and the sport program in the eyes of the community.

Placing a limitation on the number (as well as type) of fundraising projects that school groups might implement during a school year can prevent the situation in which ten different groups attempt to sell Xmas ornaments during the month of December. It also prevents the situation in which ten car washes are held during the first week of school. Such examples of *overkill* can be prevented if all potential plans have to have prior approval through one central office or *clearinghouse.* This clearinghouse can be a committee or an individual, such as the athletic director, the director of development or the office of public relations, etc. In an organization of any size, but especially in a school, there is always a need for coordination of *all* fundraising activities, as well as an understanding of what is appropriate in light of the history, the philosophy, and the existing circumstances within the organization and the community.

> **PRINCIPLE # 109:** Don't pick up "nickels" when others can pick up "quarters" or even "dollars"

Picking up "Nickels," "Quarters," or "Dollars"

Similarly, another type of overkill is exemplified when a coach, administrator or sports booster approaches local businesses to raise so-called "nickels" (small dollar amounts) for a particular sport, followed by the chief sport administrator hitting the same local businesses for so-called "quarters" (moderate amount of funds) for the overall athletic program. These efforts are then followed by the development officer, the principal or the president approaching these same businesses for the so-called "big bucks"—only to find the community businesses most unreceptive to such repeated requests for funds from the same organization. Community people and businesses can become "tapped out" (figuratively and literally) by such repeated requests or "hits."

Limitations as to Who May Be Solicited

There may be specific individuals, groups or organizations placed "off limits" as potential donors for sport fundraisers. This is frequently done so that representatives of the same organization do not repeatedly approach these donors. Rather, they are reserved for visits or solicitations by the representatives of the higher administration—the so-called *heavy hitters*.

> **PRINCIPLE # 110:** Don't complain that others approach potential donors if you had not shown initiative in contacting the same donors

On the other hand, there is always the possibility that the sport fundraiser may initially face a negative response on behalf of the central administration but, through persuasive arguments, may make a case to have the specific sport fundraising effort approved. This was the case at a well-known university (NCAA Division I), located in the Midwest. The university administrative hierarchy, the institutional fundraisers, balked and complained to the President that the athletic staff had approached a national beer distributor, located in their state, for corporate sponsorship, trade outs, and numerous other fundraising activities. The potential consequences involved hundreds of thousands of dollars going to the athletic department over the next three to five years, with the promise of much more to come.

The university development people advanced the argument that **they** were *going* to approach the same prospect (beer distributor) in the future and that this prospect rightly belonged to the overall university development apparatus. As such, they argued, this prospect should be off limits to the athletic fundraising staff.

The athletic director countered that position by advancing the argument that the university, as well as the beer distributor, had both been in existence for many, many decades and, up to that point in time at least, the university development staff *had failed to even ask* the beer distributor for any money. Thus, it was argued, the beer distributor should be considered as fair game. It was the athletic director who was able, in the short span of several months, to conclude a sizeable and long-term financial arrangement with the company. A multi-year arrangement that would result in literally hundreds of thousands of dollars in cash plus an equal amount of contributions in the form of equipment, supplies and services, including radio and television time, accruing to the athletic program on an annual basis was due to the initiative and creativity of the athletic department. In this particular case, the argument advanced by the athletic department prevailed.

CONCENTRATE ON THE PROJECTS THAT WILL PRODUCE THE MOST BENEFITS

One has to be choosy in selecting which fundraising projects and which promotional activities to undertake. Promotional activities and special events can be designed to raise money, increase attendance, improve image, and provide recognition to team members, coaches, boosters, and sponsors.

> ***PRINCIPLE # 111:*** *Don't waste efforts or time on "nickel and dime" fundraising projects*

One must concentrate on those fundraising activities that will generate the greatest number of dollars, services, and products from donors. Brent Steurwald, AD at Shenendehowa High School in Clifton Park, New York, echoed this sentiment when he was quoted as saying: "We absolutely decided that we were not going to 'nickel and dime' it . . . I wasn't going to ask my wife to bake cookies and sell them . . . We ran fund-raising events that had extremely high return with minimal amount of effort" (Cohen, 1991, p. 25).

There must be meaningful outcomes in light of the *total* resources expended. Spending too many resources on fundraising activities that generate few dollars, or on promotional activities that are only marginally successful, is foolish. Since time and effort is finite, the activities undertaken must be not only successful but also meaningful in terms of actual dollar value received—in cash, services or products. Administrators must learn to place a dollar value on the time and effort of their staff and then use both effectively and efficiently in promotional and fundraising efforts. It is necessary to set priorities in terms of where to allocate resources and efforts for the maximum impact, whether that impact is money or public exposure.

Chapter 6: Strategies and Tactics of Raising Money

> **PRINCIPLE # 112:** *Repeat successful fundraising or promotional activities are easier to complete than new ones—and take less time and effort*

Generally speaking, the number of special fundraising projects should be limited to those that will generate at least 10% to 15% of the annual net donations needed. Thus, seven to ten distinct fundraising activities during any twelve months period should be the maximum number of projects attempted. **Ideally**, the number should be much less (*each generating at least 20% of the money needed—thus, a maximum of five projects total*), with the dollar value per project much greater.

The second time around is always easier. This is especially true if careful and accurate records are kept of the activities previously implemented. The key is to maintain written documentation of previous fundraising and promotional attempts. This documentation serves as a guide for the future so that successful efforts may be replicated, while unsuccessful ones can be eliminated from further consideration. Much time and effort can be saved by repeating what had proved to be successful in the past, since the initial planning, work, and evaluating has already taken place.

> **PRINCIPLE # 113:** *Emphasize the positive aspects resulting from the fundraising drive or project rather than the negative consequences, should the attempt fail*

Another reason why a repeat project is often easier to implement, especially if the previous experience was highly successful, is that members of the public or various constituencies have an expectation of what the repeat activity will be like. And if it was a satisfying experience the first time, there is a predisposition to participate the second time around. Frequently, word of mouth advertisement helps to publicize the positive nature of the event or project. Good old fashion *word of mouth* is one of the best forms of advertising as well as motivating others to be more receptive to participate in a fundraising or promotional project.

SOLICITING AND GETTING POTENTIAL DONORS TO ACTUALLY CONTRIBUTE—GETTING THE JOB DONE

Prospective contributors, whether individuals or persons representing organizations or businesses, like to hear about the positive consequences that will result from the successful conclusion of the solicitation. Thus, the emphasis should be on the positive, that is, the meeting of the programmatic needs that will be possible with the contributions sought. Negativism or the veiled threat that dire consequences will result should there be insufficient contributions only reinforces a negative image of the sport area. The solicitation should be upbeat. Highlight the value of the sport activity and how the existence of the program or sport will meet the needs of the participants, the sport programs as well as the overall goals of the sponsoring organization.

> **PRINCIPLE #114: Take advantage of national matching gift programs**

Companies like Kodak and Xerox, as well as a whole host of other large and small companies throughout the United States, have created national corporate matching gift programs. These programs provide funds to match donations made by the employees of these firms to non-profit organizations with certain restrictions and specified dollar limitations. A matching gift program can often be one of the most cost-effective fundraising projects that can be implemented.

Some companies even provide more than a one-to-one match while others match contributions by retirees, outside directors, and even spouses in addition to employees. And, some companies provide some unique caveats for their matching gift programs. For example, Hewlett-Packard has a special program that encourages employees to pool their gifts for even great impact. KPMG Peat Marwick as early as the mid 1990s had a program which provided double or triple the employee gifts (with some restrictions). And IBM matches cash gifts at a 3 to 1 ration toward equipment (Matching Gifts, 1995, p. 2).

> **PRINCIPLE # 115: A matching gift program is one of the most cost-effective fundraising projects possible**

Altogether, there are well over 1,000 companies and some 5,000 subsidiaries in the United States that match employee contributions to specific not-for-profit. In 1954 corporate matching of employee contributions was initially introduced on a national scale. Between 1954 and 1990 over $1.2 billion dollars have been donated in this country through matching gifts to schools (including sports programs), cultural groups, public radio and television, hospitals, health social service groups, civic organizations and the United Way (7 Ways to Double, 1991). Today that figure is substantially higher.

The Council for Advancement and Support of Education (CASE, Suite 400, 11 Dupont Circle, Washington, D.C. 20036) serves as the National Clearinghouse for Corporate Matching Gift Information and publishes numerous pamphlets, leaflets, and books on the topic of matching gift programs. Today there are well over 1,000 companies that participate in the matching gift program for institutions of higher education. Altogether, CASE publishes four different leaflets listing companies possessing matching gift programs for (1) higher education, (2) elementary and secondary schools, (3) nonprofit cultural organizations and (4) hospitals, health, and other organizations.

Although the following statement may seem obvious, it is worth repeating again, and again, and again. It is imperative that one possesses integrity. A person's word is indeed one's bond, or should be. This is especially true in the area of fundraising. Maintaining the highest ethical standards, exhibiting complete honesty, as well as an openness in all that one does, helps create that all important positive image, which, in turn, helps to establish and sustain credibility.

> ***PRINCIPLE # 116: Maintain an open door policy in all that one does***

One way to facilitate the cooperative nature of working relationships is to assume a completely *open* and honest position in everything that one does. The one sure method of creating suspicion, apprehension, distrust, and doubt is to attempt to deny access to someone for any purpose. The fiscal books and all records should be *open* to all, literally. Maintaining an *open* door policy, holding meetings *open* to all, and being willing to respond directly to any and all questions, are positive elements in the creation of a positive image and reputation. This holds true for public and private schools as well as for youth sport teams and recreational organizations.

Although this degree of openness might seem, at first glance perhaps, as bordering on the inane, in reality, it is a sound judgment. Conducting one's activities in such an obvious non-secretive fashion, assuming such an open posture and projecting a honest image leads to a building of credibility and trust, which in turn, can form the basis or foundation for a positive and lasting relationship and a more productive fundraising effort on a continuous or periodic basis.

> ***PRINCIPLE # 117: People "buy" ideas from those they trust or those in whom they have confidence***

The one indispensable quality that each person has is one's credibility, one's truthfulness, if you will. This credibility (or integrity) is absolutely essential for long-term success in sport fundraising. Without it, one is doomed to fail. Building this trust, establishing this credibility, reinforcing this confidence, is the continual challenge and task of those involved in the institution, program or organization. One must work for the so-called long haul. There are no quick fixes in terms of building a deserved reputation of high integrity. In this same vein, one should not be a *flash in the pan* but one who is in the program for the long term, earning the respect of others by one's honest and forthright actions and decisions.

The worse case scenario would be when those involved in the promotion and fundraising activities are viewed with distrust and suspicion and having a lack of integrity. For the end result will be an inappropriate promotional effort and a failed fundraising attempt.

Types of Consumers

Sutton, McDonald and Milne (1997) identified four distinct classifications of consumers. These groups are referred to as: (1) non-aware consumers, (2) aware non-consumers, (3) misinformed non-consumers, and (4) media consumers. The names aptly describe the types of consumers or would-be fans of sport and recreation organizations, programs and activities.

The challenge is to generate some type of promotional or motivational scheme that would attract individuals to be more involved with the sport or recreation program. One strategy proposed by Sutton, McDonald and Milne (1997) is to implement a promotion or marketing project that would encourage individuals to "sample" the event or activity that your organization sponsors. Examples would include discounted prices, multiple admissions, sponsored bought tickets, premium give-a-ways, and special pre-game, half time or post-game activity or entertainment.

Advertising in non-traditional areas can also be effective in attracting the attention of would-be fans and consumers. Once new consumers are on site, efforts should be made to make them feel comfortable and at home. For example, special PA announcements welcoming them to the event as well as providing special welcome booths within the facility with special information and/or give-aways for first-time attendees can be very effective. The welcome booth can be used to secure the names and addresses of people in attendance on that date. A key to maintaining contact with these first-time consumers is to obtain the names and mailing addresses of these individuals so that the sport or recreation organization can maintain contact with these new consumers and would-be fans via the U.S. mail, phone and/or e-mail (Sutton, McDonald and Milne, 1997).

The Major Motivating Factor (Hot Button) of Prospects

> **PRINCIPLE # 118:** *Find the HOT BUTTON(S) of the potential prospect*

This so-called **hot button** is the major motivating factor that causes the potential contributor to become an actual contributor. One method is to create a sense of urgency on behalf of both the sport program and the prospective donor. This may be accomplished by establishing specific dates (deadlines) for securing specific sums of money. Or it may be accomplished by establishing financial goals within a certain period of time.

Chapter 6: Strategies and Tactics of Raising Money

Find out what turns the individual "on." What motivates the person to action? What are the needs of the person that can be satisfied by contributing to the sport program? This type of information is essential. This data must be ascertained and acted upon if one is to be successful in motivating one to action, i.e., deciding to actually contribute, in some fashion, to the sport or recreation program.

> **PRINCIPLE # 119:** *Identify and match needs of donors and constituencies with the program benefits provided by the organization*

In attempting to determine what motivates contributors, it is prudent to use sensitivity, awareness, empathy, intelligence, and respect in search of the prospective donors' needs. Various publics will have different characteristics, wants and needs (Moore and Gray, 1990).

A key element in obtaining a commitment from a prospect is determining what will make the person willing to act NOW in a manner beneficial to the sport program? *When there is a match or fit between the needs of the prospective donor and the benefits derived from contributing to the sport program the end result, usually, is a contribution of some fashion.*

> **PRINCIPLE # 120:** *Sell the "Sizzle"—as well as the "Steak"*

When asked to promote, publicize and market a need, it is wise to point out the *benefits* that will accrue to the sport program and/or to the donor. This is commonly referred to as selling the "sizzle, as well as the steak." It is the *benefits*, those that accrue to the sport program and those which accrue to the benefactor, which can be the motivating, attracting factors that resulting tangible assistance.

For example, when selling season tickets (the "steak") it is wise to promote the excitement and enjoyment ("sizzle") of the games. Sport organizations sell tickets, admission to athletic contests, to individuals, groups and organizations. However, the enjoyment and pride that the individual purchaser will experience by attending the games and by wearing the complimentary hat and jacket (both possessing the sport team's three color logo) that are given free to those purchasers of season tickets comprise the benefits, i.e., the "sizzle." Mere admission to the games is considered the "steak." The "sizzle" is the accompanying excitement, the enjoyment, the comradely and the pride one takes in the team during game day and by wearing the athletic program's stylish apparel.

The purpose of a feasibility study (conducting market research) is to investigate whether or not the project or activity will be successful—prior to actually committing the full resources and effort of the organization behind the project. In fundraising, it is nothing more than a way to test a potential fundraising program (service or product) to determine its potential. It is a means to diminish the downside risk in any one endeavor, through market or consumer researcher on a limited population (Frank, 1989). It is a trial effort.

Such research can assist the fundraiser by (1) surveying fans to determine what will help attract more of them to the sporting events, (2) developing a spectator or an audience profile so that it is possible to provide a more effective presentation to attract sponsors as well as advertisers, (3) measuring the potential effectiveness and/or actual effectiveness of a specific promotional campaign, and (4) assisting in fine tuning various promotional and marketing strategies.

A feasibility study for an athletic department should reveal characteristics of the community in which the project is to be conducted, as well as any special considerations that could affect the program, e.g., competition from other sources—schools, other sport programs or activities, service clubs, charities, etc. Feasibility studies are not the exclusive domain of professional sports or large athletic programs in major universities. To the contrary, small colleges as well as high schools and youth sport programs as well as recreation programs can take advantage of this strategic planning tool. There are several ways to accomplish this. Sport or recreation organizations can use their own staff or volunteers to complete feasibility studies. Of course, college or university athletic departments have only to go across campus and request assistance from the department of business or marketing within the same institution. There are numerous marketing classes conducted on college campuses throughout the country. The students in these classes are frequently looking for real-life projects to participate in for college credit.

PRINCIPE # 121: *For major fundraising projects—investigate the use of a feasibility study*

The potential fundraiser or promoter should contact the professor of such a marketing or advertising class/course and request assistance from selected students in the advertising/marketing class in terms of conducting a feasibility study. This study would not only assist the potential fundraiser but which would provide very valuable assistance and further hands-on experience to the students. Since the university or college students would most likely be juniors or seniors and would be working closely with their professor the likelihood of a meaningful and helpful feasibility study is enhanced.

Another way to secure a feasibility study is to solicit assistance (in the form of a contribution) from professionals who are involved in marketing and in conducting survey research. What better way to be able to obtain a feasibility study than to go to the recognized experts, those who conduct such studies for a living, and request such assistance as a donation.

Sometimes coaches and fundraisers find themselves in graduate school taking classes in administration, business, advertising or marketing. What better opportunity for the would-be fundraiser to kill two birds at one time than to conduct a feasibility study as part of the graduate class assignment as well as to reap the tangible benefits that such a study would provide. The point of the matter is that fundraisers and promoters should not shy away from utilizing the feasibility study as a meaningful tool. It can have a significant impact upon many fundraising projects.

Of course, it is not necessary to conduct a feasibility study or to do market research each time one wants to initiate a fundraising project. But, it is useful and worthwhile if one is to be involved in a single, major fundraising activity that will consume a significant amount of the organization's resources (time, money, effort, etc.).

Many feasibility studies are miniature attempts of the real thing. The feasibility study is followed by an assessment of success and failure, and can involve face-to-face interviews with selected members of the constituency, sometimes coupled with actual requests for contributions from selected members of the constituency. Such requests can be by means of actual physical, face-to-face meetings, mailings, e-mails, or phone calls.

The process of identifying characteristics of prospects (segmentation) should be systematic and done by professionals familiar in marketing research techniques or social science research. Such expert assistance should be sought out if the potential fundraiser lacks such expertise. In a college setting, the easiest way to obtain descriptors (age, sex, annual income, occupation, education, etc.) of any given segment of the population is to ask students in advertising and sport marketing classes or a professor to undertake this research as part of the class project (hopefully at no or minimal cost).

> **PRINCIPLE # 122:** *Keep the duration of any specific fundraising project to a limited, specified time period*

Or, the fundraiser can search for the information at the local library, the Chamber of Commerce and at the town hall or municipal building. "By pooling the obtained information, a fundraiser can obtain a picture of the total lifestyle pattern of prospective donors so that soliciting can be accurately targeted and motivating/cultivating techniques appropriately developed and scripted" (Buell, 1984, p. 616).

A specific, separate fundraising project, excluding such major efforts as capital campaigns, etc. should be conducted within a specific time frame. Generally speaking, the effort should be 4-6 weeks in duration. This is recommended because in fundraising activities that last longer than 4-6 weeks, it becomes very difficult to maintain and sustain the high level of energy needed for successful completion of the project. Also, it becomes too easy to put the work off until a later time. Most of the work will be completed within the last 30 days prior to the event anyway; human nature being what it is today. And, in some fundraising projects, such as candy sales, etc., the complete *selling window* should be restricted to a maximum of 7 days.

In any fundraising activity, the organizers should seek to spread the risk and minimize the actual involvement, while still sharing meaningfully in the income generated. That is, secure others as partners to assume some of the risk, as well as garner some of the rewards, so that both the effort, as well as the downside risk or exposure, are minimized (McKenzie, 1985).

Also, never begrudge others from reaping a reasonable profit when they co-broker a fundraising effort. As long as the sport program obtains the benefits sought, what does it matter what the so-called partner(s) gain?

For example, teams can enter into an agreement with a service club for the club's members to sell general admission tickets. The service club might net 25% to 35% of whatever the service club is able to sell in the way of tickets. The motivating factor on behalf of the service club is the potential profit from selling the tickets. The sport program will benefit as well through the 65% to 75% profit from the sale of tickets—with little effort and less downside risk on behalf of the sport entity.

Fundraisers would do well to adhere to the *KISS* philosophy when considering the advantages of simplicity of a fundraising. The *KISS* philosophy (*keep it simple and short*) holds true for most promotional and fundraising efforts. Simple fundraising and promotional activities are often the most successful. Short time frames are ideal.

> **PRINCIPLE # 123:** *Spread the risk, minimize the responsibility, and share the benefits*

Combining an athletic contest with fundraising for charity

The intricacies involved in complicated, dragged out projects often take away from the ultimate objectives with the process becoming the central issue rather than the actual objective, that is, raising money for the sport program. Besides, overkill via over complication can doom a potential fundraising effort before it ever gets off the ground. In fundraising, less is sometimes best.

An accepted principle in fundraising is to strike when the iron is hot. This simply means that the timing of the fundraising activity is *everything*. Witness the successful advertising, marketing, promotion and sale of such timely items as the pet rock, cabbage patch dolls, and the sensational hoola hoops.

Timing is crucial if the effort is to take advantage of a real or perceived need, a conducive climate or a receptive atmosphere.

A classic instance in which a college failed to act when timing was of the essence involved the winner of the $2,000 top prize in an athletic raffle. The winner, one of the community's leading business leaders, indicated to the school's sports information director that he was going to donate the $2,000 back to the organization. He indicated that when the President of the college arrived at his place of business to have their photo taken together (commemorating the winning of the $2,000 jackpot) that he would hand the check back to the President, with the stipulation that the money go back into the coffers of the sport support group (SSG).

However, due to an oversight, the President was not asked to visit the businessman. And, after a few months, this jackpot winner, in a conversation with a member of the support group, mentioned that he had given his wife the money as he thought that the college did not want the $2,000 since they had not bothered to contact him after he won the grand prize to make arrangements for the photo taking session. In this instance, the failure to follow-up cost dearly, both in terms of public relations and in terms of hard, cold cash.

THE QUIET PHASE OF MAJOR FUNDRAISING

The so-called *quiet phase of major fundraising* refers to the efforts by the organization engaged in raising funds to solicit contributions on the QT, very quietly, without major fanfare. This is done for several reasons. *First*, to determine whether such funds are capable of being generated. And, *second*, to be able to proclaim, when the official announcement of the big fundraising campaign is made (when the campaign is officially "kicked off") that a sizeable portion of the goal has already been raised. Nazareth college, a small, co-ed, liberal arts college located in upstate New York (Rochester) utilized this technique in 1996 when it announced a major campaign to raise $10 million dollars for its endowment for student scholarships, as well as for other areas of need. The president of the college at that time, Rose Marie Beston, indicated on the day that the announcement was made that the institution had already raised some $4.7 million of the goal during what she termed the "quiet phase" of the two-year campaign (Caputo, 1996).

> **PRINCIPLE # 124:** *Know where the majority of funds are coming from prior to announcing a general (major) fund drive*

In announcing a goal to the general public for any major fundraising activity, it is advisable to already have a sizeable amount collected (or committed in advance). The reason for this is that with proper planning one should know who are the prospective givers (heavy hitters). And, these individuals and organizations should have already been approached and have committed themselves. Thus, shortly after the announcement of the major fund drive the organizers can truthfully announce that one-third of the goal has already been reached. Again, this is a great motivator and generates even greater enthusiasm and support for the fund drive.

Prior to announcing the dollar goal, the 10 major donors and the next 100 largest donors should have been contacted and donations actually received or the pledges obtained. Having these gifts (or pledges) in hand is important so that specific amounts of current contributions can be publicly announced at strategic staggered intervals during the campaign.

Successful fundraising activities indeed spawn additional successful projects. The reputation that an organization earns through putting on successful fundraising projects only enhances its future efforts in generating additional monies through other promotional and money making activities. The successful atmosphere surrounding individual fundraising projects lends credence to these same or other projects being repeated in the future. Again, success breeds success. Success brings an expectation of success. And expectation of success facilitates future efforts.

The worse possible scenario in the world of fundraising is to actually attempt to raise funds but to fail and to be viewed by the public(s) as having failed. Members of the community often take a dim view of failure on behalf of those involved in fundraising for sport or recreation causes. Granted, not every attempt at fundraising will be a howling success. However, it is better not to even attempt to raise funds unless one is fairly confident of at least breaking even and not causing an embarrassment to the total sport or recreation program and the sponsoring organization.

Nothing turns off constituencies and members of the public more than a poorly orchestrated fundraising effort. This is especially true if it is perceived that the major reason for the failure of the effort is the incompetence or lack of expertise of the organization's staff. It becomes too easy to make that jump from the feeling of inadequacy of the staff in generating monies to the opinion that the staff might be inadequate and/or incompetent in their other areas of responsibility. Hence, becoming involved in raising money for sport or recreation is not something one should jump into without careful thought.

The practice of sprinkling so-called "ringers" within a crowd of prospective contributors is a time proven success strategy. One example of the use of "ringers" will suffice. However, the tactic has limitless possibilities within the world of fundraising.

> **PRINCIPLE # 125:** *Use strategically placed "ringers" to motivate others to action in meetings that are organized for the purpose of raising money*

The athletic staff planned a semi-formal dinner gathering of individuals who might be interested in becoming initial members of the school's booster club. Prior to the dinner festivities, the athletic director visited with several key community leaders as well as the superintendent and the principal. After the dinner, the athletic director was involved in delivering the pitch about the advantages of securing memberships within the newly created booster club and explaining the various levels of membership within the club.

When the athletic director announced that memberships were now going to be sold—the community leaders, including the superintendent and the principal, were most visible and vocal in their demonstration of support for the booster club. In fact, these individuals were among the very first group of people rising from their respective tables, which were situated throughout the large dining hall, to head toward the front of the room where the memberships were to be sold. These community leaders (these "ringers"), by their actions and their visible support, motivated others within the large room to likewise join these leaders in rising from their respective tables to head toward the front of the room to secure their respective memberships.

> **PRINCIPLE # 126:** *The public is fickle—they frequently overlook past successes but rarely forget (forgive) failures*

People tend to follow the actions of others who act in a specific manner, especially those whom they respect and/or those whom are of the same or higher social strata. Humans have been likened to a herd of cattle, unflattering but perhaps all too true, when it comes to being motivated to act when in a crowd. Like the group of cattle following the leader to some destination, people also tend to follow the action of others, especially if these other individuals have influence within the community or possess power or prestige. Thus, the use of these "ringers" to help motivate others to a specific course of action can be, if utilized properly, most effective and efficient.

One of the common faults of inexperienced, as well as experienced fundraisers and promoters, is attempting to do too much in terms of available time and resources. Trying to do too much can result in the significant lessening of quality of what is undertaken. This attempt to "be all things to all people" has scuttled many a would-be successful fundraiser. Priorities need to be established so that tasks that are "doable" with a minimum quality level can be undertaken.

An example of this can best be illustrated by explaining the strategic planning process that one school experienced. The newly organized booster organization decided at an early organizational meeting to follow the tactic of assuming responsibility for a few fundraising projects, but doing them in a correct and first-rate fashion. The first goal was to initiate a major membership drive for the purpose of generating three types of support: (1) moral support, (2) financial support, and (3) physical (personnel) support. Only after the initial membership drive was successful and there was the confidence that the membership drive on an annual basis would be successful, was there an effort to examine other means for generating additional dollars for the sport program.

The next project initiated was a major golf tournament in the spring of each year. After two years of an ever-successful golf tournament, which created much needed financial support and much positive public relations, the booster organization launched a major, annual, fundraising project, a project that grossed some $10,000 big money in its initial year. After this project had experienced a history of success and all details were worked out, the boosters then turned their attention to yet another annual fundraiser.

After five years, this booster organization had four major, annual fundraising activities that generated thousands and thousands of dollars. The key to this success story rested in the organization's leadership. Individuals who insisted that quality rather than quantity, that substance rather than fluff, would be stressed in terms of all of the fundraising and promotional activities.

When fundraising activities lack the minimal quality level that would be expected, in any respect, it is the public that seems to remember the faults. Indeed, the sports public has a rather short memory when it comes to successes, but a long memory for failures. In fact, the sport public can be extremely unforgiving. This is evidenced by the philosophy of "what have you done for me lately?" It seems that it only takes one error or failure to overshadow the benefits from 100 successes. Since there is a tendency for the public to freely criticize errors and since errors are more likely to occur when sport personnel are stretched too thin in terms of their capabilities, it seems only logical to see to it that one has sufficient time to complete tasks, as well as accessibility to appropriate tools or resources.

> **PRINCIPLE # 127:   Don't kill a fly with a sledgehammer**

It is very important to match appropriate solutions with specific problems, needs or objectives. *Overkill*, in terms of inappropriate allocation of resources, is a wasteful management error. For example, a printed high school basketball brochure need not consist of 64 (or 32, or even 16) pages of four-color, very high quality, glossy paper. Perhaps an 8 or 4 page brochure (organized, illustrated, and printed in a first class fashion) might meet the needs of a secondary school program and more closely match the resources of the athletic department.

Another example involves the case of the athletic director attempting to sell, door-to-door, $50 advertisements for a sport program. This is a chronic waste of skilled manpower. This is not a task that requires the time and effort of a highly trained, educated, and experienced sports administrator. There is a definite need to set *suitable prioritie*s and to elect *appropriate courses of action*, as well as *resources*, geared to accomplish *specific **and** appropriate results*. Only in this way can one anticipate success within the fundraising arena. One does not need a Mercedes to drive to the grocery store when a Ford will do the trick, and consume a lot less in terms of total resources.

ASKING FOR THE MONEY OR A DONATION

One of the cardinal sins in sales or fundraising is to fail to ask for the donation or money or whatever it is that is being sought or solicited. An example will suffice. In a study of college graduates, 26% of all respondents who have been to college indicated they have made some sort of donation to the undergraduate school they attended (Lindenmann, 1983, p. 18).

However, of those respondents who said they *had not made a donation*, 25% said that they had not been asked. It is difficult to get the money if one does not ask for it. Naturally, there are skills and tactics and techniques to be utilized in "asking" for the contributions so that it does not seem so obvious. However, the fact remains, one usually has to ask for the donation if one is to receive it.

> ***PRINCIPLE # 128:*** *In asking for money—specify a specific amount or an amount within a specific range*

In soliciting cash contributions—be specific, or nearly so. That is, ask the prospective donor for a specific amount if you have a reasonable knowledge of what that individual can afford to contribute. Or, on the other hand, it might be appropriate, for a variety of reasons, to provide to the potential contributor various options, levels, or ranges at which a contribution can be made. In this way, the individual donor has the option of choosing the most appropriate level at which to make a contribution. The more options or levels of contributions available, the greater the potential donor response.

Naturally, one needs to ask for the money. However, merely asking for the contribution is not all there is to it. There must be provided the means for the potential contributor to actually consummate the giving of the gift that is to be contributed. This is true whether money, objects of value or services are being contributed. People tend to shrug off appeals to action if a *means of action* is not provided and readily available. This means providing an immediate opportunity for the contributor to act, to do something, to give something to someone, to sign something, to mail something back in a stamped envelope, to drop a contribution into some receptacle, etc.

> ***PRINCIPLE # 129:*** *Provide a vehicle or means by which potential contributors can actually consummate the giving of a contribution*

Don't be afraid not to take "NO" for an answer. However, also be smart enough to accept "NO" when further attempts might result in negative feelings and a poor image. One should not be a *hard sell* type of promoter or salesperson. There may be other more appropriate opportunities for future sales—so one must not burn any bridges. Instead, cultivate the individual or the organization for future solicitations. However, keep the person or group somehow involved in the meantime through the use of mailing lists. That is, use one's web site and send newsletters, e-mail messages, conduct phone calls, personal contacts, involve them in special promotional activities, as well as periodic free tickets to special events, etc.

One must be trained in overcoming objections to the sales pitch or presentation and request for contributions and support. One should never *fear* rejection by prospects. Most important of all, rejection should never be taken personally. Rejection or the refusal to "buy" or to contribute or to become involved, on behalf of prospects is merely some of the possible consequences of the total sales and promotional processes. There is no inherent implication that either the fundraising project or the salesperson is not of value or worth.

Objections raised may be the result of skepticism or ignorance or just natural reluctance to making any type of commitment. One of the key ingredients in salesmanship (asking for money) is being able to meet and overcome objections by prospects. Overcoming objections can be facilitated by: (1) knowledge and confidence in the product or service one is "selling," (2) persistence, (3) possession of a positive attitude, (4) overall confidence in one's ability or position, and (5) being professional in the sales approach, including the actual "closing" of the sale.

Too many coaches, athletic administrators, and booster club members claim that all so-called donations or payments are tax deductible when, in reality, this is not always the case. To qualify for tax deductibility, contributions to booster club organizations or to sport programs need to meet very specific and rigid requirements. The buying of Christmas ornaments by well meaning supporters or fans from team members does not necessarily qualify for a legitimate tax deduction. One important rule boosters need to follow in the solicitation of all funds, when there is any question as to whether or not any donation is tax deductible, is to indicate to the donor that the determination of whether or not the contribution is tax deductible is up to the donor (and the donor's legal counsel).

> **PRINCIPLE # 130:** *Continually expand the prospect pool—*
> *never put all of your "eggs" in one basket*

Always have additional prospective donors "waiting in the wings" to be contacted should the current prospects not result in contributions. To achieve this goal, fundraisers should employ the technique of "snowballing" when seeking additional prospects whom they may solicit. Specifically, this means asking those satisfied with the sport program or who otherwise have an interest in the welfare of the program (booster club members, friends of the sport program, contributors, members, parents, etc.) for referrals, that is, names of 3 to 5 individuals to add to the so-called prospect list. This is an established practice in the general sales profession, a common tactic in the prospecting process. The end result is a continual expansion of the number of possible contacts who can be approached for solicitation purposes.

> **PRINCIPLE # 131:   *Provide for an equitable exchange for contributions made by donors***

Sport programs should attempt to provide to donors a fair, but generous and appropriate, slate of benefits in exchange for contributions made to the program. The major challenge facing sport promoters is the determination of the value, in the form of benefits, which should be returned to donors in exchange for the contributions made by them.

Athletic programs in colleges and secondary schools generally tend to return to donors, in the form of various benefits, somewhere in the neighborhood of 5-10% of the actual value of the donation. Such benefits might include, but not be limited to tickets, premiums, special privileges, etc. In such a situation, if a contributor donated a steer worth around $800, the donor might receive approximately $40 to $80 worth of so-called benefits in return.

SELF PROMOTION IN A PROFESSIONAL MANNER

There is an old proverb that is most applicable in the fundraising and promotional arenas. It goes like this. If a tree falls in a forest and if there is no one there to hear it, does it make any noise? The answer, in terms of promotions and fundraising, is a resounding **NO**. Unless the constituencies are aware of the positive aspects of the sport or recreation programs, most of one's efforts fall upon deaf ears.

Thus, it is therefore essential that those involved in the sport and recreation arenas take great pains to spread the good word to all constituencies in terms of the positive elements of the sport entity. However, not only must a continuing and conscientious effort be made to make others aware of the advantages and achievements of one's programs and activities, but great care must be taken lest the attempt to spread the good word be viewed in a negative, self-serving and destructive manner. Of course, it goes without saying that the self-promotional and public relations effort be based on absolute truth and accuracy.

Conveying the Perception of Individual Competency

Being perceived as professional, as knowledgeable, as competent is really at the crux of every sport and recreation administrator's success. Being good, being competent is one thing. Being recognized as being good and competent in one's job by others (especially by those who count) is another. **It is up to those involved in fundraising, publicity and promotions to take steps to insure that the perception of their levels of competency and knowledge and effort accurately reflects realty.**

Perceptions Do Count—Whether Accurate or Not

This is because perceptions count. Sometimes, perceptions are more important than reality. How the sport and recreation professional is viewed by higher-level administrators, those in authority, *and* by people in the community will go a long way to determine just how successful the individual will be and how long one might be in that position.

Managing by Being Seen—MBBS (Stier, 1999)

> **PRINCIPLE # 132: Walk around and be seen as a competent manager**

The basis for success of many sport and recreation promoters, fundraisers and publicity personnel is represented by the acronym **MBBS**, which stands for *Managing by Being Seen*. This acronym represents a philosophy of administration and management that denotes an *attitude of active involvement* by the administrator as well as a conscious *desire to be seen by others* doing what any knowledgeable, caring and competent administrator should be doing under similar circumstances.

MBBS conjures up a vision of the manager or administrator being seen by others actually doing something, actually performing managerial duties and leadership-type tasks. It means that individuals are deliberately made aware of the person's administrative skills and managerial efforts. It also involves recognition by others of the high competency level, motivation and accomplishments of the administrator—all because of conscious decisions and deliberate actions of the administrator.

Being a competent, professional and caring manager or administrator or leader is, in and of itself, often not sufficient for true success. One also has to be viewed by others, both in and outside the organization, as a competent, professional and caring manager/administrator/leader. Towards this end, *it behooves the administrator or manager to take special steps to insure that one is seen doing one's job in a satisfactory manner*.

Most people will have perceptions of the person in charge of the fundraising project or promotional effort regardless of what this person does or doesn't do. Hopefully, the opinions and perceptions of these individuals toward this decision maker will be both accurate and positive. It only makes sense for the administrator to act in a deliberate manner to help consciously cultivate a positive image and reputation among a wide range of individuals, constituencies and publics. To do otherwise would not only be counter-productive but foolhardy (Stier, 1999).

REFERENCES

Advertising. (1989, May 3). *NCAA news*, *26*(18), p. 5.

Bronzan, R. T. (1984, May). Fundraising today demands better ideas. *Athletic Business*, *8*(5), 12-18.

Buell, V. (1984). *Marketing management: A strategic planning approach.* New York: McGraw-Hill Book Co.

Caputo, M. (1996). Nazareth seeks $10 million. *Democrat & Chronicle*, p. C-1.

Charleston RiverDogs. (2000, June 8). *USA Today*, p. 19-A.

Cohen, A. (1991). Money comes into play. *Athletic Business*, *15*(2), 25-28, 30-31.

Frank, N. (1989, March). Consumer research—A valuable tool for sports marketers. *Team Marketing Report*, p. 6.

http://www.efundraising.com/enewsletter/newsletter_03_2001.htm (2001)

Lindenmann, W. (1983). Who makes donations? National survey provides need data. *Caser Currents*, *9*(2), 18-19.

McIntyre, M., & Anderson, J. (1987). Development—An old word with a new meaning. *Journal of Physical Education, Recreation and Dance*, *58*(1), 72-75.

McKenzie, W. (1985, August). 10 Rules for fundraisers. *Athletic Business*, *9*(8), 20-25.

McMillen, Liz. (1990). A study to determine the cost of raising a dollar finds that average college spends just 16 cents. *The Chronicle of Higher Education, XXXVII*(1), A31.

Matching gifts—Another way to support the Brockport College Fund. (1995, spring). *Kaleidoscope, VIII*(2), 17.

Moore, Deborah, B., & Gray, Dianna, P. (1990). Marketing—The blueprint for successful physical education, *Journal of Physical Education, Recreation and Dance*, *61*(1), 23-26.

NYSAHPERD Link, (1999). New York State Association for Health, Physical Education, Recreation and Dance, *IX*(2), 2.

7 ways to double your dollars. (1991). Council for Advancement and Support of Education (CASE).

Stier, Jr., W.F. (1997). Avoiding Major Mistakes in Fundraising. *Athletic Management, (IX)*1, 220-21.

Stier W.F., Jr. (1999). Look at Me! *Athletic Management, XI*(6), 20, 21.

Sutton, W., McDonald, M., & Milne, G. (1997). Escalating your fan base. *Athletic Management, 14*(2), 4, 6.

DISCUSSION QUESTIONS

1. Define the terms *supermarket approach* and the business *revenue approach* to fundraising while providing examples of each.

2. Explain what is meant by the statement that *one should strike when the iron is hot* in terms of fundraising.

3. Explain strategies for *asking for the money* and include the negatives associated with this process.

4. Outline the essentials of a *feasibility study* and explain when and how it should be used.

5. What are ringers in fundraising/promotions and explain how they may be used.

7 | SINGLE PERSON CULTIVATIONS

Use half-time at athletic contests to honor former athletic standouts

CHAPTER HIGHLIGHTS

This chapter will emphasize:

- The *single person [face-to-face] cultivation* and *appeal* method of fundraising
- The challenge of cultivating prospective major donors
- The possible need to collect sales tax on items sold as part of a fundraising project
- The advantages and disadvantages of both the *take-order* tactic of selling and the *point-of-sale* type program.
- The dangers associated with conducting fundraising projects on a too frequent basis
- A successful *direct mail* approach to generate money
- A successful *telephone solicitation* campaign
- How to develop a script to be used in a *phone-a-thon*

> **PRINCIPLE # 133:** *Fundraising efforts can be divided into four distinct categories*

Four Models of Fundraising

Today, the vast majority of all secondary schools nationwide are involved in some type of outside fundraising to supplement their sport budgets. In fact, between 20 percent and 50 percent of these athletic programs' budgets were generated via outside fundraising campaigns of one kind or another. At the turn of the century, it was estimated that over 80% of all secondary schools in the United States were engaged in outside fundraising activities to supplement the athletic budgets (Stier, 2000a).

When thinking of becoming involved in fundraising it is often useful to attempt to classify fundraising activities and efforts into distinct categories. The author, in chapter 1 of this book, arbitrarily has categorized such fundraising efforts into four general methods for generating financial support for the sport program (Stier, 2009). These four methods include:

1. Single person [face-to-face] cultivation and appeals
2. Profit centers
3. Corporate sponsorships
4. Special fundraising projects, promotional tactics and ideas

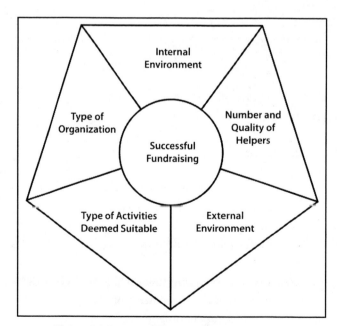

Figure 7.1 Factors Affecting the Level of Success of Fundraising Projects

The first two categories of generating revenues will be discussed in detail within this chapter. The topic of *corporate sponsorships* will be covered in chapter 9 while the topics of *special fundraising projects, promotional tactics and ideas* will be addressed in chapter 12. It is important to remember that the selection of appropriate fundraising projects or efforts depend upon a number of factors, figure 7.1.

SINGLE PERSON (FACE-TO-FACE) CULTIVATION AND APPEALS FOR RESOURCES

There are five generally accepted means by which individuals may be approached in the solicitation of money, services, and products either on a *straight contribution* (solicitation basis) or on a *purchase* ("supermarket" basis). These include (1) person-to-person (face-to-face) solicitation, (2) door-to-door appeals, (3) direct mail, (4) e-mail, and (5) the use of the telephone.

Person-to-Person Solicitation or Single Person Cultivation

The eyeball-to-eyeball or person-to-person solicitation is frequently referred to as the door-to-door approach for grown-ups. This approach is a flat-out request for contributions for a worthy cause. It is a person-to-person contact on the street, at civic club luncheons or in the office. By far, this is one of the most productive and efficient means of gathering resources that can be used.

> ***PRINCIPLE # 134: Establish convenient categories of "giving" to facilitate contributions***

It is frequently helpful to establish donor classifications as part of a planned giving campaign ($100, $250, $500, $1,000, $5,000, etc.). Examples include such easily distinguishable names as the Gold Club, Silver Club, the President's Club, The Varsity Club, the Coach's Club, etc.

Often, it is necessary to conduct some good old-fashioned research about the prospect prior to contacting the prospective donor. This can be cut short by taking advantage of other people's knowledge (common contacts, centers of influence) of the potential contributor. The immediate goal is to be able to properly cultivate, educate, and share pertinent information about the sport organization, its mission, and its activities with the prospect for the purpose of converting the prospect into a donor.

Alumni Outreach Efforts—Endowment Outreach Efforts

Both *alumni outreach* and *endowment outreach* efforts are very common at the college level and are becoming more acceptable on the private secondary school level. In terms of endowment outreach efforts, these are attempts to generate funds, grants, and long-term commitments from businesses, graduates, "friends" and other individuals and groups. The interest generated from these endowment funds are then utilized annually for general operating purposes and/or capital expenditures. Such efforts are an attempt to insure fiscal longevity and responsibility for the entity being supported.

Cultivating Prospective Major Donors—Big Ticket Donors

In working within the sport world in promotion and fundraising, it is necessary to recognize that many of the people we come in contact with are successful business people (both men and women). And, as such, these women and men expect proper (professional, first class) business relationships and interactions. Similarly, there are expectations that those involved in fundraising and promotional efforts will demonstrate specific competencies. That is, they must demonstrate professionalism and a high level of sophistication at all times in their representation of the sport arena. Needless to say, use of common business etiquette is an absolute must. This involves basic politeness in terms of meetings, telephone usage, written communication, office management, etc.

Solicitors must be willing and able to fully discuss with the prospect the needs and strengths of the organization, the institution, the program, as well as how the money will benefit the program and the participants. This is extremely important in dealing with big-ticket donors. When wealthy people contribute to charitable causes they tend to lean toward organizations or programs that they consider to be prestigious. In fact, Ostrower (1996) claims that those who are wealthy not infrequently use the act of giving or philanthropy as a means of social climbing and networking among the socially and financially elite and, as a result, tend to donate to those causes that are deemed by society as prestigious, celebrated and prominent.

PRINCIPLE # 135: *Avoid cold calls like the plague in soliciting big dollars*

In attempting to solicit large sums of money, avoid cold calls whenever possible. Instead, contacts or *centers of influence* should be utilized to pave the way and to open the "doors" to potential contributors and supporters, whether they be individuals or corporations. The strategy of utilizing third party *centers of influence* to gain access to individuals and organizations (as potential contributors and donors) is a valid one. In the area of high finance and big time donations, it is absolutely essential that cold calls be avoided at all costs. The time and effort it takes to cultivate third party *centers of influence*, for the purpose of gaining access in a receptive atmosphere to heavy hitters (contributors), is well worth it when one considers the potential ultimate payoff, i.e., large and significant contributions of money, goods and/or services.

Utilizing the "Solicitation Kit" as Part of the Sales Approach

Many times it is beneficial to take advantage of a sales tool commonly referred to as the *solicitation kit*. The content of the so-called solicitation (information or promotional package) kit should consist of a clear statement as to the organization's *mission statement*, as well as a "brag sheet" on the athletic program (Stier, 1990). Additionally, one or more of the following could be included as part of the solicitation kit:

1. Background information about the organization and its activities, a rationale for its existence, as well as the stated objectives and goals
2. A one page list of specific needs—prioritized
3. Gift range table—money, equipment, time and other resources
4. An invitation to become affiliated with the organization, present and future
5. Summary of justification for support that can include a list of accomplishments of the program as well as the values and benefits that can accrue to the participants, school(s), the community, and to the business sector, etc.
6. A list of specific benefits that can go to the contributing corporation or individual
7. Background information concerning the solicitor(s)
8. List of officers and prominent members of organization (and their achievements)
9. Description of the roles of the coaches and other staff
10. List of top contributors—individual and corporate (with range of gifts)
11. Photos, press clippings, brochures, and pamphlets on the organization and the sport programs and activities
12. Explanation of the organization's programs and services provided to various publics
13. Financial efficiency of the organization (how much it costs to raise "X" number of dollars)
14. The percentage that the soliciting organization's *own people* have contributed

---

PRINCIPLE # 136: *Don't insult your prospect by asking for too little*

When dealing with the so-called big-ticket donors, one needs to be assertive in actually *asking* for money, *and* for a sufficient amount, *and* for a specific purpose. In attempting to decide how much to ask—it is best to ask for too much than for too little. Nothing insults a potential donor, especially a heavy hitter, *than asking for too little money.*

Knowing your prospect, doing one's homework prior to approaching a prospect in terms of the needs of the prospect, the desires of the prospect, the limitations of the prospect, and the prejudices of the prospects, prevents this embarrassing situation from developing. Often, the fundraiser is unsure about the amount of money the potential donor might feel comfortable in contributing. In this case, one might present a range of possible donations or involvements from which the potential donor might select the most appropriate. This gives the potential donor the opportunity to select the most suitable degree of involvement with the fundraising and/or promotional activity.

Car wahses—both "free" and for a minimum cost are a favorite of high schools and colleges

Door-to-Door Solicitation and/or Selling

Literally almost anything can be sold on a door-to-door basis. Like the sale of Girl Scout cookies, which earn millions of dollars (168 million boxes at $2–$3.50 a box in 1996 estimated at close to 200 million boxes) annually for this national organization, sport and recreation organizations can reap sizeable rewards for a well thought out and planned program of door-to-door solicitation and/or selling. There are numerous companies that produce a wide variety of candies and other goodies that can be sold as part of a fundraising program.

One such company is *Mrs. Sittler's Candies*. Located in the state of Illinois, the company sells on an annually basis, thousands and thousands of pounds of chocolate covered candies and peanut brittle. For the most part, this candy and peanut brittle is advertised, marketed and sold through the efforts of various scout groups, school organizations and little league athletic groups (Drotning, 1981). Another company, Nestle-Beich, a subsidiary of Nestle Foods located in Bloomington, Illinois, is one of this country's largest manufacturers and seller of candy for the fundraising market/arena.

The World Wide Web has numerous suggestions and ideas for possible fundraising sales efforts. The *Fundraisingdepot* is one such site that periodically offers helpful hints as well as a list of companies that serve as sources for products, services and ideas that might be used by groups interested in generating additional monies via the fundraising route. The following is a list of hints provided by this site in 1998 (http://www.fundraisingdepot):

1. Establish a goal before starting—how much needs to be raised and for what purpose

2. Develop a detailed plan—include those steps that must be accomplished
3. Create a time schedule, a timetable that outlines what steps must be done by different people assisting in the fundraising project
4. Choose an appropriate project—one that your group is capable of completing
5. Do one project at a time—don't make things more complicated than needed
6. Be excited and enthusiastic—in whatever fundraising project you initiate
7. Promote your project—promote, promote and promote your project via as many different means as appropriate
8. Remember that fundraising is a serious business—treat your effort as a serious mini-business requiring good business and financial decisions
9. Believe in yourself—think that you will be successful, work hard and diligently and you will be successful
10. Select a reputable company or business from which to purchase your supplies and equipment that are required in your fundraising efforts.

Many fundraisers involve the selling of items such as candy or some other food or snack item. Non-edible items such as candles, Xmas ornaments, cards, etc., can also be sold. The total fundraising candy market in the United States is extensive, approaching three-fourths of a billion dollars annually, according to Paul Fine, vice-president for marketing for Nestle-Beich (Fine, 1992, May 28, personal communication). Today, that figure is substantially higher. A company that claims to be the largest nationwide fundraising organization working with schools and youth groups in this country is QSP, Inc., a subsidiary of The Reader's Digest Association, Inc. Twenty years ago they provided over $85,000,000 in profits to various groups, organizations and individuals in a single year through the sale of both edible and non-edible items (The Nation's Leading, 1990). Today, it is estimated that this figure exceeds $110,000,000 in profits.

Yet another fundraising company is Benchmark Products, located in Mansfield, Ohio. There are numerous companies today that provide a wide range of quality edible and non-edible products on a wholesale basis to sponsoring groups (many of which are sport or recreation teams as well as other school sponsored groups). These groups then resell the items on either a *take-order basis* or on a *point-of-sale* type program.

> **PRINCIPLE # 137:** *Door-to-door sales are made via the take-order method or the point-of-sale method*

The take-order selling program involves having athletes or other individuals approach prospective purchasers with a catalogue and take orders for the items. Later, when merchandise is delivered to the athletic fundraising coordinator the items are hand delivered to the buyers. The point-of-sale program has the seller actually possessing samples of the merchandise and selling the items on the spot. The money is collected, then and there, when the purchaser takes possession of the item(s).

Of course there are numerous companies manufacturing and/or selling candy as well as other items as part of a fundraising effort throughout the United States (just search the World Wide Web). The trend in recent years is for fundraising product companies to diversify and expand their product line. Thus, as a result, these companies are able to provide on a wholesale basis not only candy but a wide range of other edible products, such as cookies, pizza, donuts, etc., as well as a whole host of non-edible products to local fundraising groups *to be resold at premium retail prices* to the general public (for a tidy profit).

Using such programs and products from any number of these national and regional companies can generate sizeable profits depending upon the number of participants taking part in the selling campaign and their effectiveness in obtaining multiple sales per purchaser. In 2001 there was an estimated $1.7 billion net profit as a result of fundraising efforts by sport teams, schools, school groups and other not-for-profit organizations (http://www.efundraising.com).

Such solicitations can be either on a *cold call basis* or as a *follow-up* to a previous contact made by mail, by e-mail, by phone, exposure to media, or by a personal contact. Previous knowledge on behalf of the potential contributor as to the worthiness of the cause and the benefits that will accrue to the sport program significantly increases the potential for success. This emphasizes the need for sufficient publicity and public exposure.

Depending upon the specific situation, such as the item being advertised, marketed, publicized, and promoted, the sponsoring organization, the purpose for the solicitation, local conditions, etc., such appeals can result in approximately 25% to 50% of those persons contacted actually making some type of contribution/purchase. Naturally, the cause must be worthy and a good case (justification) must be made for the potential prospect to actually initiate a contribution and/or make a purchase of an item or service being advertised, promoted and marketed. Thus, in the case of advertising, publicizing and marketing items for sale, it is imperative that an appropriate product (good quality and value for the price) be secured to sell to the publics.

Using Youngsters as Salespersons

Young people are frequently utilized to sell, on a door-to-door basis, products and services. Two of the concerns that administrators should be aware of in respect to such sales are (1) the safety factor and (2) the liability exposure for the sport organization and organizers that might result if accidents befall youngsters engaged in selling, especially door-to-door. The health and safety of the individual is always of paramount importance and must never be compromised. The state of New Jersey has had for decades a statewide law that prohibits children to be alone when selling candy, cookies or other items on behalf of any charity or non-profit organization (Flanigan, 1998). This is perhaps a sad sign of the times in which we presently live but it is reality and organizers of fundraising projects must remain cognizant of the safety issue in all that they do.

> **PRINCIPLE # 138:** *The health and welfare of youngsters, those involved in selling (fundraising) on behalf of sport and recreation organizations, remain paramount*

Factors to consider when involving youngsters as part of the sales team include, but are not limited to, weather conditions, the time of day the young people are expected to sell, the available adult supervision and the area in which the young people will attempt to sell/market their wares. Adults must provide adequate supervision and constant monitoring of the efforts of young participants while they are actually involved in the selling process to insure that their welfare is not jeopardized in any fashion. Naturally, one must be cognizant of various community laws that restrict or prohibit door-to-door sales—regardless of the purpose or the organization that is sponsoring the effort.

Sales Tax and Selling Merchandise for Non-Profit Organizations

The tax laws are many, complicated and confusing. In terms of state tax laws and regulations, they are also frequently different in the various states. There may be different interpretations regarding tax laws, both federal and state. This is especially true when one considers the regulations pertaining to the collection of sales tax when non-profit organizations conduct fundraising activities. The question of whether or not it is necessary to collect sales tax frequently arises when the sponsoring organization is involved in selling tickets to events, merchandise or concession items as part of the fundraising effort. The county tax collector as well as the State Department of Revenue will be able to answer many questions in this regard. Again, a competent attorney or accountant should always be consulted if one is to obtain an expert opinion in this frequently complicated arena.

An example of the potential trouble that non-profit organizations can get into when there is confusion as to how tax regulations are to be interpreted can be seen in the case of the Girl Scouts and the collection of sales tax on the sale of girl scout cookies in the state of Maine. The question of whether non-profit organizations, such as Girl Scouts, schools, selected athletic teams and sport programs, should be paying sales tax on the sale of products like cookies, candies, candles, etc., was brought to the attention of the national media in the mid-1990s. In the state of Maine, the tax people revealed that the Girl Scout organizations in that state were being billed some $180,000 in unpaid taxes on sales totaling more than $3 million during 1995. The state tax assessor, John LaFaver, claimed that the sales of cookies by the group had evolved into much more than a "casual sale" and that as a result the 6% tax was due. However, a Maine Superior Court justice ruled that the Girl Scouts were exempt from the state's sales tax (Cookie tax, 1995).

Maine is not the only state to attempt to collect such a tax. Hawaii was successful in instituting and collecting a "cookie tax" on the sale of Girl Scout cookies and collected some $63,150 from the group in 1994 (Tangonan, 1995). The moral of this story is that each organization should pay particular attention to the legal requirements, such as sales tax, pertaining to the sale of merchandise by the group—and act accordingly with the best legal advice possible.

> **PRINCIPLE # 139:** *Although the tax laws are many, complicated and confusing— ignorance of such laws is no excuse*

Parents and sport organizers must be reminded that students who sell can quickly wear out their welcome within a community if the practice of using youngsters is inappropriately implemented or becomes overused. A community can quickly become saturated with door-to-door canvassing (even for worthy causes). There is a danger of too much of a good thing in three respects. *First*, there is a danger of the people in the community, the prospective contributors or purchasers, being inundated with so many requests for funds that there is a negative reaction by these individuals and groups. These individuals and businesses become tired and irritated with repeated requests for financial support of the same sport organization regardless of the apparent worthiness of the project.

The *second* area of concern involves the young sellers and their families. Fundraising efforts can also become abusive from the perspective of overusing people who form part of the sales force. Just as the people being repeatedly asked to contribute or buy something from the students can react negatively to such requests, so too can the students themselves and their families react negatively. Sometimes this reaction can be very vocal and violent. On the youth sport level as well as in the junior and senior high schools, parents and their children can easily become resentful of the time commitment expected by the athletic program in the soliciting of funds and/or selling items on behalf of the sport program. Too much of anything can become old very quickly. The consequence can be a bitterness or jealously on behalf of the families.

Today, when the child becomes involved in selling cookies, cards, calendars, candies, gift-wrapping or whatever, it is often the mother and/or the father who also joins the sales team and helps sell the product, typically at work. "What used to be the child's merchandise to sell has become more and more a parent's responsibility. And that's bringing more fundraisers out of neighborhoods and into offices" (Neuborne, 1997, p. B-1). While many parents don't mind this type of responsibility, for others it can become an unwelcome burden.

This is especially true if there are a number of athletes within a family and each of them become involved in selling merchandise or soliciting funds within the community. Or, if other organizations also expect these same students to participate in similar door-to-door canvassing in hopes of generating monies, the problem is exacerbated further. There is indeed a limit as to the number of selling efforts or campaigns ("hits") that parents and the local businesses can endorse (or endure).

More and more parents are becoming actively involved in the fundraising activities of their children—much more involved. This increased involvement is the result of (1) time pressures (it is easier to do the job themselves so that they will have more time with their children), (2) security concerns, (3) financial concerns that if the parent doesn't help the money won't be raised and there is a real need to generate additional funds for the organization or group, and (4) outside pressures from school and peers to have a successful fundraising effort.

The *third* area of concern centers around the practice of having students on the college level involved in selling merchandise as part of fundraising project. This type of situation needs to be closely monitored. All too frequently these students (especially athletes) tend to approach coaches and teachers within the institution in an effort to "move" whatever it is that they are selling at any point in time. The consequence may very well be the creation of ill will towards the athletic program. Many athletic departments have a policy prohibiting students from approaching staff members within the school in order to prevent just that type of negative fallout.

A *final* warning concerns the issuing of *quotas* to students or groups of students. These quotas often place inordinate pressure and sometimes inordinate expectations on the youngsters (as well as upon their families). And, the consequences can often negate, in terms of public relations, any benefits that might result from the actual generation of monies for the sport project.

Direct Mail Appeals

A direct mail solicitation for funds should not be overlooked either as a supplemental or primary method of generating much-needed funds for one's program. One of the challenges associated with direct mail as a fundraising effort is securing a suitable and an updated mailing list. How do you obtain the list of names and addresses to send the promotional or solicitation piece? Do you create your own lists or do you pay commercial firms for a list that has been commercially put together? Lists are commercially available, that is, available from any number of professional list brokers, companies or firms that are in the business of supplying lists for almost every conceivable category of people, business and company one can think of. Other lists can be created by the sport or recreation organization itself.

> **PRINCIPLE # 140:** *The list of prospects, to whom direct mail will be directed, can be generated internally or through professional companies that maintain all types of national, regional and statewide lists of names*

Direct mail efforts for generating monies for a variety of causes, both for profit and not-for-profit organizations, are a $40 billion dollar business in the 21st century (Stier, 2000b). Even as early as the 1990s direct mail made up 26 percent of the total money spent on advertising in the United States. White (1991) claimed that direct mail is one of the truly effective ways to solicit positive responses from *targeted audiences* in terms of generating monies through donations as well as through purchases.

Direct mail can be used for all sorts of purposes, from selling or renewing season tickets, soliciting fundraising contributions from previous and new donors, promoting special events, publicizing group ticket sales, and, of course, securing sponsors or business partners. Some direct mail efforts involve an envelope while others utilize a self-mailer (thereby saving the cost of the envelope). The type of printed piece that will comprise the actual direct effort can be almost any type, depending upon the budget and the purpose behind the direct mail project. Whether you pay for the return postage or not is another individual decision you will have to make when you get involved in direct mail.

Many professionals involved in the direct mail business have expressed the opinion that prepaying the return postage is justified by the higher rate of return when such an option is exercised. With today's advantages in terms of computers and software, "individual" letters can indeed be mass-produced for direct mailings. Another decision that has to be made is whether to use window envelopes or regular envelopes to mail out your direct mail piece (if an envelope is being used). And yet another decision that must be made by the sport or recreation administrators is whether first class postage is paid for each piece or the bulk rate method is used to mail the piece. All of these decisions will depend upon each organization's particular situation and circumstances. There is no one "correct" answer for every organization or every situation as all of the above factors must all be considered if one is to develop an effective and efficient mail order campaign for one's sport or recreation program.

Acceptable Return Rates for Direct Mail

> **PRINCIPLE # 141:** *For any given population a return rate from direct mail of 3-4% is considered acceptable*

In terms of return rates, many consider a return of 3-4% an acceptable yield rate of return for a given population, although the rate could be much higher if the population you are mailing to has a vested interest in your organization, your program or the activities you are promoting. Thus, you need a somewhat sizeable population pool to make the direct mailing effort worthwhile (White, 1991, Stier, 2000c). One way to increase the likelihood of significant returns in a direct mail campaign is to use a culled, qualified list of prospects. For example, a list of hot prospects consisting of previous contributors might significantly increase the yield or return to as much as 50% or even higher. The better the list the higher the yield.

Creating a Mailing List

There are numerous ways to begin to create a so-called database or names, addresses, phone numbers and other pertinent data about individuals and/or businesses and organizations. Gathering information from the local phone book is one way. Another method is to copy information from flyers or newspapers in your local community—information that might include data such as the names of local businesses as well as the names, mailing addresses and phone number of owners/managers.

Involving an honor guard prior to the athletic contest is the norm

Also, you can use information that can be collected as a part of doing business, such as (1) collecting and maintaining a database of season ticket holders, (2) a record of membership in your booster club or sport support group (SSG), (3) a list of vendors, (4) a list of parents of athletes and former athletes, (5) an alumni list, and (6) a record of people who have attended a game, contest or recreation event and who had filled out a card with their names, address and phone number in an effort to be eligible for a randomly chosen prize to be given away during the evening festivities. There are innumerable methods and strategies that may be used to create and sustain lists of people who might be future recipients of a mailing campaign for fundraising or for some other promotional and publicity purpose.

Using Computer Software to Manage a Mailing List

Once a list of names and other pertinent information has been created, the data can easily be managed, maintained, manipulated, and periodically updated with the aid of computers and modern software. Software such as *Microsoft*™ *Access*™ can be utilized to maintain mailing lists that contain all kinds of pertinent and personalized information, information that may be used and included in each letter mailed to individual recipients. For example, this software can be used to generate "personalized form letters" in which the recipient's name (as well as other personalized data and information) can be strategically placed throughout the letter creating the impression that the letter has been individually prepared and typed to the recipient (when in reality the identical generic letter might be sent to 10,000 recipients—with each letter personalized and individualized with the recipient's name, and other pertinent information).

The Sales Piece

> **PRINCIPLE # 142:** *With direct mail the two essential components are the sales piece and the address label*

The direct mail fundraising effort must make it clear as to the purpose(s) of the campaign as well as how the money to be raised will be used for the benefit of the program or participants. The written communication is a *sales piece* representing you, the program and the activities or events sponsored. As such, special care must be paid to the outside envelope, the enclosed cover letter, the contents (brochure, etc.), the response piece, and the return envelope. All must be coordinated and each must be professionally prepared, superbly written, and expertly printed.

Some general guidelines (Yiannakis and Braunstein, 1983, p. 83) that are helpful in making a direct mail appeal successful include:

1. The appeal should ask for a specific figure
2. The requested amount should be in so-called round figures ($25, $50, $100, etc.)
3. The communication should provide for a convenient means of responding (self-addressed, stamped reply envelope)
4. The request for funds should include opportunities to make contributions in cash, pledges, gifts in kind, deferred giving, endowment contributions, memorial giving, as well as for designated purposes

One of the biggest challenges involved in a direct mail appeal is creating an effective fundraising letter. Kuniholm (1990) suggests six characteristics of such a letter. These include:

1. Create an eye catching opening paragraph
2. Include a statement that is designed to convince the would-be donor to read the rest of the solicitation letter
3. State how a specific problem can be solved through a donation or contribution
4. Provide information that will clearly make the reader aware of the purpose of the letter, i.e., solicitation of a contribution so that the reader is not confused as to the true nature of the letter

5. Identify the reader's interests, concerns or priorities (as they relate to the solicitor's program or activities

6. Explain a notable event or activity that has recently taken place in your organization or program

Additionally, an effective fundraising or solicitation letter should certainly include a personalized greeting ("Dear Philip" or "Dear Joanne"). And, of course, a handwritten note as a "P.S." (Post script) at the end of the letter puts the finishing touch on the personalization effort with the direct mail appeal (McDermott-Griggs & Card, 1992).

Direct Mail via the Piggyback Strategy

Sometimes direct mail requests can be "piggybacked" with other written communications to various constituencies. For example, bank statements might include an enclosure from a local sport group seeking funds or contributions from the bank's customers for the worthy purpose. The advantages are obvious and numerous. In this situation the bank provides the bulk of the work, pays the expense of the initial mailing and provides the population to be solicited. The sport program might be asked to provide the insert, if even that, thus taking advantage of the bank's mailing via the "piggyback" tactic.

> **PRINCIPLE # 143:** *Some direct mail pieces can be inserted along with other pieces of mail in the same envelope, thus the name "piggyback"*

When attempting to arrange this type of "piggyback" arrangement it is not unusual for 2-4 months to pass before all of the details are worked out to everyone's satisfaction. Even once an agreement has been reached it is necessary to allocate some 2-4 weeks "lead time" in terms of providing the necessary printed information to the organization that has agreed to accept and distribute your insert. The point to remember is that this type of arrangement is not something that can be accomplished overnight. It takes time and a significant amount of planning. But the results can often be well worth the effort, especially when one considers the amount of money saved through such an arrangement and the extent of distribution achieved (prospects reached).

Telephone Solicitation

Appeals for support via the telephone can be very productive provided there is adequate planning, supervision, and follow-up of the activities. In fact, many athletic administrators feel that when properly run, phone-a-thons are the quickest and easiest way to raise dollars and increase one's donor base (Ritrievi, 1989).

The key is the proper use of volunteers as callers or solicitors. Parents, athletes, coaches, booster club members, alumni, school officials, as well as influential community members, all make potentially effective and efficient solicitors. Whether students, alumni or others are staffing the phones, always have supervisors and refreshments available during the phone-a-thon activity.

Naturally, adequate facilities with a sufficient number of telephones are absolutely essential. It is best if there are sufficient phones in one general location so that trained leaders can properly monitor the phone marathon. The number of phones will determine the number of solicitors needed for the phone-a-thon. If you are limited as to the number of phones available, callers/solicitors can work in shifts on the same day or on different dates.

A key component to a successful phone-a-thon is providing appropriate and timely orientation and training for each caller. While the team of callers is being confirmed and the availability of phones secured, it is necessary to complete research into potential prospects and to develop a *prospect list*, i.e., names and phone numbers of those who will be called. The list might include alumni, former athletes, vendors, supporters, season ticket holders, fans, etc. Advanced publicity can be of immense assistance in getting the word out to the potential prospects that the telephone solicitation will take place. Also, it is fruitful to coordinate or match the solicitors with those potential prospects with whom the solicitors might have something in common.

For example, athletic coaches might be paired to call former athletes whom they had coached. Highly successful, well-known business people would be assigned to call other business executives. And, potential alumni donors and former players might be divided or classified by the decade in which they attended—1950s, 1960s, 1970s, 1980s, 1990s etc. Another common tactic is to plan for two separate and distinct phone campaigns each year, one for the renewal of *previous donors* and the other for soliciting *new donors*.

> **PRINCIPLE # 144:** *Phone-a-thons typically call for scripts to be followed by solicitors*

Each caller should be provided cards or lists with names, addresses, and telephone numbers of prospects, along with an adequate supply of pens or pencils, stationery, envelopes, and pledge cards, etc. In addition to the pledge cards, *detailed directions* are provided in terms of what to say (a "script") when the prospect initially comes to the phone (introduction to the cause), how to respond to objections (overcoming hurdles), suggestions as to ways of closing (asking for the money), and instructions on completing the paper work following the conclusion of the phone call (adequate follow-up). Adequate follow-up is essential regardless of whether or not the prospect actually makes a pledge because one needs to make plans for subsequent phone-a-thons.

The script might contain information similar to:

"Hello, this is _____. I am a student-athlete on the football team at ABC high school. This evening the athletic department is conducting a phone-a-thon to raise money for a new scoreboard for the football program. In addition to myself, there are a number of other students, coaches and alumni calling former players, general alumni and supporters in an effort to raise money for the scoreboard. We like to have you help our athletic program by contributing a *gift* of $75."

It is essential that the caller can adequately explain how the funds raised will be utilized —whether for equipment, recruiting, special trips, scholarships, etc. It is also important that the solicitor be knowledgeable with the organization sponsoring the phon-a-thon.

If the potential contributor has previously donated, the caller should know this fact and should mention the previous gift and thank the person. When there are so-called "giving categories" the solicitor should ask for an amount greater than the donor had given previously. If the potential donor is unable or unwilling to contribute at a specific level, the caller should not be afraid or embarrassed to ask why. Also, the caller should then ask for a contribution at the next lower level. As a last resort, one should ask for some nominal gift so that the individual ends up giving something to the worthwhile program.

> **PRINCIPLE # 145:** *Phone-a-thons involve prescreening the prospects to whom calls will be made*

Frequently, neophyte solicitors are allowed to watch more experienced brethren as part of the formal orientation and training process. And, these beginning solicitors are frequently encouraged to participate in role playing, with input and evaluations provided by experienced solicitors, prior to actually making the initial calls. Again, adequate and timely education and training coupled with actual practice become the watchwords.

In terms of the date and time of the actual calls, there are two common tactics. The *first* approach is to have the calls made during a specific time period on certain dates. For example, for 4 hours on a Saturday and a Sunday afternoon, and from a central location where all of the telephone solicitors can make their contacts. The *second* alternative is to have the calls made on an individual basis. In this situation the telephone solicitors are given the names to call, along with other pertinent information and directions, and are allowed to make the calls at times and sites convenient to them—anytime, for example, during a 2-3 week period.

In the latter instance, there is less immediate supervision and less personal support provided to the solicitor. These two disadvantages have to be weighed against the flexibility enjoyed by the solicitors and in terms of the opportunities to actually *reach* prospective donors and contributors via the telephone at differing times.

REFERENCES

Cookie tax. (1995, January 24). *USA Today*, p. 6-A.

Flanigan, P. (1998, October 28). FBI profiler of criminals tells how his idea was born. *Democrat & Chronicle*, p. 2-B.

http://www.fundraisingdepot.com/cgibin/webc.cgi/25successtip.html?sid=9V8Ekc01SCTp315 (1998).

http://www.efundraising.com/enewsletter/newsletter_03_2001.htm (2001)

Kuniholm, R. (1990, January). Direct mail that delivers: How to write effective fund-raising letters. *Case Currents*, 31-35.

McDermott-Griggs, S., & Card, J. (1992). Creating a successful fund-raising letter. *Journal of Physical Education, Recreation and Dance, 63*(1), 57-59.

The Nation's Leading Youth Fund-Raising Company. (1990). Ridgefield, CTK: *Reader's Digest*.

Neuborne, E. (1997, January 22). Parents work the workplace as fund-raisers. *USA Today*, pp. B-1, B-2.

Ostrower, F. (1996). *Why the wealthy give: The culture of elite philanthropy*. Princeton, New

Ritrievi, C. (1989). Dialing for Donors. *College Athletic Management* (CAM), I*(10)*, 56-57.

Stier, W. F., Jr. (1990). ADs walk fine line on promotions. *Athletic Administration, 25*(4), 18-19, 21.

Stier, W.F., Jr. (2000a, November 30). *Fund-Raising and Promotion Secrets for the Busy Athletic Administrator*. Presentation made at the 19th National Athletic Business Conference, Orlando, Florida.

Stier, W. F., Jr. (2000b). The New Paradigm of Sport Marketing, Promotions and Fundraising in the 21st Century. *PROCEEDINGS*. The 2000 Seoul International Sport Science Congress—*New Paradigms of Sport & Physical Education in the 21st Century*, Seoul, Korea.

Stier, W.F., Jr. (2000c). Fund-Raising and Promotion Secrets for the Busy Athletic Director. *PROCEEDINGS—The National Athletic Business Conference, Athletic Business*. Wisconsin: Madison.

Stier, W.F., Jr. (2010). *Fundraising projects for sport, recreation, leisure and fitness programs*. Boston, MA: American Press.

White, J. (1991). The direct route. *College Athletic Management, III*(1), 40-43.

Yiannakis, A., & Braunstein, S. (1983). *The Complete guide to successful fundraising*. North Palm Beach: American Sports Education Institute.

DISCUSSION QUESTIONS

1. Explain in general the four distinct models of fundraising and provide an example of each.

2. Explain the differences in soliciting big donors compared with small donors. What strategies would you employ with each?

3. How would you use utilize the *solicitation kit* as part of your sales approach? Be specific in explaining the kit itself and its content.

4. Describe some of the things you would have your group **do and not do** when involved with *door-to-door sales* both in terms of the *take-order* method and the *point-of-sale* method of selling.

5. Outline how you would plan and implement a phone-a-thon.

8 | PROFIT CENTERS FOR FUNDRAISING

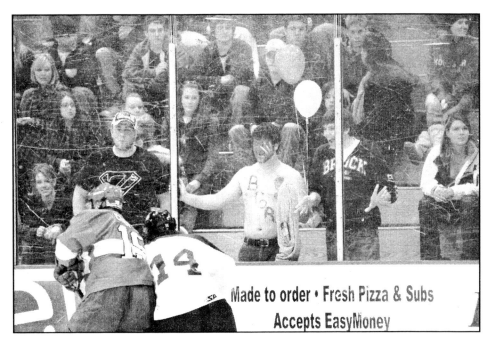

Some sports attract rabid fans and require effective crowd control

CHAPTER HIGHLIGHTS

This chapter will emphasize:

- The *profit center* method of fundraising
- The three general courses of action relating to tickets that have proven successful in terms of increasing attendance at sporting events
- A variety of ticket plans to generate resources
- How to organize concessions operations for a sport or recreation program
- The type of decisions that must be made in terms of creating and producing a printed program and other printed pieces for sale or free distribution
- The importance of team mascots, logos, and colors when creating a fundraising and promotional campaign
- The importance for sport entities to license sports logos, symbols, and names

PROFIT CENTERS

Profit centers are those areas or aspects of a sport program that have the capability or potential for generation of a positive cash flow (income), a genuine profit, for the sport program. Profit centers are stand-alone activities (mini-businesses) that generate money (Stier, 2009).

Types of Profit Centers

> **PRINCIPLE # 146:** *Increasing attendance at contests directly increases potential for other profit centers*

Depending upon the type of athletic program, the skill of the available leadership, the level at which the sport program operates, the size of its following, the basis of its support, and its competitive success, as well as many other factors, there are generally ten areas that may be considered potential profit centers. These areas include, but are not limited to, the following:

1. Ticket sales
2. Concessions
3. Program sales
4. Merchandise and Product sales
5. Car Wrapping and Moving Billboards
6. Parking fees
7. User fees for facilities and services
8. Vending machines—profit sharing
9. Luxury box seating
10. Parking condos

Many of the profit centers depend upon specific traffic patterns in order to have sufficient numbers of people to take advantage of the availability of the items or services that are for sale or use. For example, unless there are people in attendance at games, the likelihood of much money being generated from ticket sales, parking privileges, as well as the sale of merchandise and concessions, is minimal. Therefore, it is essential to do those things that will result in attracting more people to games if it is the objective to increase money generated from the various profit centers that can exist at game sites.

If the athletic team is not winning, or if the team's performance is truly an embarrassment, one might think twice before going out on a limb and exerting extraordinary effort and resources in encouraging spectator attendance. Frequently a spectator's first impression is truly a lasting impression. One gets only one opportunity to make a first impression. This is not just a catchy phrase, but is an important factor to consider.

There must be something worthwhile to promote and to attract the interest of the public. If spectators, especially first time visitors, don't like what they see, they just won't come back. They frequently don't come back even when the team improves. However, on the other hand, if the team is somewhat competitive and exciting to the spectators, the time is ripe to begin to promote and place special emphasis on getting people to attend the contests.

SUCCESS BREEDS SUCCESS

Scheduling of opponents can be an effective method of controlling the potential for promotional activities. Likewise, the scheduling of specific opponents can have a direct impact, either positive or negative, on the profitability of various athletic profit centers, such as tickets, concessions, parking, sale of merchandise, etc.

What if part of the home schedule consists of a number of "bunnies" coupled with some very attractive home contests? In this situation in which only a part of the home schedule is competitive, there are generally two avenues to pursue. *First*, one can create a "mini home schedule" that can be promoted as a **super** home schedule while downplaying the "bunnies" or mismatches. The *second* avenue open to the sport ticket promoter is to attempt to combine some of the team's strong or natural rivalries with the "bunnies" in ticket combinations and promotional packages. In this way, potential ticket purchasers are required to buy tickets to both types of contests, thereby increasing the likelihood of greater attendance (and possible increase in the profit centers) at some of the less competitive contests.

> **PRINCIPLE # 147:** *Always publicize where the proceeds from profit centers will go (a positive selling point) and publicize the items which are for sale*

In promoting the availability of one's various profit centers, it is a good principle to consistently emphasize the fact that the proceeds (profits) go to support a worthy cause (the sport or recreation program or activity, etc.). This awareness campaign can be coupled with the publicity that is generated in support of the actual items that are for sale. This can be effective whether the items are tickets, concessions, parking space, merchandise or programs. One method of inexpensively promoting such items, as well as the charitable cause, is to send flyers to alumni, fans, businesses and other prospects advertising a few of the items or services and informing them where they may be purchased. Additionally, obtaining permission from local grocery stores and other retail businesses to insert flyers into shopping bags or on the back of cash register receipts is an excellent method for mass distribution to the general public.

How can a sport program take advantage of some of these inherent profit centers that might exist within its domain? There are no simple answers to this all-inclusive question. Rather, depending upon the specific circumstances that exist for each athletic program and sport team, one can evaluate ideas and suggestions that have been utilized in other athletic arenas for possible use (adoption and adaptation) in one's own situation. However, the following information and suggestions regarding various profit centers will reveal many common principles that are applicable for almost any athletic program.

TICKET SALES

Establishing a Plan of Attack in the Structuring of the Ticket Operation

The first task at hand is to establish realistic ticket prices. There needs to be flexibility in terms of ticket prices for various age groups. There is also a need for diversity in the promotional activities involving tickets to sporting events. The question "what type of fringe benefits should accrue to the different ticket purchasers," such as preferred seating, reduced prices, special gifts, unique entertainment, etc., needs to be answered.

In selling and promoting sports tickets, i.e., establishing a ticket selling campaign, one must determine who the prospective purchasers are, the starting and closing dates of the sales effort, and the appropriate sales techniques. For example, will the promotion, sales and marketing campaign involve use of the U.S. mail, door-to-door solicitation, use of the phone, assistance from booster club members via person-to-person solicitation, etc., or some combination of all of these?

> **PRINCIPLE # 148:** *There seems to be little crossover between men's and women's fans when it comes to attending sporting events*

There seems to be little crossover between men's and women's fans within the same school or sports program. It seems that fans tend to form rather strong allegiances and they will follow one sport but not all of the sports within an athletic program. This is an important principle when attempting to sell and "move" tickets to women's sporting events. Rick Klatt, the Director of Sports Promotion for both women and men at the University of Iowa, was quoted as saying that: "People go to men's games because other people are there and people go to women's games because they want to be there" (Lamphear & Frankel, 1990, July, p. 28). The same attitudes prevail today.

Thus, when attempting to move tickets to women's sporting events the promoters need to realize that it is not necessary to attempt to compete with the men's programs for the same spectators. Rather, the promoters for the women's programs should attempt to identify and reach those potential spectators who can be influenced to support the women's programs and teams because of the quality of those activities.

Decisions Relating to the Method(s) of Selling Tickets and the Pricing of Tickets

Other factors to consider in terms of the ticket operation include the actual pricing of tickets as well as special advertising, marketing and promotional strategies of the sport activity or contest. One promotional tactic involves the availability of special types of tickets (a tiered system). For example, there may be special tickets for reserved seating or preferred seating. And, special packages can be made available for season tickets holders. Finally, teams can provide combination (coupon) ticket packages for multiple numbers of games in the same sport or involving multiple sports.

PRINCIPLE # 149: *Look to technology to increase service and positive public relations to fans, spectators and consumers alike*

Some professional teams, the Cleveland Indians for one, have installed special turnstile scanners similar to those used in supermarkets. The turnstile scanners at the ballpark serve several functions such as collecting marketing information and voiding lost tickets for fans who are then able to easily secure replacement tickets (Thumbs-Up, 1998).

Whether or not to have *advance ticket sales* is an important decision. There are several advantages of being able to sell game tickets in advance of the actual date of the contest. Generally speaking, ticket managers provide for advanced tickets sales in order to:

1. Serve as an insurance policy against a losing team
2. Protect against a poor-drawing visitor or bad weather (outdoor teams)
3. Create a positive cash flow prior to the start of the season
4. Create enthusiasm in the community for upcoming season
5. Inform the community of needs of program
6. Inform the public of the existence of the entertainment value of the sport activity

> **PRINCIPLE # 150:** *Empty seats costs money in terms of lost revenue—attempt to put such seats to good use*

A great deal of the promotional activities involved with sport programs center around attempts to increase attendance. Such efforts can be implemented around special activities (programs, events) that are attractive to the general public, as well as around reduced or special price incentives that serve as the carrot or an attracting factor. Whatever specific tactics are used, the objectives include (1) maintaining the support of fans and spectators, (2) introducing potential new spectators to the program, (3) increasing attendance, and (4) putting the potential empty seats to some productive use, now and sometime in the future.

One shouldn't be afraid to discount or give tickets away. People who come as spectators frequently purchase concessions. These same people also tend to purchase merchandise if appropriate items are for sale. And, of course, such individuals might come back and be a paying customer sometime in the future. An early study reported by Friedman (1989) revealed that discounted game tickets are the most effective way to influence fans to attend a professional or college sporting event. This technique might also have similar, practical results at the high school level.

There are innumerable promotional plans that can be used to prop up and increase athletic attendance at sporting events. These tactics, which have proven successful at different times within a variety of athletic programs, revolve around three general courses of action. These include:

1. Establishment of **special or group rates** (discounted)
2. The use of **free tickets**
3. **Promotional activities** associated with the marketing and sale of tickets to specific segments of the community
4. **Advertising tactics** related to the sale of tickets

The examples provided below under each of these three categories are not all inclusive. In reality, one is limited only by one's imagination and by what one can learn from others who are in similar situations and who have implemented successful promotional programs dealing with ticket promotions.

Establishment of Special or Group Rates (Discounted)

1. Customer appreciation day/night in which a sponsor buys tickets (often at discounted prices) and which are given away to the customers of the sponsors
2. Family (immediate family) ticket discounts to provide for the needs of those with large families—an attempt to attract youngsters to the contests

3. Free or reduced tickets to everyone whose last name is SMITH or JONES or whose last name begins with a specific letter, etc.
4. Free or reduced prices when accompanied by a full ticket purchaser
5. Reduced prices for groups of four or more (even if one of the "guests" happens to be a stuffed animal or cardboard figure)
6. Kids' night—children free with accompanying parent
7. Availability of discount prices for specific games—for off nights
8. Discount ticket (coupons) books for families
9. Guest night—2 tickets for the price of 1 or 3 tickets for the price of 2
10. Coupon discount with the purchase of a ticket
11. Group sales at a discount—discounted tickets to youth oriented organizations such as youth sport groups; to service clubs like the Lions club, Kiwanis and Elks; to specific corporations or groups such as the phone company, gas company, electric company, board of Realtors, labor unions, etc.
12. Merchants are given tickets (coupon book) at a discount
13. Provide merchants with so many game tickets for every $50 of contributions to the sport program

> **PRINCIPLE # 151:** *When coupons are used, consumers desire either to save money or to experience something new (Perry, 2000)*

The Use of FREE Tickets

1. Tie in with local businesses to give tickets away to special populations
2. Give tickets away via the community Welcome Wagon to new individuals and families in town—an excellent method of introducing the sports program to newcomers in town
3. Free tickets to worthy causes such as hospitals, scout groups, etc.

Promotional Activities Associated with the Advertising and Marketing of Tickets

1. Offer local groups the opportunity to sell tickets for a percentage of the gross sales
2. Ask every vendor who sells to your school to buy 2 season tickets and/or 250 general admission tickets to your games

3. Sell advertisers a package deal including sponsorship of a game, plus game tickets and an ad in the program and/or signage within a sport facility

4. Arrange for community groups (youth hockey club, little league, midget football) or businesses to sell tickets and receive a cut of sales price (20% for example)

5. Sell tickets to a game accompanied by a free (or reduced) ticket to the local theater or bowling alley or golf course

6. For every ticket a person buys to the theater, bowling alley or golf course, the purchaser receives a free or reduced priced ticket to one of the selected sport contests

7. Install *promotional turnstile advertising* so that every person who enters the sport facility can glance at the marketing and advertising copy on the turnstile

---

PRINCIPLE # 152: *Take advantage of the individuals who attend the contests— build a prospect list from the names of those individuals who purchase or inquire about tickets*

Use your ticket sales as well as phone or written inquiries to help create a list of backers and supporters by building a mailing prospect list. Then use the list to further promote the sport program by mailing newsletters, ticket information, as well as a whole host of special promotional materials. The names and mailing addresses of individuals who have attended a sporting event or who are potential supporters are very important in terms of future communication attempts. They are also important in terms of future purchases of tickets and sport paraphernalia.

The mailing prospect list can be built through a variety of means. *One method* is to encourage spectators to complete a short questionnaire, designed to obtain such pertinent information, at an athletic contest. This questionnaire can also be used in a contest, for example, a raffle for prizes, thus insuring that more people will complete the form. *Another tactic* is to just to ask spectators to complete an opinion survey in an effort for the sport or recreation organization to be able to better meet their needs.

A *third method* is to simply provide a means by which spectators can drop in a business card, or just sign their names and addresses on a pre-printed form and drop it into a box provided for that purpose. The sport administrators can then mail to these individuals a carefully designed form soliciting information. A *fourth* technique is to re-

Signage is an important element in promoting one's program and activities

cord the names and address of any individual who orders tickets to contests or who contacts the athletic office for information, for any reason whatsoever.

The ultimate objective is to obtain a current list of individuals who might be interested in the sport program and teams. Great efforts should go into maintaining an up-to-date listing of those who are prime candidates as spectators, fans and supporters.

CONCESSIONS

The overriding consideration when contemplating involvement in the area of concessions is whether or not the end results are worth the effort and resources that must be put into the total concession operation. If the paid sport staff members are involved in the concessions arena, then the cost of their released time must be accounted for and factored into the total cost of the concessions operation. However, if volunteers are responsible for the general operation of concessions, then there are no real, significant costs, in terms of salaries for staffing the concessions area.

Whether the athletic concession area is staffed by salaried athletic personnel, by volunteers or by an outside firm, it is the total financial, promotional, and public relations effort that must be taken into consideration. If such financial, promotional, and public relations benefits of the concession activity do not justify the time and effort required for the management and supervision of the concessions area, **then it would behoove the sport organizers or boosters not to become actively involved with concessions**. The major justification for maintaining a concession operation is to generate a profit, both in terms of money and in respect to positive public relations, for the sport program.

Generally speaking, operators must be concerned with (1) the commitment to be successful in operating the concession concern, (2) proper staffing, (3) proper training and evaluation of staffing, (4) cleanliness, (5) quality and quality control, (6) menu selection, (7) food preparation and service, (8) adequate space, (9) promotion and marketing of the operation, and (10) advertising (Hilkemeyer, 1993; Waldo and Murray, 1996; Stier, 2000d)

Operational Aspects of Running Concessions—Points to Consider

One of the first decisions that must be made involves the determination of the menu itself. What will be the mainstay of the menu? What will sell? What will produce the greatest profit? What snacks will be provided? When will the concession stand be in operation? Is there ample storage for inventory?

Particular attention needs to be paid to low food cost items as well as items that provide for a high net profit with as little work as possible. And, don't forget about food items that are indigenous to your area, to your part of the country (Hilkemeyer, 1993). The degree of skill required in the preparation of items must also be taken into consideration.

> **PRINCIPLE # 153: Net profits from concessions (food and beverage operations) are derived from volume**

Items like cold drinks, cotton candy, popcorn, snow cones, hot dogs, nachos, and the like, are not time intensive in their preparation and enjoy a high profit margin for the concession operation. Special attention, especially in today's world of health and food consciousness, must be paid to the ingredients (salt and cholesterol) in the food that is for sale.

However, the concession operators need to be aware of local ordinances that have a direct impact on their operation. Some municipal laws require that packaged snacks require a vending license in order to sell. Hot dogs and nachos, in some locals, are included under restaurant codes and the operation of the concession stand must meet the local code standards. Foods that are cooked in grease, such a hamburgers and French fries, might require the sponsoring organization to follow very strict restaurant *and* fire codes that could include venting hoods, fire extinguishers, specific amount of square footage in the cooking area, etc. (Cohen, 1992).

> **PRINCIPLE # 154: A streamlined menu can result in excellent and speedy behind-the-counter service**

In recent years concession menus have become more and more complex and extensive. As a result, cashiers have a challenge in adequately performing their responsibilities. Thus, more and more, concession operators have replaced "cigar box" cash boxes and have instead invested in electronic cash registers or at least basic adding machines. One of the reasons behind this shift towards a wider menu selection has been the demand by potential customers. Today, the typical sports concession stand may have 20-25 items while in years past the average concession operation might have offered only a basic menu of soft drinks, beer (if allowed), popcorn, hot dogs, hamburgers and candy. However, with that said, do not attempt to offer "everything" on the menu to the consumer. There is still a need to consciously keep the menu streamlined lest one attempts to offer everything under the sun (Ferguson, 1990a; Ferguson, 1990b; Stier, 2000a).

Once the menu has been determined, the appropriate pricing of each menu item must be made. The goal is to make a reasonable profit. Pick and choose what you will provide and then serve quality items speedily and in a pleasant and clean atmosphere (Holtzman, 2001). This means that the profit margins (money remaining after cost of sales and merchandise is deducted) must be high enough to warrant the involvement (time and effort) in concessions. Running a concessions stand is not a get-rich scheme. It takes hard work, dedication, advance planning and an understanding of advertising, promotion and marketing to the public. Patience and persistence also are great assets.

Monitoring the concession operation is a major challenge. There are many factors that must be paid close attention to if the concession stand is to be successful. One of the major areas that must be constantly monitored is the supervision and training of workers. The National Association of Concessionaires, as well as area restaurant associations and various concessionaire suppliers, have training aids and advice to assist the new and experienced workers (Bigelow, 1989).

> **PRINCIPLE # 155:** *Proper selection, training and supervision of personnel will go a long way to insure correct operation of the concession stand, including minimizing theft of loss of funds and inventory*

Proper selection of staff and adequate training are two important factors in insuring honesty of the concessionaire workers, both those who volunteer and those on salary. Close supervision and established work rules will go a long way to prevent skimming of profits by those individuals working in the concession stand. The maintaining of cleanliness is yet another major challenge. How the concession operation is viewed by the public in terms of cleanliness will determine, for the most part, how successful the operation will be. No one will want to purchase food items at a site that is not clean. No one wants to be served by an attendant who has dirty hands.

> **PRINCIPLE # 156:** *Service* **and** *quality* *are the two watchwords associated with concession operations*

Today the watchwords are *service* and *quality*. If the concession stand cannot meet the ever-increasing standards in terms of expectations of the customers the result will be an ineffectual and inefficient operation. The result will be lost profits and negative public relations.

The establishing and following of proper accounting procedures are essential ingredients of any successful concession stand. Hiring, training, motivating and keeping qualified, friendly workers are difficult tasks for the managers of the concession stand. Ordering and storing an adequate supply of all items, food and drink items as well as non-food items, must be done well enough in advance to insure that the items are on hand for the actual athletic event. Nothing could be worse than for the day of the sport event or contest to arrive and for the concession workers not to have the proper items on hand, ready to be sold.

There are four essentials necessary for any concession stand to be successful. *First*, there must be appropriate items to sell for a fair price. *Second*, there must be adequately trained and professional salespeople to work the concession stand (including the various machines) and to serve as a clean-up team. *Third*, there must be people at the event who desire to purchase (are motivated to act) the items that are for sale. *Finally*, there is the task of assessing and evaluating (on a continuous basis) the total concession operation.

> ***PRINCIPLE # 157:** It is generally recommended that if you operate a concession stand, have it open for all contests and events, not merely for a few big games*

The need to act upon the evaluation of the various aspects of the concession stand is mandatory. Evaluation of the concession operation (stand) is facilitated by the maintenance of good and accurate records of all that is done in the concession operation. This is so that those efforts that are successful can be retained and repeated while changing and improving those areas that need a facelift.

Essentially, everything connected with the concession area should be evaluated in light of what is working well and what can be improved in the future. Here, as always, hindsight is a valuable tool. As the concession stand continues to operate and the workers gain experience and a better feel for the total operation, the concession area will hopefully be more productive, successful and profitable.

Picking Concession Food and Drink Items—Points to Consider

> ***PRINCIPLE # 158:** Don't over complicate things—make it easy for people to purchase and consume items*

In selecting the food and drink items to comprise the menu, it behooves the forward thinking promoters to answer the following questions (Cohen, 1991, May). What would the operators of the concession stand enjoy buying and eating if they were spectators? What items are easy to promote, advertise and eventually sell? What would be enjoyable selling? Which items are easy to prepare, handle and actually sell? Which items have a built in high profit margin? What brands are well known by the public and are viewed as quality items? What products have a natural appeal to the majority of people within the general geographic target area? What products can be stored without undue problems and difficulties (spoilage)? What items are easy to clean up within the facility where the food and drink are consumed? What food items can be easily and profitably advertised, promoted and sold before, during as well as after the athletic contest/event?

"Popcorn, hot dogs and nachos are concession staples, big sellers that can produce ample profits" (Cohen, 1994, p. 45). Generally speaking, some of the highest profits within the concession area are generated by cold drinks (90%), cotton candy (90%), popcorn (85%), nachos (90%), snow-cones (95%) and hotdogs (50-60%) (Cohen, 1992). It is not uncommon for hot dogs to generate half of a stand's total profit. Even pizza (heated in a microwave) has become a staple in some areas of the country.

Determining Pricing Schedule and Cost of Sales—Points to Consider

> **PRINCIPLE # 159:** *Plan on turning over your inventory once a month, more if you have a good-sized operation*

In determining the profit margins, cost of sales and overhead, a good rule of thumb is that income, minus the cost of merchandise, but prior to deducting other expenses, should not fall below 65%. In the world of athletic concessions, mark-ups in the area of 65-85% gross profit are quite legitimate. Aaron Conklin, recreation director for the City of St. Peters, Missouri, recommends that if "a concessions operation can keep its food costs and labor at about 30 percent each, and maintain its overhead and utilities at about 10 percent, they should theoretically net a 60 percent profit (Conklin, 1999, p. 57). Others suggest an overall profit target of 80%. This means that if it costs you 20 cents, you want to sell it for a dollar.

It is also wise to ask the vendor for suggestions as to the cost of the items for sale that might be appropriate in a particular geographical area. In essence, the law of supply and demand (what items customarily sell for in your area) is often a criterion for the determining the price one can change for any given item. Pricing must be competitive. That is, items should be sold for what the *market will bear* without gouging the prospective customer.

> **PRINCIPLE # 160:** *Charge a fair price for the menu items—don't gouge the customers but charge what the market will bear, keeping in mind that the customer has the convenience of having the items readily available*

In determining total *net profit*, one has to consider the amount of money that remains after all expenses are deducted. Generally speaking, a concession operation should be generating at least at a 55-60% net profit.

To achieve this, items that have a low cost to the concessionaire, items that are not complicated to prepare, items that have a high profit margin (low cost versus high sales price, such as popcorn) and items that are popular with the public should form the basis of inventory for the concession operation. A concession stand operated by volunteers, parents or boosters, which involves no cost for personnel, naturally enhances the net profit potential for the concession operation.

Popcorn, the old reliable concession stand staple, still meets all of the criteria for a great food component for any concession stand. Popcorn is something most people like and accept. It is a food item that is healthy and attractive for the consumer while being relatively inexpensive for the concessionaire. It is also easy to prepare. In short, the profit on popcorn is relatively high considering the initial cost of the item and the time and effort in its preparation for consumption (Herzog, 1990). The gross profit for popcorn generally runs as high as 85 percent over the cost of the popcorn itself and the serving container, usually a bag or cup (Cohen, 1992; Conklin, 1999).

> *PRINCIPLE # 161:* *Maintaining inventory may be the most boring task associated with concessions but it is also one of the most important— if you are expecting to make a reasonable profit*

Promoting the Concession Area—Points to Consider

The following suggestions are generally considered to be wise advice for the concessionaire in the effort to promote profitability of the operation.

1. Use point of purchase display posters and printed advertisements (obtained from supplier) as they make your product more attractive
2. Provide for safe, courteous service for the public
3. Implement weekly or even daily inventory counts of menu items to insure nothing is lost (stolen) and that sufficient inventory is on hand for consumers
4. Sales of menu items increase if the food is prepared in front of customers
5. Use value pricing and advertise that fact via display and advertising. That is, offer several sizes (small, medium and large) in some items and lower the cost per ounce of the large offerings. This encourages the customer to "trade up." There is definitely a trend for larger containers to be sold today.
6. Use professional menu boards (vendors can provide these as well) representing an adequate menu mix
7. Promote parties and group events and open the concession stand for these events
8. Put away or disconnect vending machines—don't encourage your own competition. Vending machines should only be available to sell items that the concession stand does not offer
9. Provide for a convenient, clean and neat area for customers to eat after ordering from the menu

10. Be sure that the menu is easy to read, even from a distance

11. Have a "special" on the menu. Once customers are attracted to the concessions area, they frequently purchase other items.

12. Train your staff in selling—have them ask customers if they would prefer a specific item. Have them make suggestions as to possible purchases by the customer (Cohen, 1992, January).

13. Provide an incentive bonus for salespeople

14. Anticipate rush hours and have adequate staffing—send people into the stands before the "rush" begins in order to prevent "bottle necks" at the concession stand

15. Advertise during, before, and after the game

16. Use the PA system to advertise specials periodically (and for a specific period of time, 10-15 minutes), the so-called "Zayre 15-minute In-Store Special" or the K-Mart 10-minute "Blue Light Special" promotion.

17. Keep all display items filled. Drink dispensers should be kept 75% full so as to attract attention and motivate the purchaser to action.

18. Secure an animated beverage dispenser and keep it where it can be seen. Similarly, place the hot dog rotisserie in a visible spot where customers will see it (and smell the food). Vendors are only too happy to assist in the advertising, marketing and selling of their products—take advantage of their experience and expertise.

19. Have an active, clean, and attractive concession stand, one that will attract attention

20. Have all food handlers use plastic gloves and have the concession area very, very clean

21. *Never allow concession workers to eat or to engage in horseplay while in the concession stand area*

22. Have all workers in the concession area wear professional clothing (uniforms)

23. Food should *never* be served at the wrong temperature. Food that should be hot must be hot. Food that should be cold must be cold. Nothing is worse than a cold hot dog or a warm soft drink or stale popcorn.

24. Change (rotate) some products periodically and add new items regularly

25. Maintain a close watch over *waste* (no more than one half of one percent) and of all *discounts given to staff*

26. Be careful about allowing the staff and helpers to have free samples of leftover cooked food at the end of the day as this encourages over preparation at the end of the day in anticipation of receiving freebies when there are leftovers

27. Provide a suggestion box for customers to provide ideas on how to improve the concession stand

28. After each day's activities double check how things went and examine what sold well and what didn't. Be especially attentive to leftover food that must be disposed of (wasted) so that unnecessary and expensive spoilage doesn't happen in the future.

PRINCIPLE # 162: *The bane of every concession operator is waste (spoiled food items, lost money and lost revenue)*

Gross Profit Potential for Various Food Items—Points to Consider

Be sure that you know what the items that you have for sale actually cost you (including paper goods, condiments and other extra things that you provide to your customers). If you are striving for a *cost percentage* of 25-35% or less (*the cost you paid for the items divided by the amount that you sell the items for*) on the total items that are sold at the concession stand, you will need to have some items that will have a lower *cost percentage* (such as fountain sodas, popcorn and cotton candy—at 10%) to counteract the most expensive items such as turkey sandwiches, hot dogs, bottled drinks, and chocolate candy (Holtzman, 2001).

PROGRAM SALES AND OTHER PRINTED PIECES

Team programs can be sources of sizeable profits for the sport program, depending upon a number of factors such as the printing costs, the cost of sales of such items; and, finally, how the printed piece is financed, i.e., whether or not advertisements are included within the printed piece in an effort to offset the cost of the item. In the production of an athletic program, or for any printed piece for that matter, there are several decisions that must be made prior to the actual printing of the piece.

The *first decision* that must be made in terms of printed pieces for a sport program revolves around the determination of the actual purpose(s) of the items. In addition to the traditional printed athletic program, other printed items might include team calendars, schedule cards, media guides, recruiting brochures, highlight flyers, etc.

Another decision that must be faced is the actual makeup or composition of the printed items. For example, a decision has to be made in terms of the number of pages involved, the size of the pages, the quality of the paper, the number of color inks (if more than black), the actual number of pieces printed, the number of photographs, and whether or not professional typesetting is used in printing the publication piece. And, of course, how many of the items need to be printed, i.e., the actual press run and when the printed items are needed. It is important to keep in mind that the cost per printed piece decreases as the total number of pieces printed is increased.

A *third decision* to make is whether or not to use ads within the printed piece. If ads are to be included, what shall be the going price of the ads for a full page, a half page, a third of a page, a quarter page, an eighth page, as well as the front and back covers and the inside of the front and back covers? How much can reasonably be expected to be raised through the sale of ads and what percentage of the total printed space shall be devoted to advertisements?

A *fourth decision* hinges on how the advertisements shall be solicited. That is, will members of the coaching staff seek paid advertisements? What about the athletes themselves? What role shall the booster organization or parents play in the sale of advertisements for the printed athletic program? Or, will outside professional "headhunters" whose professional job it is to raise money through the sale of advertisements be sought and hired to perform this task?

A *fifth decision* hinges on whether or not the printed item will be given away or sold. If it is to be sold, for what price? Through what mechanism will the printed piece be distributed? Will the printed item(s) be distributed at games as well as through other means (mail, etc.)? Will hawkers make the piece available before and during the contest? Will the programs be available at the ticket counter and at the ticket taking area? Can the items left over also be used for recruitment purposes at a later time for those school-based programs that are involved in the student recruitment process?

Athletic programs, as well as other printed items, can be successful in promoting the image of the sport program to the general public. Additionally, such items as team calendars, game programs and souvenir programs can be structured in such a way as to provide sizeable profit to the athletic organization. The profit potential essentially hinges upon the factors of (1) selling advertisements and (2) selling the printed programs or calendars, or whatever the printed item might be, for a specific price to the sports fans—either at athletic contests or through sales within the community.

A fan tries his luck at the free throw line dueing a contest at a basketball game

MERCHANDISE, PRODUCT SALES

Another profit center revolves around the selling of merchandise related to the athletic team or sponsoring organization. One of the earliest examples of a sporting event associated with a logo on athletic apparel was in 1852 when the first collegiate athletic contest (a rowing match) in the U.S. was held between Harvard and Yale. The losing Yale athletes wore Lacrosse shirts with the letters "YALE" on them. Today, Yale expects to earn considerably more (actually, some $250,000) for the licensing of its name and logo on a variety of sporting and non-sporting apparel. And, Harvard, the winners of that 1852 contest, expects to bring in a profit of over $1 million today. (Boola Boola, 1998; Yale Mascot Sale, 1998).

In attempting to arrive at a reasonable sales operation of merchandise there are seven essential areas that must be addressed. These include (1) selecting the merchandise, (2) pricing of the merchandise, (3) ordering correct merchandise, (4) ordering at an appropriate time, (5) advertising and marketing strategies for the item(s), (6) accounting for the funds, and (7) as handling, disposing or storage of any remaining or left over inventory.

Selecting Merchandise

What can be sold? What is marketable for any given athletic program? What do people want to buy? These are critical questions indeed. To answer the question, WHAT can be sold? The answer is ALMOST ANYTHING. For example, T-shirts, ties, sweatshirts, book bags, shirts, jackets, pants, shorts, bumper stickers, sports calendars, ad books (selling ads to businesses), caps, glasses, cups, etc. Schools and teams are putting their names and logos/mascots on almost anything and everything from computer games, to sportswear and even food companies. Literally scores of advertisements from vendors promoting items for resale will cross the desk of any athletic director during the course of a school year, illustrating literally hundreds, if not thousands, of items that can be resold through merchandising, promotional, advertising, and marketing efforts. Additionally, consideration should be given to the quality of the items, the wholesale cost to the organization, the potential selling price, the net profit and the available support of the sales force.

Use of Team Mascots, Logos, and Colors

In planning to select and/or create various items to sell, it is important to utilize one's school or club colors as well as the logo or mascot on the merchandise, see appendix D. Create an identity with the team or organization through the use of a team *mascot, logo*, and *colors* on all merchandise sold. It is important to remember that the logo, mascot, and/or symbol that are representative of the sport entity be professionally created and expertly utilized on all items of apparel for sale or distribution.

> *PRINCIPLE # 163:* *Strategically use team mascots, logos and colors to help promote and market the sport organization and activities*

Even minor league teams can experience tremendous growth in profits from merchandise sales. The Batavia, New York baseball team, the Class A affiliate of the Philadelphia Phillies, generated only $14,000 in merchandise sales in 1997 when the team was known as the *Clippers*. However, in 1998, as the *Batavia Muckdogs*, the team soared to over $91,000 in sales of merchandise in its first year with the new logo and marketing plan. A *Muckdog* is an ornery looking dog that is pictured chomping through a wooden fence. The mascot/logo has become a hit with sports fans of all ages and across all social-economic levels (Pitoniak, 2000).

In summary, items or products that are selected to be sold should be useful, sometimes unique and be a better value or at least equal value than what people normally purchase from a local merchant. If a particular product or item can't stand up to such scrutiny—perhaps the wisest strategy of the sport promoter would be to pass on the item and to look at other possible merchandise to purchase in order to resell and promote.

> **PRINCIPLE # 164:** *Whatever is to be sold should be useful, somewhat unique and either a better value or equal value than what the potential purchaser would normally buy*

Naturally, the more visible and popular the sport entity is, the more attractive the merchandise is to the general public, to fans and to supporters. Merchandise possessing the team's logo from Syracuse University or from Notre Dame has more appeal to a larger audience than a team's logo from a medium size high school. This does not mean that the high school cannot successfully market and sell various items of merchandise. To the contrary. Small schools and small athletic organizations can still successfully select merchandise that can be sold to appropriate constituencies in sufficient volume to create a meaningful net profit.

PRICING OF THE MERCHANDISE

A wise decision in the pricing of the merchandise is essential. Actually there are two goals in terms of selling any merchandise. The *first* goal is to make a profit. That is certainly expected. However, the *second* motive or objective is to obtain an ever-increasing exposure of one's program within the community and among the various constituencies. Thus, it does no good to price the merchandise so high that only a limited number of items are actually sold. It is better to sell a larger number of items at a lesser profit per item and gain additional exposure via the distribution of the various merchandise to a wider population. A 40% to 50% net profit on the sale of general sports merchandise is not unreasonable.

The twin sins of any sport promoter dealing with merchandise include: (1) not being able to secure the correct items for sale from the wholesaler, and (2) ordering an incorrect number (either too many or too few) of the items. Failing to order on time is indeed an almost unforgivable sin for the sport merchandiser. One simply must be able to make a decision and execute a commitment in a timely manner for the purchase of whatever items the organization wishes to sell. There is no hard and fast rule when it comes to ordering merchandise, but individual vendors will be able to provide the sport organizers with rather specific time requirements for particular items. The basic idea is to plan well enough in advance of the date when the merchandise is needed, thus insuring that there is sufficient time to have the item(s) shipped.

> **PRINCIPLE # 165:** *Don't order too many or too few items to resell to the public— leftover merchandise is the bane of fundraisers*

Naturally, items that are in stock and generic in nature can be provided in less time than items that must be custom made. For example, generic sweat shirts can be obtained in a much quicker turnaround time than can sweat shirts that must be screened or embroidered with the name and logo of the particular athletic team.

> **PRINCIPLE # 166:** *Pre-selling merchandise greatly reduces the risk of leftover items and financial exposure*

The number of items that are ordered rests upon a number of factors, including one's best judgment as to how many can be moved (sold) once the items are on hand as well as whether or not any items will be *pre-sold*. That is, will the money for a specific number of sweatshirts be collected prior to the placement of the order of sweatshirts? Or, will the athletic organization purchase the items and hold them in inventory while attempting to sell them? Pre-selling and collecting the money prior to placing the order greatly diminishes the risk of ordering an incorrect number of items or items with incorrect sizes.

Marketing, Promotional and Advertising Strategies for the Sale of Merchandise

How will the items to be sold be promoted and marketed? That is, how will they be advertised <u>and</u> actually sold? Will youngsters sell the items door-to-door? Can they be sold through the school store? Can they be sold at games? Will parents of the athletes be asked to purchase and/or sell such items? Who will train the sales force? Who will manage the record keeping of the sales operation? These questions must be answered in light of the resources and limitations that exist within a particular organization.

CAR WRAPPING AND MOVING BILLBOARDS

There is value in being seen, period. Witness two California companies, *Autowraps Inc.* of San Francisco and *FreeCar Media* of Los Angeles, both of which wrap automobiles with advertising copy. This *car wrapping* technology "enables cars to be wrapped from roof to rocker panel with digitally-printed adhesive vinyl wrap" (Bowles, 2000, p. 3-A). The wrap even covers the windows but does not prevent the occupants from seeing out. These moving billboards have the advantage of being mobile rather than stationery and, hence, have the potential for reaching a wider audience of potential consumers.

PARKING

Depending upon the demand, charging for parking can prove to be a most effective way in generating a significant source of income for the athletic organization or group. Of course, there are some essential ingredients that must be present in order for parking to become a moneymaker. *First*, spectators must desire (need) to find a site to park their vehicles; *second*, there must be an absence of free parking spaces (lack of competition); and, *lastly*, there must be suitable and safe parking spaces (adequate supply) available that can be cordoned off and used as a parking lot(s) for an appropriate time and for an affordable price.

The use of available parking spaces for additional income is not the exclusive purview of big-time athletic programs. Rather, schools of all sizes at every level of competition can rent out parking spaces for any type of event that attracts large crowds and where available and free parking space is somewhat limited.

USER FEES FOR FACILITIES AND SERVICES

Anytime an athletic operation has control of the indoor or outdoor facilities, in terms of scheduling the use of such facilities; and, has the authority and responsibility for renting the facilities (gyms, pools, fields, weight rooms, etc.) to outside groups or entities for specific fees, there is potential for raising sizeable monies for the athletic program. The athletic department might rent out part of the facility to any number of outside organizations such as church groups, other schools, professional, and semi-professional teams, square dance clubs, youth sport teams, etc. The list is literally endless.

> **PRINCIPLE # 167:** *User fees enable sport entities to take advantage of their facilities when not in use by one's own teams*

The idea is simple. An outside entity pays for the use of the athletic facility while agreeing to provide an umbrella insurance policy, as well as adequate supervisory and security personnel coupled with an agreement to make repairs for any and all damage caused by the group.

Another way to make money through the use of facilities is to conduct sport camps or clinics. Or, one may rent the athletic facilities to an individual or group who in turn would conduct such programs. There are various types of sport clinics, as well as summer athletic camps, which can be fairly easily organized and that can be equally popular and profitable. In the latter category, any number of sports (baseball, ice hockey, football, soccer, basketball, swimming, etc.), as well as cheerleading camps and camps organized for the training of student athletic trainers, may be established and planned for the school's facility. Other types of camps that utilize sports facilities can also be conducted. For example, weight loss camps and camps for older people have proven to be both successful and popular on college campuses.

In the area of sport camps and clinics as well as with the use or rental of facilities, there are two avenues that may be pursued. *First*, the athletic department can organize and run the camp or clinic itself. In this scenario, the organization does not have to pay for the use of a facility and can save the cost of what would have been the rental fee. The *second* option is to simply rent out the facility, in exchange for a straight fee or for a percentage of the *gross* profits, to an outside organization. In this scenario, it is the outside entity that will take responsibility for organizing and implementing the sport camp or clinic. In this second option, there is less risk involved to the organization owning the facility that is being rented out, but also less profit.

VENDING MACHINES

Vending machines, those silent and inactive sales devices, can be a boon to the treasury of any sport or recreation organization. Usually placed in schools and within and around athletic and recreation facilities, vending machines provide a profit sharing opportunity with the owner of the machines. The major questions that must be answered revolve around the exact percentage of the gross sales that accrue to the athletic organization, the location of the machines and the contents within the machines. Since the owners of the machines secure all licenses and permits there is usually no work involved on behalf of the organization where the vending machines will be placed. The only responsibility of the school or the athletic team is to provide a specific location for the machines.

> **PRINCIPLE # 168:** *Raising funds via vending machines is often called the silent (and easy) moneymaker*

The contents of vending machines today can include almost anything. Items such as coffee, soups, milk, candy, soft drinks, sandwiches, ice cream, hot chocolate, pastry, gum, fruit, etc., are all popular items that can be sold through the vending machines. Of course, items such as cigarettes, which can also be sold via such machines, must be evaluated very carefully in terms of appropriateness within an athletic or educational atmosphere or arena. And, even including candy and other snack foods in vending machines can come under criticism and can result in negative publicity for the school or the athletic organization within some communities.

Technology and Vending Machines

Technology has come to the vending machine. Witness the tactic Coca-Cola Co. has begun testing with its new vending machine—the machine is able to automatically raise the price of a bottle of Coke dispensed from the machine when the weather becomes warmer. This somewhat novel approach (charging more when people desire a cool drink as a result of warmer temperatures) is a variation of the *law of supply and demand*. In 1999, Coke chairman and chief executive officer, M. Douglas Ivester, indicated that during a sporting event with rising temperature, the spectators' desire for a cool, soft drink would be greater and that it is only fair that the cost for such a product be increased under greater demand. With the prototype machines, the escalation of the price of a Coke would be automatically initiated by the machine in reaction to the rise in temperature (Coke wants, 1999).

PREMIUM PREFERRED SEATING AND LUXURY BOXES

The idea behind preferred, premium seating is simple. Special seating, such as (1) *luxury boxes*, (2) *skyboxes* or (3) *reserved seating* close to courtside or the field, is set aside on a season long basis in prime locations for the exclusive use of patrons willing to pay for the privilege of having access to strategic, exclusive seating offering super views of the athletic competition. In addition, there are "extras" or special amenities (not available to holders of regular seats) that often accompany the executive or luxury seating accommodations associated with luxury boxes or skyboxes, such as the availability of personalized (read *pampered*) service, special foods and drinks as well as privacy. Renting the use of these executive or luxury seating accommodations can result in tremendous income to the sponsoring organization.

The history of charging for the use of seats can be traced back much farther than one would image. In fact, recent disclosures by Jim Hoobler, curator of art and architecture at the Tennessee State Museum in Nashville, has confirmed that such practices were common as long ago as 1885 when members of the First Presbyterian church (now known as The Downtown Presbyterian church) charged $25 to rent a pew in church, presumably close to the front of the church, for a six-month period of time (Back to the Future, 1995).

> **PRINCIPLE # 169:** *Exclusivity and special amenities are essential elements to the successful marketing of premium or preferred seating*

The idea of real premium seating, at least in the US, can be traced back to the 1960s when the Forum in Inglewood, Calif., introduced the " . . . *concept of exclusivity*, with so-called Senate seating and the Houston Astrodome opened with *skyboxes* almost like living quarters, with bedrooms and kitchens," said Bill Dorsey, president of the *Association of Luxury Suites Directors* (Hiestand, 1999, p. 3-C).

While in the past luxury box seating (often referred to as skyboxes) has often been thought of as being the exclusive domain of big-league (major league) professional sport teams with their large stadiums and sports complexes—*this is no longer the case*. Today, almost every professional sports stadium has preferred or premium seating in the form of so-called luxury boxes or skyboxes and every new facility will include such amenities. In fact, it is estimated that by 2015, some 500-550 sports venues will have, at a minimum, 25 suites available each. These suites will be marketed to well-heeled fans, patrons and businesses willing to pay significant sums for the privilege of using, on a season long basis (often with multi-year contracts), such preferred, exclusive seating. Even many minor league teams as well as athletic programs at various levels have gotten into the act or are considering the possibility of utilizing the idea of so-called luxury or preferred seating arrangements. For example, **Iowa Cubs**, a Des Moines, Iowa minor league baseball team, has 44 suites for its fan base.

PRINCIPLE # 170: *Luxury, premium seating is an essential element in the successful funding of almost all professional and big-time sporting events*

Today, whenever and wherever you have fans wishing to view sporting events, administrators and organizers will eventually get around to having suites to provide a special *premium space* for fans to view the games or sporting events. Exclusivity is the key to premium or preferred seating while service is the proverbial icing on the cake. As a result, premium seating can command significantly more in price than regular seating (Wong, 2000). Although some have claimed that exclusive suites should remain the province of professional sports, this has not slowed the rapid expansion of suites at all types of sport venues at all levels of competition. People like the idea of premium seating, of exclusivity. And, when there is a demand, there will always be someone willing and able to meet that demand.

PARKING CONDOS

A more recent phenomenon in terms of generating income is the use of so-called *parking condos*. Adjacent to large stadiums or field houses are built two-story, covered structures which are utilized to provide both safe and convenient parking for vehicles (cars, vans, and buses) as well as facilities for meals and relaxation before, during, and after athletic contests.

Essentially, these structures, which might be privately owned or owned by the school itself, provide opportunities for rather sophisticated tailgate parties and secure parking of vehicles by fans willing to rent such facilities on a single season or multiple season basis.

> **PRINCIPLE # 171:** Take advantage of the need by well-heeled spectators to park their cars by establishing parking condos

Such parking condos may be rented for $1,500 to $2,500 per season in 2010, depending upon the locale. Of course, the attraction of the parking condos rests not only in the availability of exclusive, convenient and secure parking for individual's vehicles but also in the fact that the two story structure contains so-called party rooms that the "owners" of the parking condos can utilize on game day for elaborate pre-game and post-game gatherings for either intimate personal get-togethers or for business gatherings. Of course, Reagan (1992) indicated that those who have leased the condos may take advantage of the party facility and the parking space throughout the calendar year.

REFERENCES

Back to the future. (1995, December 26). *USA Today*, p. 3-C.

Bigelow, C. (1989). Spicing up your concession profits. *Athletic Business, 13*(1), 42-45.

Boola Boola, Moola Moola. (1998, February 6). *Sports Illustrated, 88*(6). 28.

Bowles, S. (2000, September 15). Motorists finding logos a gas. *USA Today*, p. 3-A.

Cohen, A. (1991). Concessions come of age. *Athletic Business, 15*(5), 61, 62, 64.

Cohen, A. (1992). Cooking up concessions. *Athletic Business. 16*(1), 35-36, 38.

Cohen, A. (1994). Food fight. *Athletic Business, 18*(11), 45.

Coke wants to raise price when summer swelters. (1999, October 28). *Democrat & Chronicle*, p. A-3.

Conklin, A.R. (1999). Plugging the leaks. *Athletic Business, 23*(7), 57-61

Ferguson, M. (Ed.). (1990a). Ringing up concessions. *Athletic Business, 14*(9), 63-66.

Ferguson, M. (Ed). (1990b). Sports Marketing. *Athletic Business, 14*(10), 26.

Friedman, A. (Ed.). (1989). Consumers indicate discounted tickets (March, 1989). *Team Marketing Report*, p. 5.

Herzog, B. Snack to the future. (1990). *College Athletic Magazine* (CAM), *II*(5), 33-36.

Hiestand, M. (1999, May 26). Skyboxes gain mass appeal. *USA Today*, p. 3-C.

Hilkemeyer, F. (1993). Food for thought. *Athletic Business, 17*(5), 39-43.

Holtzman, M. (2001). Money hungry. *Athletic Business, 25*(4), 75-79.

Lamphear, M. P. & Eleanor, F. (1990). Filling the seats. *College Athletic Management (CAM), II*(3), 27-29.

Perry, P.J. (2000). Free and easy. *Athletic Business, 24*(8), 42, 44, 45.

Pitoniak, S. (2000, June 18). Baseball marketing with a bite. *Democrat & Chronicle,* pp. 1-D.

Regan, T.H. (1992, May). *Parking Condos.* Unpublished Manuscript. Columbia, S.C.: University of South Carolina, Department of Sport Administration.

Stier, W.F., Jr. (2000a, November 30). *Fund-Raising and Promotion Secrets for the Busy Athletic Administrator.* Presentation made at the 19th National Athletic Business Conference, Orlando, Florida.

Stier, W.F., Jr. (2000d). A fundraising and promotional primer for sport: Part two. *Applied Research in Coaching and Athletics Annual, 15,* 12-147.

Stier, W.F., Jr., (2009). *Fundraising projects for sport, recreation, leisure and fitness programs.* Boston, MA: American Press.

Thumbs-Up. (1998, September 19). *USA Today,* p. B-6.

Waldo, B., & Murray, W. (1996). Hungry? *Athletic Business, 20*(10), 58-62.

Wong, G. (2000). Sit-down strike. *Athletic Business, 24*(1), 22, 24.

Yale mascot sale. (1998, January 27). *USA Today,* p. 3-C.

DISCUSSION QUESTIONS

1. Why is it important to emphasize and publicize where the profits will go when raising funds? Be specific and provide examples.

2. How would you go about filling up the seats for your athletic contents? Be specific and provide a rationale for your efforts.

3. How would you go about selecting items for your concession menu? List some of the items you would select and justify your decisions.

4. What might prevent you from ordering too much merchandise to see at athletic contests and be left with leftovers (and financial loss)?

5. Explain what organizers should be alert for in raising money by means of vending machines and user fees to prevent fiscal loss and reduction of legal liability.

9 | THE ESSENCE OF CORPORATE SPONSORSHIP AND BUSINESS PARTNERSHIP

The pie-in-the-face contest is aways fun (for the fan doing the throwing)

CHAPTER HIGHLIGHTS

This chapter will emphasize:

- The need for *corporate sponsorships* for sport entities today
- The history of corporate sponsorships for sport entities
- How the NFL has become the best marketing partner among the four major pro leagues
- The essential elements of corporate sponsorships for sport entities
- The advantages (to the corporation) of securing the naming rights for sport facilities
- The different types of sponsorship or partnership arrangements that can be established between the sport program and a company or corporation

- The possible benefits that sport or recreation entities might provide to potential business sponsors
- The major national corporations that are involved in significant corporate sponsorship agreements
- The *four types of sponsorship agreements* in terms of exclusivity
- The difficulties associated with the *naming game* of facilities
- The reasons that potential corporate sponsors offer as justification for their involvement in sponsoring high school athletic programs

THE RELATIONSHIP BETWEEN HIGH EXPENSES AND THE NEED FOR CORPORATE SPONSORSHIPS

In today's climate of ever increasing costs for sports, both recreational and competitive, more and more athletic administrators and recreation managers are looking at the world of corporate sponsorships to help alleviate the enormous economic crunch being experienced at all levels. Across the board, from the very largest university sport program to the junior high school athletic program, administrators and managers are experiencing a shrinking of the purchasing dollar. Only within the past two decades has the corporate sponsorship route of fundraising really been closely examined in terms of seeking significant monies. The big-time collegiate and university sports programs as well as collegiate recreation programs are currently blazing (Stier, 2009) the trail in amateur sports and the efforts are beginning to trickle down to the smaller colleges and even the high schools and youth sport levels (Stier, 1998). As a result of the tremendous competition for sponsorship dollars, it has become more difficult to get companies to sponsor events "in this era of ever-increasing competition for the corporate dollar" (Schmid, 1995, p. 21).

Consequently, one of the major sources of revenues for big-time programs and teams (at all levels and in all sports) in the 21st century is through mutually beneficial financial arrangements with businesses and corporations. These *business partnerships* or *corporate sponsors*, as they are often called, provide much needed resources for the sport and recreation entity in exchange for certain specified benefits accruing to the business, corporation or organization acting as the sponsor or partner.

PRINCIPLE # 172: *Corporate sponsorships permeate all levels of sport*

Sponsorships have become so popular and so prevalent in our society that two would-be college students, Luke McCabe and Chris Barrett, have offered themselves to be sponsored by potential corporations and businesses. Toward this end they created a web site advertising themselves as sponsorship partners. They envision themselves sporting "corporate logos on their hats, shirts and shoes, and in their cars and dorm rooms. Luke would even consider a tattoo" (Wanted: Corporate sponsors, 2001, 7-D).

THE BEGINNINGS OF SPORT SPONSORSHIP

The use of what is now referred to as corporate sponsorships for sport and recreation programs is not really a new phenomenon. In fact, there has been a long history of businesses and corporations using sports for promotional, advertising and marketing purposes. In 1852, the New England railroad sponsored a competition in the sport of crew between Yale and Harvard. Before 1900, trains and streetcars had a close association with baseball with so-called "baseball trains" bringing numerous fans to games. After the turn of the century, Gillette began to utilize boxing to market/promote the sale of razor blades. Coca-Cola was the first to associate itself with the Olympics by sending cartons of coke on the trip transporting the US team to the 1928 Olympics held in Amsterdam. However, efforts at developing corporate sponsorship or affiliations did not involve significant monies until relatively recently. For example, even as late as the mid-1970s, General Motors turned down the opportunity, for only $2,000, of gaining the *title sponsorship* of the New York City marathon. Less than twenty years later, in 1989, that very same sponsorship was secured by Mercedes-Benz for a quarter-of-a-million dollars (Ferguson, 1990). Today that figure is even much higher.

Although stadiums have had corporate monikers of companies named after famous men such as William Wrigley and August Busch, the so-called big-time commercial name game really didn't get a jump start until 1973 when the Rich Corporation in Buffalo, New York inked a 25-year agreement for some $1.5 million to have the naming rights to the Buffalo Bill's football stadium (then named *Rich Stadium*). The contract called for a $60,000 payment each year. It took another 15 years (1988) before Atlantic Richfield Co. as well as the Great Western Financial Corp. took the leap and put their corporate names on the basketball arenas in Sacramento, California and Los Angeles, California (The Stadium Jinx?, 2001).

Even as late as 1991 only three major league teams had sold the naming rights to their stadiums. But, by 1996 this number had grown to at least 32 facilities (19 arenas and 13 stadiums) that had sold the naming rights to their facilities to corporations (Hiestand, 1996, p. 7-C.). And, by 2001 the number of stadiums/arenas having naming rights agreement in place stood at 50—worth a total of $3.2 billion (Bayles, 2001). By the beginning of 2002 there were "62 major league stadiums sporting the names of companies, which have agreed to pay a collective $3.4 billion for the privilege over as long as 30 years" (The Stadium Jinx?, 2001, p. 2-E). Today almost every major league stadium has some sort of signage arrangement.

The trend is obvious, corporate sponsorships or business partnerships between sports and the corporate world has been on the upswing and there is no end in sight. For example, there were more than a dozen stadiums and arenas in the United States that were seriously seeking corporate sponsorships in the form of naming rights for their facilities in early 2002, including the Superdome (New Orleans), Comiskey Park (Chicago), the former Trans World Dome (St. Louis), as well as the stadium where the Miami Dolphins play their home games (The Stadium Jinx?).

> **PRINCIPLE # 173: Corporate sponsorships are a mega-bucks business in the sport world today**

In present day terms, mega-bucks agreements with sponsors are commonplace in almost every area of sport and recreation. In 1995, The Ohio State University signed a five-year, $9.25 million sponsorship agreement with Nike (Buckeyes buck, 1995). A year later, the University of Wisconsin signed a similar deal with Reebok International Ltd. for $7.9 million over five years (For the record, 1996). In 1997 Nike, this country's largest sports shoe and apparel corporation, announced a multi-year sponsorship agreement with the U.S. national soccer team. The deal reportedly had a value of some $120 million dollars. This agreement was in addition to others previously signed by Nike with soccer organizations in the Netherlands, Italy, Russia, South Korea, Nigeria and Brazil (Nike Invests, 1997). Budweiser has its name "in the lights," as part of sponsorship agreements *or* as part of advertising packages, in 84% of all professional stadiums and arenas in the United States (Who's Counting, 2001).

In 1999, Lowe's Home Improvement Warehouse agreed to a naming rights contract with *Charlotte's Lowe's Motor Speedway*. The agreement called for $35 million over a 10-year period (Lane, 2000). *CBS* signed a $6 billion deal with the NCAA for the *men's basketball tournament*, to begin in 2003. *ESPN* paid $19 million ($2.7 million annually) for its 7-year deal (that expired in 2002) with the NCAA for the rights to the *women's basketball tournament* and other championship events. At the time of this writing, CBS indicated that it would agree to the NCAA's proposal for $200 million for an 11-year sponsorship agreement for the women's tournament and 18 other NCAA championships ($18.14 million *a year*) in event ESPN did not resign with the NCAA (Martzke, 2001). Overall, such sponsorships on the planet earth in the 21st century are projected to exceed 20-billion annually (Stier, 2000a).

> **PRINCIPLE # 174: NASCAR is considered the very highest of all professional sports**

A national survey was reported September 20, 1999 that purported to indicate the rankings of various professional sports, major sport leagues and sport associations *and their desirability among current and potential sponsors*. The study found that NASCAR rated the very highest of all professional sports according to those "decision makers at companies with sports sponsorships" (Farrell, 1999, p. 2-B). NASCAR's prestige was without peer among those responding to the survey.

The "Corporate Olympics"

Perhaps the turning point in terms of big business (dollars), corporate sponsorships and the highly visible world of sport came during the 1984 Olympics in California. It was at that time that the Olympics cemented the relationship between the corporate world and sports. This was the Olympics when Coca-Cola gladly paid some $3-million dollars for the privilege of having its soft drink being billed as the "official soft drink" of the Los Angeles Olympics. As the result of the extensive corporate sport sponsorship packages at the Los Angeles Games generating some $230-million in profit, the 1984 Olympics has been nicked named the "Corporate Olympics" (Brooks, 1990).

A young fan particicpates in a rock, paper, and scissors promotion at a Western Illinois basketball game

Today, corporations and businesses recognize that having products and services associated with sports, sport activities, sport venues and sport personalities can generate sizeable increases in public exposure resulting in increase sales and mega-profits. There is a definite business (read *money*) relationship between sport entities and corporate entities in any given corporate sponsorship agreement. And, in recent years, such relationships can indeed be big business involving huge dollar amounts never before contemplated.

HOW CORPORATE SPONSORSHIPS WORK

> **PRINCIPLE # 175:** *Sponsorships involve mutually agreed upon business decisions to exchange assets and resources in a mutual satisfaction process benefiting both parties*

Sport sponsorships involve an *exchange of benefits* or *assets* both for the sport entity and for the organization or business serving as the sponsor (Copeland, Frisby & McCarvlle, 1996). This mutual trade or substitution of benefits or resources relates to *exchange theory* in which both parties are able to provide and receive or to borrow and loan (i.e., exchange) different benefits depending upon the needs of the other (Stotlar, 2001). In *exchange* for some type of asset, benefit or assistance given to sport organizations and schools by sponsors, the schools and athletic/recreation programs enter into a reciprocal agreement or arrangement for provision of a variety of benefits. The arrangement has to satisfy both sides while providing mutual help and satisfaction to each entity (White and Irwin, 1996). Typically, the sport entity receives resources (*money, goods and/or services*) from the sponsor. The sponsor, in return, receives any number of benefits—both tangible and intangible (goodwill, for example). "Those who pay the big bucks think they are getting their money's worth for stadium deals through improved name recognition and an association with active lifestyles" (The Stadium Jinx?, 2001, p. 2-E).

TYPES OF SPORT SPONSORSHIP AGREEMENTS

There are a variety of sponsorship or partnership arrangements that can be established between the sport program and a company or corporation. In exchange for entering into a sponsorship arrangement or agreement sponsors can be given different names or designations such as "title sponsor" or "presenting sponsor" or a "team sponsor" or an "event" or "game sponsor"—each representing the extent or scope of the sponsor's responsibility and the type of contribution made. Any number of benefits can accrue to the sponsors, depending on what the sponsors need or want and what the sport entity has available. Creativity is the key here in matching available (tangible and intangible) benefits with needs/wants,

CORPORATE SPONSORSHIP AGREEMENTS AND THE IDEA OF EXCLUSIVITY

Sport sponsorships or corporate partnerships can also be conceptualized in terms of their exclusivity. Sponsorship agreements may be developed in terms of being (1) non-exclusive, (2) semi-exclusive, (3) exclusive, and (4) outright ownership. There are advantages as well as disadvantages (or limitations) to each. Whether one type of sponsorship is most appropriate for one sport organization and/or for a particular business or corporation will depend upon a wide range of factors (Stier, 1999). The key for the sport administrator or recreation manager is to assess one's own situation and to make a judgment call in light of the particular situation and the circumstances that exist at the present time and/or in the future (Stier, 1996).

PRINCIPLE # 176: *Sport sponsorships or corporate partnerships can also be viewed in terms of their exclusivity*

Non-exclusive sponsorships

The non-exclusive sponsorship is, as the name implies, one in which there are any number of organizations or businesses that serve as sponsors of the sport or recreation organization and it's various programs. Under this agreement, an individual sponsor may have a wealth of other sponsors (with no restrictions) to compete with in terms of garnering promotional and publicity exposure among segments of the general public.

Semi-Exclusive Sponsorships

In this type of agreement the sponsor is given protection from having to compete against other companies (as sponsors with the sport entity) that are similar in nature or of like kind. For example, a soft drink beverage company is given assurances that there will be no other soft drink beverage company identified as an official sponsor of or partner with the sport entity. Thus, if Coke became the semi-exclusive sponsor, then Pepsi would not be accepted as an additional sponsor, although Ford Motor Company could become a sponsor.

Exclusive or Sole Sponsorships

This type of sponsorship agreement enables the business or corporation to have tremendous protection from competition from *any other organization* insofar as sponsorship is concerned. The exclusive sponsorship is just that, an agreement that allows a single entity (business or organization) to be designated as "the sponsor" for that sport organization and/or team for a specific period of time. There are no other sponsors, period.

Outright Ownership of the Event or Program

This type of situation can develop when the potential sponsor decides that the cost of the sponsorship or partnership would be so exorbitant as to be practically prohibited. In this scenario the decision might be made that it would be cheaper, in the long run, *to actually own and buy the event or program itself.* Then, it could for no additional expense sponsor itself. There is more control in this type of ownership situation. The idea is that it is hard to lose an argument with oneself. This type of situation is more common in a sport like race car driving where a corporation or business can own its own car racing team and then enjoy all of the benefits of a sponsor by taking advantage of its very own property.

Sponsorships have had a profound effect and impact upon all levels of sport programs and organizations from professional sports on down to the scholastic level (Lehr, 1994; Stier, 2000b). There is big money to be made for both sponsors and sport entities through corporate partnerships or sponsorships and it seems that everyone is getting in on the act. Competition for sport sponsorships and business partnerships is fierce and will remain so for the foreseeable future. Morris & Irwin (1996, p. 7) believe that "perhaps at no time in history has there been more competition among sport properties for corporate funding."

Corporate sponsorships in North America totaled over $1 billion in 1990, in the neighborhood of $2.4 billion in 1991, and around $3.7 billion a year later. And, of this amount, some 66% of these event sponsorships were sport related (Hiestand, 1992; Stotlar, 1993). In 1997, corporate sponsorships involving events of all kinds totaled approximately $6 billion, a 9% increase over the previous year. Sporting events of all types accounted for 65% of this dollar value. The breakdown of how the companies' sponsorship money actually is spent includes: (1) sports, 65%, (2) entertainment tours, attractions, 11%, (3) charitable events, 9%, (4) festivals, fairs, 9%, and (5) fine arts (performing, visual, museums), 6% (Corporate Sponsorships, 1997).

In terms of brand names serving as sponsors of sporting and non-sporting events in North America in the early 1990s, the company that had the *highest percentage of sponsorship agreements* with 10% was Coca Cola, followed closely by Pepsi with 8.5%. Budweiser (6.5%) and Miller brewing (4.6%) ranked third and fourth, respectfully. Nevertheless, Coca-Cola ($75 million) lost out to Philip Morris ($85 million) in terms of being the biggest spender for all types of event sponsorships (Hiestand, 1992).

CORPORATE SPONSORSHIPS AND RECREATION PROGRAMS

Opportunities for corporate sponsorship agreements for college recreational programs are seemingly wide-open since 80 percent of the U.S. college students participate in intramurals/recreational programs while only 2 percent of college students are varsity athletes. "Corporate sponsorship has raised the profile of *recreational sports* on America's college campuses relative to their educational mission," indicated Kent Blumenthal, the executive director of the National Intramural-Recreational Sports Association (NIRSA) (Steinback, 2001, p. 26). Blumenthal also added that sponsorships have " . . . brought value—added incentive to participate in programs—everything from water bottles, towels and T-shirts to the additional programs themselves" (p. 26).

Effectiveness of Sponsorship Agreements with Recreation Programs

The existence of sponsorships or business partnerships with recreation entities on the nation's campuses certainly provides a clear and significant benefit to the sponsoring organizations and businesses. In one such study conducted by a candy company (*Nestlé Crunch*) that sought to determine the value attached to a sponsorship agreement with a recreation department at a college—it was found that students who were surveyed three months following the sponsored activity were twice as likely to list *Nestlé Crunch* among their five favorite brands of candy bars as they were upon their tournament registration. Just how extensive corporate sponsorships are on our college campuses can be seen in the fact that, in 1999, a Baltimore area marketing firm, *Campus Concepts Inc.* was able to funnel over $2 million to NIRSA and participating schools in the form of cash, trips, equipment and products (Steinback, 2001).

HIGH SCHOOLS AND CORPORATE SPONSORSHIPS/PARTNERSHIPS

Corporate sponsorships have proven to be very successful even on the secondary level. Since the early 1990s there has been a discernable trend towards greater corporate sponsored regional and state sport championships. There has also been a tendency for corporations to attempt to identify (establish sponsorship deals) with individual school districts, especially those representing an affluent population base and those that had successful programs and winning records. Potential high school corporate sponsors tend to offer the following rationale for their involvement in sponsoring athletic programs: (1) community goodwill, (2) employee goodwill, (3) favorable media, (4) image enhancement, (5) increase in brand awareness (6) association with a popular, successful program, (7) desire to help programs needing financial assistance, and (8) increased sales (Dorsey, 1993; Forsyth, 2000).

The state of California has been very successful in tapping the rich and fruitful high school sponsorship arena. In fact, the California Interscholastic Federation and its Southern Section, in particular, have been true leaders, if not pioneers, in the world of soliciting corporate sponsorships on the interscholastic level. As early as 1976, the Southern Section of the California Interscholastic Federation successfully negotiated a corporate sponsorship package with Dr. Pepper in an effort to supplement its athletic awards program.

From this initial effort, the payoff in 1989 amounted to over $1.6 million dollars flowing into the high school coffers from statewide sponsorship agreements with such giants as Cocacola and Reebok for the support of the state high school championships over a three year period (Bring on the Sponsors, May 1989, p. 8). The state's year-end competitions carried names such as "CFI/Reebok Track & Field Championships."

> *PRINCIPLE # 177: High schools also have successfully utilized corporate sponsorships or business partnerships in the raising of much needed monies*

Television and the High School Sports Market

Television has long played a large part in sport sponsorship, even on the secondary level. In September 1989, two high schools in the greater Cleveland area played in the first televised contest of what was to be a weekly high school sports cable television package. The game attracted more than 8,000 fans to the stadium. However, the total TV viewing audience was estimated at more than 8.5 million with some half-a-million people in the state of Ohio itself (Brewington, 1989).

In 1990 it was reported that corporations in Alaska and Minnesota helped to underwrite state high school championships. Four companies in Alaska provided some $500,000 to the Alaska School Activities Association. In Minnesota, the State High School League received $275,000 from a bank holding company (Corporate Sponsors, 1990). And, the Connecticut

Interscholastic Athletic Conference has successfully sought sponsorship and donations for its state championship programs from a number of corporations, including Delta Dental, Home Entertainment, Coca-Cola, Carlson Travel Network, and McDonalds.

Dealing with high school sports on the national level, *SportsChannel American*, a joint venture of NBC and Cablevision, signed what was expected to be a multi-year television deal with the National Federation of State High School Association, to begin in September of 1989. The agreement initially called for the televising of 25 contests (both boys and girls sports). However, the venture was cancelled in the early fall of 1991.

Of course, the television coverage of high school state championships in such sports as football and basketball is nothing new. States like Indiana, California, Minnesota, Texas and Florida have been active in this regard for some years. In fact, some $540,000 was earned from the televising of the Minnesota state high school ice hockey tournament.

High School Corporate Sponsorships and the Soft Drink Industry

At the high school level, the soft drink industry seems to be the most popular type of business with which high schools tend to sign corporate sponsorships. In 1999 it was reported that some 140 districts had established corporate sponsorship agreements with soft-drink corporations/businesses. The year before, only 46 districts had signed such accords (Cohen, 1999). Webster New York's school district, in cooperation with the town of Webster, entered into negotiation with Pepsi for a *pouring rights* (corporate sponsorship) agreement in 2000 that promised to generate around $3.5 million over the next 10 years in exchange for exclusive rights to sell the soft drink within the school district and on the town's properties (Kohlstrande, 2000).

Jefferson County School District (Colorado) with 17 high schools was among the first school districts to ink a truly major financial contract with a national sponsor. The 10-year deal with US West Communications Group provides for a $2 million package for the district that allowed the telecommunications giant to become the strategic supplier to the district. In addition, the agreement also called for the company to rename the stadium used by the district. Although Jefferson County School District was one of the largest corporate sponsorship deals between a high school athletic program and a corporation, at that point in timeit was not the only mega-bucks agreement between a high school and a corporate entity in this country. There have been similar agreements cropping up all over the country in recent years. The Madison (Wisconsin) school district is another that has enjoyed a significant financial bonanza as a result of signing a corporate sponsorship agreement with Coca-Cola. The three-year contract calls for up to $1.5 million in benefits accruing to the district's students, teachers, programs, etc. (Cohen, 1999b).

Advertisers versus Sponsors

> **PRINCIPLE # 178:** *Advertisers are not necessarily the same as sponsors*

One must keep in mind that companies and corporations that *advertise* in sport and recreation publications or choose to provide advertisements on behalf of such organizations (and their programs/activities) are not necessarily *sponsors* in the true sense of the word. Companies advertise (become advertisers) because they need to expose their products, goods and services under favorable conditions to potential customers, current customers and past customers. Advertisers need to promote and tout their "wares" as well as their image and reputation before the eyes, touch, taste, ears and noses of the public.

While sponsors also wish their potential and current customers or clients to become aware of their products, goods and services (just like advertisers); sponsors have another very important objective in mind when they enter inter a sponsorship agreement with a sport or recreation entity. Specifically, companies that seek to become an official sponsor desire to create a *very real* and *easily recognizable link, association or affiliation* with the sport or recreation organization, its programs or activities, and/or its personnel. In addition, through the sponsorship relationship, the company that becomes an official sponsor desires to be easily distinguished or differentiated from other companies that are not granted the prestigious title of *sponsor* (Brooks, 1994).

Advantages Accruing to Sponsors of the Buffalo Bills

When the Buffalo Bills (NFL) secured, in the summer of 2000, 15 major sponsors for their preseason football camp held in Rochester, New York, it was a further sign of how much sport sponsorship had evolved during the preceding decade. In the past, the Bills had a much smaller list of minor sponsors when the team trained in Fredonia, New York. However, the move of the training camp to the Rochester facility in 2000 also brought a change in the outlook toward corporate sponsorships. From the Buffalo Bill's perspective, Rochester was the second-largest fan base outside of Buffalo and the team sought to take advantage of that fact. From the sponsors' perspective, it was a great marriage in that "The Bills are the preeminent sports marketing machine in this area . . . they've become an important part of the social fabric of this region, and helping them stay on top is exciting for us and (makes good business sense)", reported Phil Yawman, senior vice president of corporate development for Choice One, a sponsor that inked a five-year marketing/promotional partnership with the NFL Bills (Roth, 2000, p. 9-A). Prospecting for Would-Be Sponsors

One source of potential sponsors is to identify those companies that are currently involved in sponsoring sport or recreation type organizations, programs or activities. *Another* tactic is to determine those businesses, corporations and organizations that might have a natural tie-in, shared aims or an element of commonality with your entity. A *third* tactic is to become aware of those businesses or organizations that might have a (similar) target market that your sport program or recreation organization also reaches—so that you can develop a tailor made sponsorship proposal that would create a bridge or connection between your target market(s) and the potential sponsor's target market(s). And, *lastly*, examine those companies that serve as vendors for your sport or recreation entity as suppliers of goods and services for your organization, personnel, participants, programs and activities.

Food and Beverage Companies as Potential Sponsors

At the local level, food and beverage companies have been prime sponsorship prospects for many years for any sport or recreation program. One reason for this is that their corporate parents frequently provide monies in their budgets to support the local markets. Thus, it behooves the sport administrator to closely work with the local arm of national food and beverage corporations in the solicitation of corporate dollars through sport sponsorships. In 1989 it was estimated that one-third of the NCAA Division IA schools were actively involved in some kind of local corporate sponsorships (Berg, 1989). In the early years of the 21st century that figure is much, much higher, probably as great as 75% for all NCAA Division I schools (Stier, 2000c).

> *PRINCIPLE #179:   Beverage and food companies are traditional sport sponsors*

In 1989 over 4,000 companies formed a funding pool for corporate sponsors, an increase of 150% over the previous year *and* a gain of 3,700 from 1982. Of the $2.55-billion dollars available in special events marketing and funding available from corporate sponsors, *some 65 percent of those funds were earmarked for sports alone*. To keep the growth of corporate sponsorship in its proper perspective, it is interesting to note that in 1982 only 10 corporations had event-marketing departments. Eighteen years later, over 400 corporations had such departments or divisions (Wegs, 1990). And, in the early years of the 21st century it is estimated that over 700 corporations have departments or divisions whose responsibilities involve event-marketing (Stier, 2000c).

Selling a Sport or Recreation "Product" or "Service"

There are three basic elements in the successful sale of any product or service within the world of sport. *First*, corporations are involved in communication and it is sports and sport personalities that can provide the medium. *Second*, in today's society, sports provide a mechanism whereby corporations may gain access to various and differing segments of consumers (target markets). *Third*, sports enable marketers to attach a specific and desirable image to products or services that differentiate their products or services from others in the marketplace. Thus, sport sponsorship may be thought of as the selling of rights from a sport organization to a corporation or business whereby the business may utilize any of the images and symbols associated with the sport for the benefit of the business (Brooks, 1990).

Two universities that had been early leaders in terms of soliciting significant corporate sponsorships for their collegiate athletic programs were the University of Denver (Krupa, 1988) and the San Diego State University (SDSU). The University of Denver had been very successful early on in putting together a corporate sponsorship program involving sixteen (16) major donors—both local and national. In subsequent years, Denver has been the beneficiary of an excellent sponsorship relationship (agreement) with Coors Brewery. In recent years, the university was able to offer excellent and extensive signage opportunities to various sponsors for each of its seven athletic venues, all under one roof within its new facility—Daniel L. Ritchie Center for Sports and Wellness (Conklin, 1999b).

At the NCAA Division IA level, Fred Miller, the former athletic director at San Diego State University, had likewise been in the early forefront of corporate sponsorship, in the 1980s, in an attempt to subsidize the athletic department's limited financial resources. Through an innovative corporate sponsorship program the Aztecs grossed $1.2 million dollars in 1988 and 1989 from sponsors such as Coca Cola, Texaco, and Dodge (Special Report, 1989). By 1991, SDSU's sponsorship involvement included Avis, Texaco, Chrysler-Dodge, Volkswagen, USAir, Marriott Hotels, and State Farm Insurance. And, sponsorship of one San Diego State University football game ranged from $10,000 to $16,000 while a single basketball sponsorship cost between $4,000 and $8,000 (Goldberg, 1991).

In later years, institutions continued to expand corporate sponsorships to include larger and larger sums of corporate monies. In 1995 the University of Colorado signed a six-year corporate sponsorship agreement with *Nike Inc.* for some $5.6 million in cash as well as complimentary apparel and equipment (SWOOSH, 1995). And, in 2002, when the University of Maryland moved into its new athletic facility there was also a new name, *Comcast Center*. The name was part of a $20 million corporate sponsorship package with the telecommunications giant (Person to Person, 2000).

PRINCIPLE # 180: Corporate sponsorships are not limited to sport teams but include conferences and associations as well

With some 85% to 95% of the nation's biggest athletic programs running in the red, corporate sponsorships are being viewed as a viable method of blunting the financial crunch facing our nation's university sports programs. Many plans were being presented in the 1990s in an effort to overcome this financial crisis. In fact, in 1990, Fred Miller (SDSU) proposed that 23 out of the 105 or so institutions with sports programs classified as NCAA, Division

IA enter into a corporate sponsorship consortium to attract national sponsors for both football and basketball at these big-time sport schools.

One of the reasons why so many corporations and businesses are seeking to become involved in corporate sponsorships with colleges, universities and even secondary athletic programs is that many corporations have been priced out of the so-called "sponsorship arena" by the NFL, NBA, MLB, and the NHL. Another reason is because businesses and corporations are keenly aware that such association or affiliation with sports in general, specific sports programs, and individual sports personalities can be good for business in terms of increased awareness of products and, most importantly, greater sales of products and services. *It boils down to money, period.* It is estimated that corporate sponsorship of a team or specific contests has the potential for improving the way in which fans view the sponsoring company's products by nearly 20-30 percent.

THE CHALLENGE OF THE *NAMING GAME*

The *naming game* has become very prominent in many segments within the business world. This desire to be involved in the use of naming rights is evident both inside and outside of the world of sport and recreation. Note the wide range of efforts to utilize the *naming rights* of different physical facilities, parts of different buildings, as well as major items of equipment by different organizations, businesses and corporations.

> ***PRINCIPLE # 181:***   *Seemingly, there is nothing sacred when one considers the naming game—the* **naming rights** *for everything and anything can potentially be sold*

Name Changing of Facilities

There are numerous examples of educational institutions as well as municipal governments that seem willing (even eager) to change (*rename*) the names of existing facilities as part of a new corporate sponsorship agreement with a big-name company or a big-spending donor. Changing the name of a facility when a new big time donor or corporate sponsor comes along is sometimes touchy. This is *especially true when the facility has already been named after an individual, deceased or living.*

This was the situation when Oregon State University *renamed* its football stadium. The stadium was called for many years *Parker Stadium*. It was named after a big-time donor/benefactor from the 1950s who was elected to the football Hall of Fame. The name was changed to *Reser Stadium* in honor of a current big-time donor who gifted the school with $5 million over the future five years and who also agreed to give the school an additional $15 million over the following fifteen years (The *Name-Change* Game, 1999).

Opponents who are against such name changes claim that once a site has been named for someone then tradition requires that the name not be changed. The opposite view was expressed by the AD at Oregon State University, Mitch Barnhart, who was quoted as saying: "The opponents who don't want you to change will say, 'What about tradition?' I look them right in the eye and say, 'What about the student-athletes?'" (The *Name-Change* Game, 1999, p. 12). Barnhart indicated that he has no qualms whatsoever doing whatever it takes to help pay off the athletic department's debt, balance the sports budget and help finance the construction of new athletic facilities.

Some contests between periods require quick cleanup efforts by the staff

The city of Rochester, New York, ran into unexpected opposition and severe negative public relations when it tried to rename the then 41-year old *Community War Memorial* (sport and conference center), after the facility was renovated and expanded. The asking price was $2 million. Almost immediately, representatives from three war veteran groups strenuously objected to the changing of the name, charging that the city was insensitive to the thousands of vets who served and died for their country (Bellaby, 1996; Negrea, 1996). Finally, after much negotiation, a compromise was reached with the official name change being *Blue Cross Arena at the War Memorial*.

A similar situation surfaced in Denver where the city fathers wanted to change the name of *Mile High Stadium*. Many citizen groups criticized this move. However, the opposition was to no avail—a $120 million deal was eventually made with Invesco. The new name of the stadium, which officially opened August 25, 2001, was officially designated as *Invesco Stadium at Mile High* (McCarthy, 2001).

> **PRINCIPLE # 182:** *There is a big difference in providing a name for a yet unnamed facility, and* **changing the name** *of a facility that already has been christened with a name*

Selling the Naming Rights to Parts of a Facility

A team that has not followed the more familiar path of selling the naming rights to the entire stadium is the Cleveland Browns (NFL). With the advent of a new stadium in 1999, it was announced by Browns' owner Al Lerner that instead of selling the naming rights to the stadium itself, it had been decided to sell the naming rights to the stadium's four main gates for an undisclosed sum to four corporations—The Cleveland Clinic, CoreComm, National City Corporation and the Steris Corporation. The owner said that he just felt that the name of the stadium should remain *Cleveland Browns Stadium* and nothing else. Although he was not adverse to involving sponsors, Mr. Lerner indicated that he wanted the sponsorship agreements to be involved in areas or facets of the facility other than the name of the actual stadium (Browns owner, 1999).

DETERMINING THE VALUE OF THE NAMING RIGHTS TO THE DONOR

In terms of determining what the benefits might be worth to a potential sponsor, Jackson (1988, p. 18) suggests to look at the going rate (dollar value) of other sponsorships for similar events that are being marketed and promoted in the area. When comparisons are possible and suitable, one needs to be willing to negotiate and be even somewhat arbitrary. Being flexible in this area of establishing the final cost to the sponsor, as well as creating the components of the benefit package for the potential sponsor, is a must.

> *PRINCIPLE # 183:* In determining the pricing structure examine the **inventory of benefits** *available to the sponsoring organization and establish a reasonable charge in light of the actual value of the benefits*

Pricing Structure of Benefits Associated with Corporate Sponsorships/Business Partnerships

In today's marketplace, it is highly advisable, if not essential, to be able to provide the potential sponsor with adequate data about the sport program's ability to reach specific (target market) consumers. Irwin and Stotlar (1991) emphasized that corporations need to know the return value derived through both (1) the number of exposures generated, and (2) the number of exposure recipients. Thus, coaches and athletic administrators must be able to conduct meaningful and fruitful research in terms of the types of individuals who attend the sporting events and their purchasing habits and capacities.

Additional types of information that sponsors are interested in securing include: age, gender, income levels, and home addresses of contest patrons, fans and spectators. This information falls under the category of *patron demographics research*. *Psychographic market research* deals with the attitudes, opinions, and lifestyles (revealing interests, values, and activities) of those attending the sporting events. Sponsors are interested in such information as the data enables the sponsors to determine whether the patrons, fans and spectators fit the demographic "model" that the corporations are targeting.

Another area of data or information that can be helpful for sponsors is information that indicates the cost-effectiveness of the advertisement or association. A study by Stotlar and Johnson (1989) revealed that spectators at college stadiums were able to successfully recollect the advertisements on scoreboards located in the stadium or arena upon leaving the facility. In fact, nearly 70% were able to identify the advertisements; with 77% remembering in football stadiums while 62% of those in basketball arenas could do likewise. Plus, nearly one-third of the products purchased at the stadiums and arenas were bought *as a direct result* of stadium advertising. The conclusion of this investigation was that stadium and arena advertising (frequently included as part of a corporate sponsorship package) can indeed be effective in motivating consumers at the event to purchase the advertised products.

And, since it is of the utmost importance for the sport administrator to have access to this data in approaching potential sponsors, it may be necessary to conduct periodic survey research of fans, spectators and patrons. The crux of the matter is that sport marketers, fundraisers and administrators must be armed with appropriate information and hard data prior to attempting to convince corporations and business that it is to their benefit to become corporate sponsors.

REFERENCES

Bayles, F. (2001, January 17). Subway in Boston faces corporate renaming. *USA Today*, p. 3–A.

Bellaby, M.D. (1996, December 1). War memorial still without a sponsor. *Democrat & Chronicle*, p. 1–B.

Berg, R. (1989). The money game. *Athletic Business, 13*(9), 28, 30–34, 36, 38, 40.

Brewington, P. (1989, September 1). TV's focus: What's good in prep sports. *USA Today*, 2-C.

Bring on the sponsors. (1989). *Athletic Business, 13*(5), 8–10.

Brooks, C. (1990). Sponsorship: Strictly business. *Athletic Business, 14*(10), 59–62.

Brooks, C.M. (1994). *Sports marketing*. Englewood Cliffs, NJ: Prentice Hall.

Browns owner sells rights to gates only. (1999, June 30). *Democrat & Chronicle*, p. 8–D.

Buckeyes buck. (1995, December 29). *USA Today*, 1–C.

Cohen, A. (1999). Schools for sale. Athletic Business, 23(7), 32–33.

Conklin, A.R. (1999). Dollar signs. *Athletic Business, 23*(7), 45–50.

Copeland, R., Frisby, W., & McCarville, R. (1996). Understanding the sport sponsorship from a corporate perspectives. *Journal of Sport Management, 10*(1), 32–48.

Corporate sponsors in Alaska, Minnesota. (1990). *Athletic Director, 7*(10), 12.

Corporate sponsorships. (1997, April 17). *USA Today*, 1–B.

Dorsey, V.L. (1993, October 20). Gifts can help ease 'financial burden'. *USA Today*, p. 12–C.

Farrell. G. (1999, September 2). NASCAR wins with sports sponsors. *USA Today*, 2–B.

Farrell, G. (2000, June 7). Welcome to Atlanta's airport, brought to you by . . . *USA Today*, 1–B.

For the record. (1996, June 7). *USA Today*. 9–C.

Forsyth, E. (2000). Tackling sponsorships. *Athletic Business, 24*(12), 89–96.

Goldberg, M. (1991). Brought to you by. *College Athletic Magazine (CAM), III* (3), 4–5.

Hiestand, M. (1992, December 8). Sports sponsorships weather recession well. *USA Today*, 6–C.

Hiestand, M. (1996, October 8). Creative packages spur stadium sponsorship. *Democrat & Chronicle*, p. 7–C.

Irwin, R., & Stotlar, D. (1991). Putting up the numbers. *College Athletic Management (CAM), III*(5), 5.

Jackson. B. (1988). An event marketing primer—Part II. *Athletic Business, 12*(9), 18–19.

Kohlstrande, J. (2000, November 16). Money from pop rights could pour into Webster. *Democrat & Chronicle*, 3–B.

Krupa, G. (1988, April 1). Promise and pitfalls of sponsorship. *Sports Inc.*, 19–21.

Lane, M. P. (2000). Editor's column. *Team Marketing Report, 12*(9), 2.

Lehr, R. (1994, Spring). Sports marketing: Schools should consider all factors before enlisting corporate support. *Interscholastic Athletic Administration,* 12–13.

McCarthy, M. (2001, March 16). Critics target "omnipresent' ads. *USA Today*, p. 6-B.

Martzke, R. (2001, February 20). CBS has $200M women's NCAA bid. *USA Today*, p. 1–C.

Morris, D., & Irwin, R.L. (1996). The data-driven approach to sponsorship acquisition. *Sport Marketing Quarterly, V*(2), 7–10.

Negrea, S. (1996, March 6). Vets vow to fight arena's renaming. *Democrat & Chronicle*, 1–B.

Nike invests $120M into U.S. soccer team. (1997, October 23). *Democrat & Chronicle*, 3–C.

Person to person. (2000). *Athletic Business, 24*(4), 25.

Roth, L. (2000, May 26). Bills lineup entices camp sponsors. *Democrat & Chronicle*, 1–A, 9–A.

Schmid, S. (1995). Let the games begin. *Athletic Business, 19*(1), 21.

Special report. (1989, January 9). *Sports Inc.*, pp. 27–28.

SportsManagementClub.com (2002, April 8). [monthly newsletter, April 2002].

Steinbach, P. (2001). Intramarketing. Athletic Business, 24(1), 26, 28.

Stier, W.F., Jr. (1996). An Overview of Administering Competitive Sport Programs Through Effective Marketing, Fundraising and Promotion. Applied Research in Coaching and Athletic Annual. 11, 116–128.

Stier, W.F., Jr., (1998). Sport promotions, sponsorships and resource generation for the 21st Century. *Applied Research in Coaching and Athletics Annual 1998, 13,* 191–210.

Stier, W.F., Jr. (1999). A fundraising and promotion primer for sport: Part One. *Applied Research in Coaching and Athletics Annual 1999, 14,* 219–242.

Stier, W.F., Jr. (2000a, August 26). *Current Situations and New Directions for Sport Management: From the Perspectives of Cultural Differences.* Presentation at the 2000 International Sport Management Congress, Seoul Korea.

Stier, W.F., Jr. (2000b). Fund-Raising and Promotion Secrets for the Busy Athletic Director. *PROCEEDINGS—National Athletic Business Conference.* Wisconsin: Madison. Athletic Business.

Stier, W.F., Jr. (2000c). The Past, Present and Future of Sport Management. *PROCEEDINGS—Current Situations and New Directions for Sports Management: from the Perspectives of Cultural Differences.* Presentation at the 2000 International Sport Management Congress, Seoul, Korea.

Stier, W.F., Jr. (2009). *Fundraising projects for sport, recreation, leisure and fitness programs.* Boston, MA: American Press.

Stotlar, D.K. (1993). Sponsorship and the Olympic winter games. *Sport Marketing Quarterly, II*(1), 35–43.

Stotlar, D. K. (2001). *Developing Successful Sport Sponsorship Plans.* Morgantown, West Virginia, Fitness Information Technology.

Stotlar, D. K. and Johnson, D. A. (1989). Stadium ads get a boost. *Athletic Business, 13*(9), 49–51.

SWOOSH. (1995, October 10). *USA Today*, p. 1–C.

The *Name-Change* Game. (1999). *Athletic Business, 23*(9), 12.

The stadium Jinx? (2001, December 25). *St. Petersburg Times*, 1–E, 2–E.

Wanted: Corporate sponsors for 2 affable spokesguys. (2001, February 7). *USA Today*, 7–D.

Wegs, M. (1990, April). Corporate Sponsors—A New Athletic Partnership Unfolds. *Athletic Director, 7*(4), 18–21, 38.

White, A.B., & Irwin, R.L. (1996). Assessing a corporate partner program: A key to success. *Sport Marketing Quarterly, V*(2), 21, 24–28.

Who's Counting. (2001). *Athletic Business, 25*(9), 11.

DISCUSSION QUESTIONS

1. Outline the history of sponsorships for businesses and sports.

2. Explain the fundamental elements of corporate sponsorships.

3. Explain how corporate sponsorships work in terms of the concept of exclusivity

4. Outline some strategies for obtaining would-be sponsors

5. Describe how naming rights may be used for fundraising and share potential challenges that might face organizers in terms of naming a facility for the first time and attempting to rename a facility.

10 | Creating Corporate Sponsorships and Partnerships

Pancake breakfasts seem to be a favorite of booster clubs

CHAPTER HIGHLIGHTS

This chapter will emphasize:

- Five primary reasons why corporations seek to become official NCAA sponsors
- The importance of the media is in the world of corporate sponsorship
- How to work with both franchisees *and* franchisers as potential sponsors
- The six questions that should be asked when approaching businesses as potential sponsors
- The image of the potential sponsor is all important to the sport entity
- How to package the typical sponsorship proposal
- The quantitative and qualitative Information needed by the sponsor

- How to price appropriately and fairly a potential sponsorship agreement (that is, creating an *equitable exchange process)*
- How *tradeouts* work between sport entities and businesses
- The concept behind the use of *gifts-in-kind*
- The financial picture associated with the naming of buildings
- The current trend in sponsorships for corporations to enter into all-school (full-program) arrangements with big-time NCAA schools
- How to securing sponsorships is not the same as seeking a donation
- Ways to counteract slippage among sponsors
- Why it is best for the sport organization to always do more than promised in any sponsorship agreement
- The objective measurements revealing the effectiveness of sponsorship agreements

WHY CORPORATIONS DESIRE TO BECOME SPONSORS

Corporations and businesses decide to become sponsors for sport and recreation organizations and events for a variety of reasons. *One* reason is that sponsorship of an athletic program or sport team or event enables the corporation to zero in on a particular *demographic factor(s)* in terms of current and potential consumers. To have an effective sponsorship situation there should be some connection between the people (participants, spectators, fans) at the games or events and the sponsor's wish to have its name and products/services exposed to these same individuals. If a company desires to concentrate on a particular market (their *target market*) and if the demographics of the individuals (age, sex, social class, salary, marital status, education, etc.) associated with the sport organization is similar to the target market(s) of the corporation—then there is a possibility for a good match and perhaps an excellent opportunity for a mutually beneficial (tit for tat) sponsorship agreement to be the result (Kuzma, Shanklin, and McCally, 1993; McDonald & Sutton, 1999b;).

Another reason why a business may desire to become a sponsor or business partner with a sport organization, program and or event is because of the desire to be somehow associated, in the eyes of the public(s), with the wholesome reputation and image of the sport entity. This is because, in effect, sponsors are borrowing or piggybacking upon the image and reputation of the sport (and its programs, activities and people) when the sponsorship or partnership agreement is consummated. This is a two-edged sword, however, as the eventual outcome can become a negative situation for the sponsor—if the reputation or image of the sport entity is discredited or tarnished in any material fashion, such as in a national recruiting faux pas, a financial scandal, a sexual harassment or physical abuse indictment (Stier, 1997).

Generally speaking, sponsors typically desire one or more of the following eight objectives: (1) greater and more intensive *exposure* of corporate name and products, etc., (2) extensive *publicity* among targeted populations, (3), positive *public relations* (4) affirmative *association* or *affiliation* with a sport entity or personality, (5) increased *awareness* by the public,

(5) greater *brand recognition* (6) *frequency* in terms of advertisements, etc, (7) greater *duration* of advertisements and logo, and (8) increased *visibility*. All of these things have one thing in common, that is, the sponsor wants its name out in front of people; the public; the consumer; the potential, current and past customer—all in a favorable light, over and over and over again (for long period of time) for the purpose of inducing these people to "buy into" the sponsor's image and reputation and to purchase the sponsor's products, goods and/or services. The end result, from the corporation's perspective, is increased revenues and increased profits (Stier, 1999b).

> **PRINCIPLE # 185:** *Three major goals for corporate sponsors are increased exposure to publics, **increased revenues** and **increased profits***

Official NCAA Corporate Sponsors

There are five major or primary reasons and four secondary reasons for corporations to become *official NCAA sponsors*. These include: (1) desire for affiliation with sports, (2) advantages of media exposure, (3) access to intercollegiate sports, (4) tickets access to NCAA championships, and (5) product/service exclusivity. The four secondary reasons are: (1) increase in consumer base, (2) tie-in programs, (3) Image enhancement, and (4) coincides with peak advertising.

How Sport Entities Could Improve Their Relationships with Sponsors

A national survey was conducted by the National Sports Forum that dealt with the reasons why major corporations are involved in corporate sponsorship agreements with sports and sporting events and what these corporations expected from such agreements. Almost two-thirds of the respondents indicated that they wished that sport organizations did a better job of understanding their company's business and marketing goals. A same percentage also desired more interaction between themselves (as sponsors) with the fans and spectators (Corporations say "Show Me", 2001).

> **PRINCIPLE # 186:** *Attempt to create a retail application with the corporate sponsor— make sure there is a good fit with the sponsor's sales objectives*

Walker & Stotlar (1997, p. 123) identified four specific objectives or goals of sponsorships. *First*, the desire to increase sales. *Second*, the advantages of enhancing the image of the sponsoring organization or business. *Third*, the need to boost awareness of the sponsor (and its products and services). And, *fourth*, the desire to increase the motivation of the employees within the sponsoring organization. The profit motive is often the prime moving force behind modern day corporate sponsorship packages.

CORPORATE SPONSORSHIPS AND THE MEDIA

The very real and tremendous impact that the news media has upon people and the individual person's decision making ability (choices) is an important consideration when corporations evaluate any potential corporate sponsorship agreement. The media is very, very powerful in terms of creating and reinforcing public opinion. And, the media covers sports and sport related activities very, very closely. It is this connection, this very real linkage between the media and sport that helps fuel the corporate sponsorships of today. Extensive exposure within the electronic and print media has tremendous potential for influencing the opinions, attitudes and decisions of the individual consumer in our society towards the company, the organization, the activity, the program, the products, the services, and the individual(s) being covered (or exposed) by the media.

EVALUATING AND SELECTING AN APPROPRIATE SPONSORING ORGANIZATION

> *PRINCIPLE # 187: Sponsorships involve an exchange of benefits to both parties—the "secret" is to find out the needs of both sides and then to satisfy those needs*

Almost any type of business can become a corporate sponsor for a sport or recreation organization or program. Some of the popular product categories (of businesses) over the years that NCAA institutions approached and signed as corporate sponsors of their intercollegiate athletic programs include soft drinks, fast food , financial institutions, auto dealers, airlines, grocery stores, gas and oil companies, travel agencies, beer companies, rental cars firms, and motels/ hotels. Perhaps one of the reasons why more schools get involved with soft drink and fast food firms than beer or cigarette companies hinges upon the ever increasing concern over the appropriateness of using such firms as sponsors of school sports (political correctness).

Doing One's Homework

It is necessary to do one's homework before approaching the so-called big-ticket donors (sponsors) directly on an individual basis (Lachowetz, Sutton & McDonald, 2000). It is helpful to understand the type of activities that might be favorably looked upon by the potential donor/partner. Additionally, it is helpful to know the type of contributions that the donor has made previously to other charitable causes and what type, if any, of sponsorship agreement has the corporation engaged in previously? And, finally, knowing the purposes for which the donor or business made contributions or signed sponsorship agreements is most helpful as is the knowledge of the amounts donated or the size of the corporate sponsorship package.

There should always be an attempt to match what the sport program or activity is attempting to accomplish with what the potential donor wants to support and has supported in the past (Kuzma, Shanklin and McCally, 1993). This can be accomplished by a thorough examination of the donor's beliefs and feelings towards the type of program one is involved in and the achievements and involvements of the sport program. This researching of information pertaining to potential donors can be facilitated by seeking information from mutual friends (centers of influence), gathering information from the local library, city hall and from the local chamber of commerce (How to secure, 1995).

> *PRINCIPLE # 188:* *Create a compatible match between the needs and activities of the sport program and the interests and needs of the corporation or business*

Attempt to make a match between the corporation or business whose social image is compatible (closely aligned) with your program. For example, companies that create or market products for women might be receptive to women's sports programs. Similarly, corporations that perpetuate the sport image (soft drink companies) might be receptive to supporting the sport teams within your organization. Manufacturers of weight equipment or football equipment may be potential advertisers for and/or contributors to football programs. Corporations marketing tennis equipment might be more willing to contribute to tennis programs than to become involved in supporting baseball teams.

The objective is to develop a plan that matches the sport program (and/or its goals) with the sponsor, that is, to help reach the goals of the sponsor, as well as the goals of the sport activity or recreation organization. To do this, it is necessary to correctly assess the general goals and purposes of the potential donors, whether or not they are individuals or businesses, so that a correct match between the donor and the requesting organization can be made. It is also beneficial to remain flexible in discussions, deliberations, and in negotiations.

FINDING A SUITABLE SPONSOR—
SOLICITING ORGANIZATIONS, BUSINESSES OR INDUSTRIES

The larger the organization, business or industry, the greater the likelihood that the final decisions, as to which worthy cause will receive specific donations or which corporate sponsorship agreement(s) will be consummated, will be removed from the local level, i.e., from the responsibility of the local manager or administration. Conversely, it is the smaller organizations and businesses that are able to have decisions relating to contributions made at the local level, often without significant delays. Remember, the person to whom you might be making the initial presentation of your proposal may not be the final *decision maker* (Forsyth, 2000).

Approaching the Key Decision Maker (Power Person)

> **PRINCIPLE # 189:** *Always try to make your proposal to the ultimate* **decision maker** *in the corporation, the individual who is able to make the final decision as to the acceptability of any sponsorship agreement*

In some instances you will be required to make your presentation two, three or more times before the proposal actually gets in front of the *decision maker*. And, in some instances, your presentation may be limited to a lower echelon person in the corporation and that person will take your "pitch" to the higher administration, the actual decision maker(s). In this latter situation, it is your prepared sponsorship (printed and professionally prepared) proposal document that will be your major sales tool (pitch) in your absence.

Working with Franchisees and Franchisers

Local franchisees of national chains sometimes have in place a policy or practice of only becoming involved in local sponsorships, endorsements or advertisement schemes *if the arrangement is made at the regional office or even the national level*. This frequently makes it more difficult (but not impossible) for the sport marketer to reach the eventual decision maker within the business or corporation. It becomes too easy for the representative of the local franchisee to indicate that no decision can be made locally and that the sport representative will have to contact the "national" or the "regional" office.

> **PRINCIPLE # 190:** *Some local franchisees are forbidden to enter into a local sponsorship arrangement—rather; the decision for sponsorships is left up to the regional or national headquarters*

On the other hand, sometimes the local franchise is free to enter into a sponsorship, promotional or advertisement arrangement with a local sport or recreational organization on its own, at its own discretion. Another possibility is when a group of local or area (independent) franchisees agree not to enter into individual or solo arrangements with any organization or individual seeking sponsorship. Instead, they require that any such sponsorship, advertisement or promotional agreement be agreed to by all of the local or area franchisees. In this situation, it would not be possible to obtain a sponsorship on behalf of a single McDonald's restaurant, even though several different owners might represent the stores in question. Instead, such a sponsorship package would involve all of the area's McDonald's restaurants and would have to be approved by each marketing director representing each of the different franchisees.

A number of franchise owners of McDonald's in the Rochester, New York area reportedly pooled their local advertising and marketing monies and coordinated their marketing efforts through one advertising firm. As a result, representatives of sport organizations approaching an individual McDonald's franchise owner would be directed to contact the advertising firm handling all of the McDonald's marketing activity for that geographical area. In this example, any benefits accruing to McDonalds would have to benefit all of the franchise owners in the area and not the single McDonald store in closest proximity to the sport organization. Such an arrangement enables the franchisees to get more value for their marketing and advertising dollars but it also makes it more difficult for an individual sport organization that has only limited appeal to or connection with all of the stores.

Other firms, such as Ponderosa, required individuals wishing to make a specific proposal for a sponsorship agreement or affiliation to contact the chain's national office where many decisions regarding sponsorship involvement for the local level would be made. And, in other instances, some local franchise owners or their managers have been able to make their own decisions regarding sponsorship affiliations, such as the upstate New York Arby's Roast Beef outlets. For example, in the late 1990s, the local Arby's restaurant in Brockport, New York, became the exclusive corporate sponsor for all of the intercollegiate athletic sports programs at the State University of New York campus located in that same city.

A Citizens National Bank representative accepts a "Game Sponsor Certificate" at a Werstern Illinois University basketball game

Don't hesitate to use a *ringer* or a *center of influence* in getting access to the right power person (decision maker) in the sponsor's organization. Such an individual can also be invaluable in getting preliminary information about the company or individual and, finally, in actually arranging a meeting between the sport representative and the person to whom the proposal is being pitched.

Questions to Consider when Approaching Potential Sponsors

There are eight questions to answer when considering approaching businesses, corporations, and industry in an effort to secure sponsors. These are:

1. What type and amount of assistance should be sought (cash, "people" support, services or other assistance, such as introductions to third party potential donors)?
2. What kind of information do you seek to find about these potential donors?
3. What type of contributions has the donor or company previously made?
4. What type of sponsorships has the company previously agreed to?
5. Who might be able to help you gain access to the appropriate decision makers?
6. What kind of information do you provide to the potential donors?
7. Who in the organization should initially be contacted in the solicitation effort?
8. Who in the organization is the final decision making authority in terms of consummating a sponsorship agreement?

CONTROVERSIAL SPONSORSHIPS AND SPONSORSHIP AGREEMENTS

When considering what kind of companies might be suitable as corporate sponsors or business partners it is wise to remain aware of potential controversies that may arise when certain type of businesses are considered. There are some companies that might be thought of as *too controversial as sponsors* because of the type of business they are in. For example, companies whose products and services include tobacco, alcohol, certain type of magazines published, firearms, gambling, etc., might not be considered as appropriate sponsors and business partners for some sport or recreation programs, activities and events. The negative backlash from segments within the community as well as from potential and current consumers would be so severe that the use of such products or services would be prohibited (Stier, 1998).

> ***PRINCIPLE # 191:*** *Companies that sell alcohol and/or tobacco or offer gambling might cause controversy if sponsorship agreements are entered into by sport entities*

A survey in 1992 found that 86% of event managers (sport and non-sport alike) would not accept tobacco marketers as corporate sponsors. This is an increase over 1990 when the percentage was only 62%. In addition, this 1992 study also found that approximately half of the sport event managers seeking sponsorships would not accept an alcohol sponsor and one-third would reject even the beer or wine markets as corporate sponsors (Hiestand, 1992).

Another source of problems with sponsorships is the *over dependency factor*. This refers to the situation in which sport organizations and recreation programs become so dependent upon the financial support and resources provided by outside organizations that should such financial support be withdrawn or reduced the result would be disastrous. One of the very real dangers, especially as it relates to competitive athletic programs, is the situation in which outsiders (contributors, sponsors, etc.) attempt *to control* or *micro-manage* portions of the program under the veiled threat of loss of the (essential) financial resources provided by the sponsor. Yet another danger is that the sport or recreation entity *becomes totally fiscally dependent* upon the financial well-being and generosity of the corporate sponsor or partner. And, thus, when the financial climate is not rosy, there is the potential for a reduction in sponsorship monies flowing from the business partner to the sport organization, program or event. Such an event can prove to be catastrophic for the sport entity.

> ***PRINCIPLE # 192:*** *State attorneys general can void corporate sponsorships entered into by state universities if such agreements fail to pass the State law or are not in the best interest of the State*

There are numerous examples, at all levels of sport and recreation, where events, programs and contests have been cancelled or downgraded due to the pullout of a sponsor—for whatever reason. Many within the sport and recreation profession decry the over dependence upon outside sources for the financial wherewithal to support the sport/recreation programs, at even a minimal level. Some administrators believe that when sport and recreation organizations and programs become so dependent upon outside funding, outside resources, that without such funding or resources there is a very real possibility of cancellation of events or even entire programs, perhaps it is better to reassess the whole sponsorship arena.

Potential Problems with Sport or Recreation Sponsorships (and Granting of Naming Rights)

> ***PRINCIPLE # 193:*** *A perennial danger of naming a facility for a corporate sponsor is the potential for the sponsor to defame or tarnish the reputation of the sport or recreation entity*

This two-way match between the potential sponsor and the sports entity also involves consideration of local and national mores, customs, and expectations in which the sport organization finds itself. One example that involved a major university in the East ended in a failed attempt with a potential corporate sponsor. In this situation, the university attempted to enter into an agreement with a major gambling casino in Atlantic City, New Jersey.

The proposed corporate sponsorship, when announced by the publicity departments of the university and the casino, raised an uproar, both locally and nationally. There was a wide spread concern raised among alumni and others associated with sport in general and the institution in particular. The school and the athletic administrators took a beating in the local and national press. The proposed sponsorship quickly became a very hot potato. As a result, the proposed sponsorship never came to fruition. Both the university and the casino recognized that the negative, national publicity over the suitability and appropriateness of a so-called "marriage" between amateur sport and a gambling casino was detrimental to the interests of both the university and to the casino. The decision was made to cut the university's losses (negative publicity) and to back off from the planned arrangement.

This is a good example of a corporate sponsorship match that did not meet the needs of either the university or the casino. In fact, it did the opposite. The negative publicity associated with the questioning of the appropriateness of such a tie-in between a university sports program and a gambling casino created harmful publicity and brought up a potential negative image in the eyes of the public. In the end, both the casino and the athletic entity elected to back off and not consummate the relationship, thus, supposedly preserving the gulf between sports and the world of gambling.

The same type of situation can involve a single donor. A good example of this was the John E. du Pont situation that took place at Villanova University. In the late 1980s Mr. Du Pont donated some $5 million to Villanova University to build a recreation center and the center was promptly named the *Du Pont Pavilion*. However, when Mr. Du Pont was convicted of third degree murder of a wrestler, David Schultz, the university faced a quandary. What to do with a highly visible recreation center now named after a convicted murderer? In this instance, the school simply changed the name of the facility to *The Pavilion* (Cohen, 1999).

THE SPONSORSHIP PROPOSAL

The sponsorship proposal is a professionally prepared, printed or typed report or document (including a cover letter of introduction) that representatives of the business or corporation can read to find out all kind of information about the sport entity and the proposed corporate sponsorship agreement. *It is a tool* to be used in support of your formal presentation to representatives of the potential sponsor. When you are developing such a sponsorship proposal be sure and include information about your sport organization, its programs and activities, as well as the people involved—paid and volunteer personnel as well as fans, supporters, spectators, patrons, etc. The information presented within the document should be accurate, well-organized, succinct and easy to read.

Packaging the Sponsorship Proposal

> **PRINCIPLE # 194:** *Fluff enables reality to be noticed—therefore, don't hesitate to use fluff to promote and publicize your sponsorship proposal as long as it is done in good taste*

How the sponsorship proposal is packaged (presented and organized) is often as important as what is inside the document. In today's marketplace it is essential to have a written document as part of the proposal effort (Brooks, 1994). The proposal is a carefully prepared and researched document; it is a *selling tool* for the sport organization. Typically, today's proposal is a 3-D proposal, that is, possessing three-dimensional qualities such as a brochure, videotape, a film, photos, testimonials, etc. Make sure it is professionally designed, organized and presented. Make it noticeable. Remember, **fluff enables reality to be noticed** (Stier, 2010).

In attempting to sell a corporate sponsorship program, the packaging of the actual sponsorship plan itself is very, very important (How to secure, 1995). Similarly, the manner or fashion in which the plan or proposal is presented is equally important for positive results. That is, the plan outlining the proposed strategies, the activities, the efforts, etc., must be created, packaged, and presented in such a fashion as to place the most favorable light on the plan and those individuals presenting the plan. The individuals who have responsibility for making the decision (or recommending the decision to higher authorities) regarding the extent of the corporation's involvement in the sponsorship plan should be favorably impressed with the presentation and the packaging of the plan as well as the plan itself. *Professionalism is the watchword here.*

> **PRINCIPLE # 195:** *The packaging is almost as important as the content— in the creation of a proposal for sport sponsorship*

The packaging of the proposal and the manner in which it is communicated can have a direct relationship on successfully communicating a positive and accurate image of the sport program to potential sponsors. The ultimate goal is to successfully explain the purpose(s) and the needs of the sport program as well as the components or factors affecting the sponsorship plan to representatives of corporations, businesses, and industry so that intelligent decisions can be made—hopefully in favor of the sport program.

Although it is essential in many instances that a first-class sponsorship proposal (pamphlet, kit or printed brochure) be created for use by solicitors when dealing with prospective donors, it must be remembered that a promotional or informational brochure *is only a tool* to be used in conjunction with a professionally trained (volunteer or staff personnel) solicitor. In the opening section of your sponsorship proposal be sure to succinctly introduce yourself. Provide a brief glimpse into what your organization is, what it does, and what valuable service or products it provides. This is not unlike a mission statement with an added blurb in terms of the value of your organization and its services/products, etc.

It is important to remember that the printed document, brochure or "package" should not be created with the intention that the "piece" be the only contact that a prospective donor will have with the program. The brochure is not a substitute for a professional person-to-person contact by a trained and experienced solicitor who is well versed with the specifics of the sport organization and the skills of salesmanship. Brochures and pamphlets are important but one should not rely upon them exclusively to sell the concept or the program. The major purposes of the brochure or pamphlet are threefold:

> *PRINCIPLE # 196: Don't let a brochure be a substitute for a knowledgeable person-to-person contact*

1. To provide written communication that will provide insight into the program, the needs, the accomplishments of the athletic operation, the proposed plans, etc.
2. To provide answers to frequently asked questions in an honest and forthright fashion, in advance
3. To address potential objections or controversial, negative aspects or questions, in advance

COMPONENTS OF AN EFFECTIVE SPONSORSHIP PRESENTATION

When planning your formal presentation don't forget that what takes place prior to the actual face-to-face interaction is often as important as the actual formal presentation itself. In fact, the sale is frequently made well before the actual presentation if the presenter does one's homework properly and in advance. Sometimes what is referred to as an introductory or so-called "credential meeting" is held with the sponsor's representatives. At this time sport administrators attempt to present their credentials and to explain their capabilities to those to whom the idea or proposal is to be introduced. However, don't lose sight of the ultimate objective, i.e., *to sell the idea of a sponsorship package* to the business, corporation or organization. It is to your benefit, in terms of credibility, to be able to demonstrate early on an accurate understanding of the needs of the potential sponsor.

Toward this end, Betsy Komjathy, who is an expert in making presentations and is a partner with communication skills company Rogen International, suggests calling a few days prior to the initial meeting and asking a few questions so that the upcoming meeting might be more fruitful and productive. Ask specific, insightful questions (without sounding like an interrogator) to help you zero in on what is important for the client or company representing a potential sponsor or business partner. Demonstrating an in-depth knowledge of the potential sponsor illustrates your competency and thorough preparation. If you aren't perceived as having sufficient and adequate knowledge about the potential client or sponsor, you are more likely to be negatively viewed because of a lack of such insightful questions and knowledge—and your presentation will likewise suffer (Komjathy, 2000).

When making a presentation, time is of the essence—literally. You typically have about five minutes, or less, to get the person's attention and to make your point. Otherwise, you will tend to lose your attentive audience. Additionally, keep to your central points; don't complicate the issue(s) with extraneous information, communications and ideas. Schibsted (2000) suggests presenting, at the most, one major concept or central point as well as four satellite thoughts; otherwise the essential message may become lost in the cluster and confusion of conveying so many thoughts or facts.

> **PRINCIPLE # 197:** *Stick with the essential point and skip the extraneous information, facts, and thoughts when presenting the sponsorship proposal or plan*

Typically, formal presentations to would-be sponsors should be short (and to the point). The first few moments of the presentation are critical (first impressions do indeed count). Remember, you don't have to tell the recipient of the message everything you happen to know. Selectively share the central information that matters the most, the information that is critical to understanding the essence of the proposal presentation and which will be most helpful in the client's understanding and decision-making process.

If the presenter wishes to liven up the presentation it may be possible to add personal anecdotes that are brief, graphic and to the point. However, keep the number of stories to a minimum. And, never bore your audience. Remember, efforts at providing a personalized touch via anecdotes are more effective if directly related to the issue at hand and if the story is believable (Schibsted, 2000).

Information/Data to be Provided to the Potential Sponsor

Provide a clear, succinct description of your organization, its mission, the scope of its activities, its history, its impact upon the community, and the important people associated with and within the entity. Take stock (an audit, if you will) of what you have to offer. What assets can you offer or provide that the potential sponsor might find attractive? What goods, products, services or association(s) can you provide (reputation, exposure, etc.)? Clearly state the potential benefits that might accrue to the potential sponsor. In return, what do you want from the potential sponsor or business partner in terms of money, services, goods, products, affiliation, etc?

Information Needed by Sponsors

Sponsors want and need very specific kinds of information if they are able to make an intelligent decision as to whether the proposed sponsorship agreement might be in their best interest. Thus, it behooves the sport promoter and marketer to not only keep appropriate and timely records and data but to be able to access *and* present data in the most favorable light. There a number of different types of records or data that you can use to help you in the sponsorship arena. Some data can be most helpful in selling the concept of the sponsorship to the business or corporation. Other data can be most helpful after the sponsorship is concluded in terms of accessing the degree of success experienced by both the corporation and the sports entity.

> **PRINCIPLE # 198:** *Accurate facts, records, statistics, data, and information are the keys to a successful sport sponsorship*

Such information is needed in order to provide an accurate picture to the prospective sponsor in terms of what reality is for the sport entity and for the sponsoring organization or business. As stated before, there must exist a good match between the sport organization and the sponsoring entity, a match that will enable both to realize meaningful and real benefits. However, in order to make an intelligent decision, a decision based on reality rather than mere wishes or fancy, it is necessary that all parties have access to accurate information, data, facts, etc. Such hard data (see chapter 9) must be able to be produced so that timely and appropriate decisions can be made on behalf of all the parties involved.

General information about the sports organization and personnel (including alumni/ae); benefits; cost figures; activities; achievements; attendance; seating capacity; product usage; ticket sales; media coverage; types of customers, fans and vendors; how the sponsorship package will be evaluated, etc., may be helpful in painting an accurate, timely and vivid "picture" of the sport organization to the potential sponsor (Forsyth, 2000). "Without such documentation about the impact such an agreement has had on the company's image enhancement, increased visibility, greater awareness among groups or constituencies, new market segments, great market share, new distribution channels, and/or increase in sales, there might be little optimism for a repeat agreement with the same corporation or business." (Stier, 1999a, p. 219).

Chapter 10: Creating Corporate Sponsorships and Partnerships 241

> **PRINCIPLE # 199:** *One must not only have hard data (facts, records, information) on hand but such documents must be readily accessible*

Quantitative and Qualitative Information for the Sponsor

Sponsors typically want to see the type of benefits that they will receive as a result of any corporate sponsorship agreement both in quantitative *and* in qualitative terms. Quantitatively, sponsors are interested in such things as *when, how long, how much, how many, and how often*? For example, how many fans attend a typical game, how often will the PA announcements involving the corporation's name be made during a game, how much will it cost the company, how long is the pre-game tail-gate party for clients of the corporation, what type of food will be served at the post game social, etc. Qualitatively, the sponsor is interested in knowing whether the *correct* people (customers, consumers, fans, prospects, spectators) are at specific events, whether the people comprising the target market are able to see (be exposed to) the brand name, or the service, or the product at appropriate times. It is up to the sport administrator to provide such data to the sponsor so that the decision maker(s) within the business can have all of the facts with which to make a correct assessment.

MEETING THE POTENTIAL SPONSOR'S NEEDS

The question you need to ask yourself is: "What can the sport entity do for or provide to the potential sponsor that will be a real benefit for the sponsor?" Whatever the needs of the potential sponsor is—meet those needs, if at all possible. The *first* step is to find out what the sponsor needs. The *second* step is to be able to meet or fill those needs, if at all possible. The third step is convincing the corporate decision maker(s) that such a marriage or a business partnership would be mutually beneficial. If a company, a potential sponsor, needs more foot traffic, then you might think about establishing a sponsorship program that includes a coupon that must be redeemed in the store since this might be very attractive to the prospective sponsor.

In attempting to find out what these potential needs might be, observe and seek input from a variety of individuals. Above all, don't be afraid to ask the potential sponsors what their needs are—and then attempt to work out a special, individualized deal with each sponsor. Be flexible. Be imaginative. Be creative. Be willing to negotiate. An excellent example of a university finding out what a local company wanted is the University of Minnesota (twin cities) which negotiated a $242,000 sponsorship agreement with Land O' Lakes, a dairy supply company. In exchange for the money the company received signage within the university's ice hockey facility as well as the right to conduct several special promotions involving the school's football team (University of Minnesota, 1998).

Failing to Satisfy the Corporate Sponsor

An example of failing to meet the needs of a potential corporate sponsor (or ticking off a prospective donor) can be seen in the activities of the University of Oregon and Nike Corporation. Phil Knight, CEO of Nike, was evidently angered over the University's joining the Workers' Rights Consortium, a labor watchdog that rejected Nike's request for representation on its board of directors. As a result, Mr. Knight withdrew a previously promised personal pledge of some $30 million that he had made to the university, his alma mater. The consortium has so upset Mr. Knight that he has also had Nike withdraw financial support from the University of Michigan and Brown University (Knight moves, 2000; Michigan, Nike, 2000). The moral of the story is to keep prospective donors happy, satisfied and content—at least until the money changes hands.

What Corporate Sponsors Look for in a Partnership with Sport/Recreation Entities

Different sponsors want different things. However, all want and deserve to get *something* for their buck. Simply put, potential sponsors are looking for tangible advantages for their company, their business, their image, their products, their services and, sometimes, their personnel (Gray, 1996). Businesses are concerned with developing an association, name recognition, a brand identity among a specific group of individuals within the population (a target market) and among those individuals who will be making decisions relative to the company's products, goods and services. They are also concerned that *the absence of their presence* within the marketplace (as a sponsor) could also be equated with a lack of name recognition, a lack of consumer support, a lack of sales, and therefore a lack of profit for the sponsoring corporation.

In general, businesses seem agreeable to entering into various types of corporate sponsorship deals because they desire to:

1. Satisfy the business need of increased sales, exposure or acceptance by current and/or potential consumers and customers
2. Meet the needs of current and potential consumers and customers of the sponsoring company
3. Meet the needs of the sport or recreation entity seeking the sponsorship by providing the entity with some assets or tools that are needed
4. Be a good citizen or neighbor in the community
5. Compete successfully in the marketplace with their competition
6. Be seen as being competitive with other companies—that is, *they would be noticed by their absence*
7. Increase market share
8. Increase name (brand) recognition

9. Increase profits
10. Increase positive media exposure within the community

> **PRINCIPLE # 200:** *Some businesses become sponsors because they fear that they will be "noticed" by their absence by the general public and/or specific target market ("keeping up with the Jones" syndrome)*

Corporations and businesses often ask themselves questions such as are provided below in an effort to discern whether a potential sponsorship agreement would be in their interests.

1. Is there a *good fit* in terms of image and reputation between the sport or recreation organization and the business entity?
2. Is there a *good match* in terms of demographic information relating to the sport or recreation organization and the target population (desired consumers) of the potential business partner?
3. How will the corporation's products, goods and services be publicized, advertised and promoted as a result of the sponsorship agreement?
4. Is there the possibility for significant *increased sales*—on and off site?
5. Is a *hospitality venue* available where clients and prospects will be able to react to the business products, goods, services as well as personnel?
6. Will there be an opportunity for the business partner to be viewed in a good light by being associated with and/or supporting a recognized worthy cause (i.e., *Boy Scouts, Girl Scouts* or *Special Olympics*)?
7. Can *product sampling* be made available at the sport or recreation site?
8. What activities can take place that might enhance brand awareness for a product or service?

FINANCIAL CONSIDERATIONS OF SPONSORSHIPS

One of the challenges facing the sport organization that desires to solicit a corporate sponsor is what to charge for the sponsorship arrangement. That is, how much should one ask for from the corporation or business in exchange for whatever benefits the sport entity might be able to provide? Also, what type of benefits can or should the sport entity provide to the sponsor in exchange for whatever is being asked from the sponsor?

> **PRINCIPLE # 201:** Charge what is customary in your area—do you homework and see what similar packages will go for and will cost.

Honoring those who have played a part in your program's success creates support for one's program

One tactic commonly used is to charge what other comparable organizations are charging, i.e., charge what the marketplace will bear. Another strategy is to charge on the basis of what you deem to be the fair value of what products and/or services you are providing, plus a reasonable profit. For example, in terms of commercial television, if the cost of a 30-second or 60-second commercial is X number of dollars and your sponsor will receive a total of 3 minutes of national TV exposure as a result of signage within the facility, you might charge the sponsor a percentage of what the television ads would have cost the firm. Yet another method is to charge what you believe the sponsor is capable of (or use to) paying.

Benefits Provided to Sponsors

Some of the more frequently used benefits (exchanges) given to sponsors y sport organizations can include such items as public address announcements, complimentary tickets, facility signage, souvenir program advertising, back-of-ticket advertising, coupon distribution at games and events, on-air broadcast mentions, booster club memberships, as well as various hospitality privileges.

Giving Away the Store—A Major Mistake in Fundraising

> **PRINCIPLE # 202:** Have an equitable exchange process—don't give away the store

Sport organizations need to be sure that the exchange agreement between the donor and the sport entity is mutually beneficial to both parties a*nd that one does not give away the store in one's exuberance to enter into a sponsorship agreement.* Such a situation did take place in one institution of higher education that fell into such a trap, twice. In the *first* instance, the football coach agreed to name, in perpetuity, an annual Most Valuable Player award, in honor of an individual who agreed to pay only the cost of the trophy to be presented each year. In this instance of a clear give-away, the football coach was so eager to enter into some type of sponsorship or exchange arrangement that he agreed to give away the naming rights for a paltry sum of something like $15 to $25 each year. Clearly, this exchange of benefits was totally out of line with the donor of the annual trophy getting the best of the exchange.

The *second* instance of a one-sided financial arrangement occurred when the school's athletic department agreed to display/hang, for a period of three-plus years, a large (and not overly attractive) sign over the entrance to the indoor basketball facility in exchange for minimal financial support by a local gas station/convenience store. In this instance, the athletic department came out on the short end of the proverbial stick because the exchange of benefits between the business and the athletic department was clearly unbalanced in favor of the former. Raymond Horton, Columbia Business School professor indicated that if you are going to sell your naming rights or enter into a corporate sponsorship, "don't settle for peanuts" (Farrell, 2000, p. 1-B).

Tradeouts

Tradeouts work well because they don't cost the sport program money in terms of hard, cold cash. Cash flow is not hindered through the use of tradeouts. In fact, just the opposite. The cash flow of a sport organization is enhanced through the use of tradeouts. It is important to remember that a tradeout doesn't cost the sport organization cash. Instead, the sport entity provides services or goods for something that is in turn of value to the sport program (Moore & McGarey, 1986). In a media tradeout agreement, the sport program offers items or services to the media that the athletic administrator has placed a cash value on. These items and/or services are put together in a package format with different cash values. For example, tickets, program advertisements, booster club memberships or public address announcements may be exchanged in return for media time on the station.

PRINCIPLE # 203: Tradeouts are attractive to sport organizations because they don't involve an expenditure of cash

---

Of course, tradeouts can be equally effective with all types of organizations including, but not limited to Radio stations, Television stations, Printing houses, Grocery stores, Hardware stores, and Newspapers.

Gifts-in-Kind

Gifts-in-kind can involve any gift that the sport program can utilize to help in offsetting the athletic budget. The list of possible gifts is almost endless. For example, donations could take the form of equipment and facility donations, program advertising, tickets, free motel rooms, free meals, sport banquets being underwritten, free advertising in the media or on billboards or on buses, donated trophies or awards, sponsorship of a recruiting film or videotape, sponsorship of a radio or TV program or series, etc.

Such items are a blessing in that, depending upon what they are, the gifts can either be converted to cash or sometimes used themselves in the operation of the sport program. For example, the sport program can use gifts of beef, pork, various commodities, airtime, ticket printing, stationery, stocks, bonds, club memberships, etc., for the purpose for which they were intended. Or, these gifts could be used as prizes or merchandise in other fundraising activities in an effort to generate other resources. Or, they could be bartered with other individuals or organizations for other items that are needed by the athletic program.

> *PRINCIPLE # 204: Securing gifts-in-kind can satisfy a sport organization's needs without having to spend money for the same items*

The advantages accruing to the donor rest in the fact that such contributions of non-cash gifts, from inventory items as well as used clothing and equipment, can reduce taxes owed by the donor as well as creating positive public relations for the contributor, whether an individual or a company. In some instances, such contributions of non-cash items also enable the contributor to make larger donations than might be otherwise impossible.

For example, corporations, under existing IRS rules and regulations, are allowed to deduct overhead costs plus 50% of the markup for the items they donate to "qualified charities serving the ill, needy, or infants." For example, in the case where a corporation had an equipment item that had cost $2,000 and that retailed for $3,000, the corporation would be allowed to claim a deduction of $2,500 (the cost plus 50% of the markup) upon donating the item to the charity (Guttman, 1992, March 16). Always check for the latest IRS rules/regulations.

There are numerous examples of large corporations making significant contributions of gifts-in-kind or non-cash items to sport related groups. Kodak, headquartered in Rochester, New York, contributed videotapes and photo films to Boys Clubs and Girls Clubs. Glacier, a bottler of spring water in California, has donated thousands of dollars worth of spring water to bike-a-thons and skateboarding contests.

One word of caution in dealing with gifts-in-kind. The determination of what is fair market value of the non-cash items donated to the charity remains the responsibility of the individual or corporation making the actual donation. It is never the responsibility of the fundraising entity to be involved in the appraisal of any donated item. Rather, the non-profit organization should merely document that a particular items was actually donated, provide a receipt and a sincere "thank-you" and leave it at that. Attempting to serve as an appraiser only muddies the water.

The Financial Picture Associated with the Naming of Buildings

The typical financial arrangement supporting the naming of a facility involves a contribution of as much as 50% of the total cost of the structure. However, many organizations, seeking an ideal situation, look for a commitment to pay for 100% of the facility. In reality, however, every situation is unique and must be judged in light of existing circumstances. Some naming rights can be had (and have been secured) for less than 50%, some for much less. It all depends upon the situation and the circumstances in existence, both for the organization with the facility and the potential donor/sponsor. An added wrinkle involved in the financial planning for most buildings involves annual maintenance/operations costs. Therefore, many fundraisers and development officers seek to raise additional monies to help pay for annual maintenance expenses. Toward this goal, many institutions attempt to raise a maintenance endowment equal to 30% of the cost of the construction of the building to insure that money is available for maintenance and repairs in perpetuity. This maintenance endowment is built into the exchange equation for the construction, maintenance *and* the naming of the building (Cohen, 1999).

When attempting to establish a sponsorship arrangement with a business or corporation one should attempt to meet the needs of both the potential corporate sponsor *and* the sport program. There are three key factors to keep in the forefront in the area of corporate sponsorships and equitable exchange agreements: (1) everything must be done in a professional manner, with class, (2) the corporate sponsor must be fully satisfied, and (3) the sport organization must receive fair value for the benefits that it provides to the sponsor or donor.

SPONSORSHIP DEALS WITH COLLEGES AND UNIVERSITIES

Many of the corporate sponsorship deals with the biggest universities provide for the bulk of the money, or at least a very hefty amount, to go to the major sports of football and basketball. Some of the most lucrative deals call for sizeable amounts of the sponsorship money to go directly to the head coaches of the flagship sports of football and basketball. Witness Michigan State's Tom Izzo's deal with Nike that paid him $200,000 annually. Although apparel agreements make up a majority of collegiate athletic sponsorship income, other sources of sponsor monies are available. For example, the University of Tennessee has a sponsorship agreement with Gatorade for some $200,000 while UCLA has a contract with Gatorade, Coca-Cola, MBNA Bank, Pacific Bell and State Farm—for a sum that approached six-figures (Williams, 2001).

Notwithstanding the sponsorship deals with Izzo and others, there is a current trend among some corporations (Reebok, for example) to severely curtail the number of previous lavish shoe or apparel deals with individual coaches and/or schools. In recent years the apparel/shoe companies have discovered that the all-school deals do not always work for the companies economically. Today, the emphasis is more on quality than quantity in terms of which schools to sponsor. This is especially true when all-school (full-program) deals are concerned. Even Nike, Inc. has reduced the number of full-program sponsorship contracts in the early 2000s to around 15-20, although the apparel company still is involved with approximately 200 athletic departments. Those contracts that call for full-program involvement involve truly big bucks. The University of Michigan's contract, for example, calls for between $25 million and $28 million in cash as well as equipment and apparel (Williams, 2001).

Securing Sponsorships for "Olympic" (Non-Major) Sports

Corporate sponsorships of non-major sports ("Olympic" sports as they are often referred to) are entered into by businesses today often with an understanding that such a sponsorship deal would enable the business to also be involved as a sponsor of the major sports of football and basketball (Williams, 2001). It is still the so-called major sports that "call the shots" when it comes to sponsorship dollars.

SPONSORSHIP—PHILANTHROPY OR A BUSINESS INVESTMENT

In the past, corporations, businesses and organizations that engaged in sponsorship type activities with sport and non-sport entities did so based upon the philosophy of giving back to the community. This *philanthropic version of sponsorship* revolved around a desire on behalf of the company or organization to contribute to the society where the organization operates and makes a profit. This strategy of giving back enables the corporation or business to provide much needed resources for worthwhile causes within a community, often creating a real, tangible benefit to the community where the organization conducts its business. Only secondarily were businesses concerned with the potential for increased awareness and recognition of the company's good deeds and philanthropic (contributions) efforts by individuals, the general public as well as specific segments of the public (Stotlar, 2001).

> ***PRINCIPLE # 205:*** *Securing sponsorships is not the same as asking for a donation*

Although donations involving sponsorship type agreements have traditionally been viewed as philanthropy by many businesses, in more recent years, there have been a shift in how some sport and recreation administrators view such involvements. This shift has seen donations being viewed more *as an investment* (from the perspective of corporate and business donors). Steve Meeker, the director of institutional advancement at Black Hills State University in South Dakota is one such administrator. Meeker was responsible for securing corporate sponsorships from the community's businesses that involved wall and floor signage at basketball games for between $3,000 and $5,000. Dave Little, the AD at the school, credits Meeker with a very progressive approach and an open mind in approaching fundraising for the intercollegiate sports program. "Some of his biggest successes have been because he has gone into the corporate marketing world with [the idea of] donations as investment as opposed to philanthropy" (Byrd, 2001, p. 33).

> *PRINCIPLE # 206:* *Many companies interested in sponsorships view the sponsorship opportunity as a business investment rather than outright philanthropy*

Viewing Sponsorship as an Investment—Not Merely Philanthropy

"Sponsorship is not philanthropy" (Brooks, 1994, p. 161). Corporate sponsorships are business arrangements and are not to be considered merely as gifts or as a form of philanthropy (Cronwell, 1995). The reason for this is simple; the individual sponsor seeks a definite return on the investment of resources that are part of the sponsorship agreement or contract. Thus, the concept of *return on investment* has replaced the concept of *philanthropic contributions*. The costs of a sponsorship to a company can involve a great deal of money, money that should be viewed as a financial investment that will hopefully generate a return on such an outlay. More and more sponsors today view such agreements in a traditional business sense (Lough, 1996, p. 11).

> *PRINCIPLE # 207:* *The* **Charitable Approach** *has been generally replaced by the* **Exchange of Benefits Approach** *for today's corporate sponsorship agreement*

Stotlar (2001) reveals that the so-called *charitable approach* pales in terms of effectiveness when compared to the *exchange of benefits approach* and suggests that one should keep in mind the ultimate self-interest of the corporation (profits) as the basis for a sponsorship agreement. Thus, in planning and organizing the sponsorship package the sport administrator should concentrate more on an exchange of mutual benefits in which the sport/recreation entity receives much needed resources in exchange for clearly identifiable benefits accruing to the business partner (sponsor) and less on the philanthropic aspect of the sponsorship agreement or the package.

SLIPPAGE AMONG SPONSORS

It is important to remember that there will always be some slippage in terms of sponsors, i.e., some sponsors will not renew for a subsequent year for whatever reason. That is why you should always be on the lookout for additional sponsors. You never know whether a sponsor will renew and if one or more do not then you need to be ready. Typically, one can tell during the time of the sponsorship arrangement what the attitude and feelings are of the sponsor's representatives if the sport personnel are sharp and keep in regular contact with the client.

Some may not renew because they were dissatisfied with the arrangement or with how things turned out. Maybe it is something you did or did not do that was the cause of a non-renewal. Maybe the client did not receive sufficient reinforcement in terms of what benefits the company received as part of the sponsorship agreement. Perhaps the economic climate might be different thereby making renewal of such an arrangement inappropriate from the sponsor's perspective. Perhaps the cost of the sponsorship has become untenable for the sponsor in the present financial climate. Maybe the sponsor just wanted to "go in another direction" with its advertising dollars. Therefore, it is important that you determine (through a person-to-person talk, if at all possible) the reasons for such dissatisfaction so that you can take remedial action, if appropriate, so that others won't follow this lead of leaving the fold.

> *PRINCIPLE # 208: Anticipate some slippage among sponsors from year to year— and plan to replace those that do not renew*

Objectively Measuring the Effectiveness of the Sponsorship Experience

Both sport administrators and representatives of the corporate sponsor need to be able to objectively determine whether the sponsorship package was a success, both for the sport entity and for the sponsor. Determine ways to objectively measure or quantify the benefits of such a sponsorship. Doing so will go a long way to convince the sponsor's decision maker(s) to renew the sponsorship agreement for a subsequent term of time.

Renewing Sponsorship Agreements

A major component of all sponsorship agreements is the *servicing of the partnership* (Titlebaum & Watson, 2001). Remember, you are always looking forward to the renewal of the sponsorship agreement—therefore, always do more than you agreed to. Keep the sponsor happy. One way to do this is to always keep the sponsor informed in a timely fashion of what you are doing for their organization, in writing, via phone and in person. You never want to lose a sponsor. To increase the likelihood of a successful renewal, it will be necessary to work as hard as you did in securing the initial agreement. Some of the information or data you can provide to the sponsor in support for your renewal negotiation could include the following (Poole, 2001, p. 10).

> **PRINCIPLE # 209:** *The first rule of sponsorship is: always be prepared to do <u>more</u> than you promise—never do <u>less</u>*

1. Gate attendance, demographics and trends
2. Local/regional/national/international news media print coverage and trends
3. Television viewership, ratings and demographics where possible and a VHS copy of the telecast, plus clips of local affiliates' coverage of the event
4. Radio coverage with a broadcast signal overlay on the sponsors' sales areas
5. Complete list of associate sponsors/hospitality suite customers and trends
6. Information on merchandising, product displays, sampling and signage with photographs
7. On-site sampling and merchandising report
8. Clip book of advertisements and property-generated promotional activities relating to the event
9. Clip book of news releases and news clips tracking back to event public relations
10. Public-address system announcements log with sponsor scripts
11. Samples of coupons generated by all sponsors and the event itself
12. A copy of the event program and poster
13. Samples of tickets, especially if the tickets included the sponsors' marks
14. Samples of media sponsor promotional tie-ins with comments on their effectiveness
15. A personal thank-you letter to the sponsor signed jointly by the sport property's (organization) senior managers
16. A snapshot report from the director as to how the sponsorship affected key performance requirements stated in the contract.
17. A statement providing an overview of how the entire sponsorship experience went, highlighting the most significant benefits accruing to both the sponsor and to the sport organization

Always keep in touch with sponsors—both in person and through the "written" word. Provide periodic reports outlining how the sponsorship agreement has been going. At the conclusion, provide a detailed, written report outlining how you have fulfilled (and gone the extra mile) in meeting the terms of the sponsorship agreement.

> **PRINCIPLE # 210:** *Be prepared to document to the sponsor the effectiveness of the agreement so as to facilitate the renewal process for yet another year*

Provide copies of all written copy used in the sponsorship program including photos, in a scrapbook, and audio as well as videotapes, to confirm that activities took place. Prepare a 3-D report to let the sponsor know that you upheld you part of the agreement. Amshay and Brian (1998) point out the importance of convincing sponsors that their money was (or will be) well spent as part of the sponsorship or partnership arrangement with your sport entity. Thus, be specific in how your sport organization has been able to do what you had claimed in your original proposal. For example, provide results of surveys that reveal the percentage of the sample population surveyed who could recall the names of the sponsors whose logos were prominently displayed within a sport venue. This would be one method of determining the success of the sponsor's placement of signs and logos. Stotlar and Johnson (1989) conducted such a study and found that recognition rates were as high as 70% for some sporting events at the collegiate level.

REFERENCES

Amshay, T., & Brian, V. (1998, July 20-26). Sport sponsorship sword cuts both ways. *Sports Business Journal*, p. 23.

Brooks, C. M. (1994). *Sports marketing*. Englewood Cliffs, NJ: Prentice Hall.

Byrd, A. (2001, June 4-10). Meeker attributes success to luck; others credit his open mind. *Street & Smith's Sport Business Journal*, p. 33.

Cohen, A. (1999). The name game. *Athletic Business, 23*(7), 37-43.

Corporations say "show me the consumer" during sporting events. (2001, Spring). *Sport Supplement, 9*(2), 7.

Cronwell, T.B. (1995). Sponsorship linked marketing development. *Sport Marketing Quarterly, 4*(4), 13-24.

Farrell, G. (2000, June 7). Welcome to Atlanta's airport, brought to you by . . . *USA Today*, p. 1-B.

Forsyth, E. (2000). Tackling sponsorships. *Athletic Business, 24*(12), 89-96.

Gray, D. P. (1996). Sponsorship on campus. *Sport Marketing Quarterly, V*(2), 29-34.

Guttman, M. (1992, March 16). It pays to be in-kind. *Sports Illustrated, 76*(10), Special Advertising Section.

Hiestand, M. (1992, December 8). Sports sponsorships weather recession well. *USA Today*, p. 6-C.

How to secure corporate sponsorship & grant funding. (1995). *National Girls and Women in Sports Day—Community Action Kit* (Supplement to *JOPERD*), S-10.

Knight moves. (2000, May 8). *Sports Illustrated, 92*(19), 27.

Komjathy, B. (2000). Prep & follow-through. *Kinko's Impress*, Issue 1, 44.

Kuzma, J.R., Shanklin, W.L., & McCally, J.F., Jr. (1993). Number one principle for sporting events seeking corporate sponsors: Meet benefactor's objectives. *Sport Marketing Quarterly, 2*(3), 27–32.

Lachowetz, T., Sutton, W A., & McDonald, M. A. (2000). Selling the big picture. *Athletic Management, XII*(6), 22, 24–25.

Lough, N.L. (1996). Factors affecting corporate sponsorships of women's sport. *Sport Marketing Quarterly, V*(2), 11–19.

McDonald, M.A., & Sutton, W.A. (1999b). Soliciting sponsors. *Athletic Management, 11*(1), 26, 28–29.

Michigan, Nike strike apparel agreement. (2000, May 16). *USA Today,* 6-D.

Moore, M., & McGarey, E. (1986). No money down—Marketing athletics on a limited budget. *Athletic Business, 10*(8), 64-67.

Poole, M. (2001, May 28-June 3). Keeping sponsors means pitching like you did the very first time. *Street & Smith's Sport Business Journal*, 10.

Schibsted, E. (2000). Timing. *Kinko's Impress*, Issue 1, 45.

Stier, W.F., Jr. (1997, October 6). *The Essentials of Corporate Sponsorship (Partnership) in Physical Education, Sport and Recreation in the Americas.* Presentation made at the International Conference on "Alianza Estratégica Para La Educación Física, El Deporte Y La Recreación" [Seminary-Workshop: "Strategic Alliance for Physical Education, Sport and Recreation], México City.

Stier, W.F., Jr. (1998). Sport promotions, sponsorships and resource generation for the 21st Century. *Applied Research in Coaching and Athletics Annual 13,* 191–210.

Stier, W.F., Jr. (1999a). A fundraising and promotion primer for sport: Part One. *Applied Research in Coaching and Athletics Annual, 14,* 219–242.

Stier, W.F., Jr. (1999b, August 13). *Fundamental Concepts of Fundraising, Promotions, and Public Relations for the Fitness/Sport Manager.* Presentation at the 8th international convention of the National Sport Council of Taiwan (in Taipei City), organized by the Aerobic Fitness and Health Association of Taiwan. Sponsored by IHRSA and IDEA—Republic of China.

Stier, W.F., Jr. (2010). *Coaching: A problem solving approach.* 2nd ed. Boston, MA: American Press.

Stotlar, D.K., (2001). *Developing Successful Sport Sponsorship Plans.* Morgantown, West Virginia, Fitness Information Technology.

Stotlar, D.K. & Johnson, D.A. (1989). Stadium ads get a boost. *Athletic Business, 13*(9), 49–51.

Titlebaum, P., & Watson, S. (2001). Money decisions. *Athletic Business, 25*(1), 34, 36, 38.

University of Minnesota: Twin Cities. (1998, January 23). *Chronicle of Higher Education, 44*(20), p. A-43.

Walker, M.L., & Stotlar, D.K. (1997). *Sport Facility Management.* Sudbury, Massachusetts: Jones and Bartlett Publishers.

Williams, P. (2001, June 4-10). Non-revenue teams rely on football, men's hoops. *Street & Smith's Sports Business Journal*, p. 29–30.

DISCUSSION AND REVIEW QUESTIONS

1. Provide some suggestions (strategies and tactics) for working with franchisees and franchisers in terms of sponsorship agreements.

2. Why is it important to reach the so-called Key Decision Maker of the entity with which you are seeking a sponsorship agreement? Explain how this may be done.

3. What can be done to lessen inherent risks associated with sponsorship agreements with certain kinds of (controversial) companies? Be specific in terms of strategies and tactics.

4. Outline how the packaging of the sponsorship proposal and agreement can play a role in cementing the agreement/contract. Describe various ways of packaging the proposal and/or agreement.

5. Explain how tradeouts work and provide examples.
    1. What type of information, facts and data is needed by the potential sponsor?
    2. Explain what organizers can expect relative to slippage among sponsors and what sport organizations can do to combat this possibility.

11 | FUNDRAISING STRATEGIES AND PROMOTIONAL TACTICS

Silent auctions, when combined with other activities can be big money makers

CHAPTER HIGHLIGHTS

This chapter will emphasize:

- The advantages of using promotional activities with one's organization
- The importance of taking *community standards* into account when planning promotional and fundraising activities
- Five questions to answer in determining whether a specific fundraising project is suitable for one's organization
- The *piggyback principle* of fundraising and promotions
- The advantages of using holidays when planning fundraising projects
- The advantages of using the committee process in planning and organizing fundraising projects and promotional activities
- The categories of promotional, marketing and fundraising activities
- The variety of gambling fundraising projects with advantages and disadvantage of each

- A sampling of special fundraising and promotional projects
- The essence of "ghost" fundraising type projects
- The essential elements of different types of fundraising auctions
- The idea behind various types of "thons" in the fundraising arena
- Several game day and half-time activities can be utilized in promoting and fundraising for one's organization
- How banquets and luncheon activities can be organized and planned to help promote and fundraise for one's organization or program

IMPLEMENTING SPECIAL PROMOTIONAL AND FUNDRAISING ACTIVITIES

A variety of promotional type activities and special events may be planned and implemented to raise money for athletics, to promote a sport program, to increase attendance, to improve an image, and to provide recognition for team members, coaches, boosters and sponsors (Stier, 1998a). The critical factor is to find what is acceptable within the community and what will generate sufficient funds in light of the expenditure of resources (downside risks). Naturally, the same caveat regarding saturation of the community with an excess amount of activities holds true for school-sponsored events, just as it does for the door-to-door sales projects cited earlier.

> **PRINCIPLE # 211:** *Community standards will determine the type of fundraising projects that will be supported by the populace*

While many activities involve little time and money, others involve significant amounts of both. Additionally, many of the ideas and projects that are presented in this chapter have the potential for significant success, both in terms of generating monies and in promoting individual sport activities. However, the actual benefits, including revenue generated, can vary for each of these projects or activities depending upon individual circumstances.

There are five questions that any person, who is contemplating becoming involved in raising money for a sport program, must be able to answer prior to actually initiating a project. The answers to these five questions will go a long way in determining whether the fundraising effort is justified and feasible, as well as aiding those involved in the shaping of the campaign or project itself, so as to increase the likelihood of eventual success. These questions include (Stier, 2000a).

1. What is the complexity (degree of difficulty) of the project? Is it very simple or complex?

2. What expenditure of effort and what resources will be necessary to complete the project?
3. How much time is required?
4. What is the degree of exposure, i.e., what are downside risks of the effort(s)?
5. What are the potential positive consequences or gain in terms of money, other resources and positive public relations?

Combining (Piggybacking) Fundraising Activities with Other Events

> **PRINCIPLE # 212:** *Combine (piggyback) fundraising and/or promotional events with other attractive activities*

The practice of combining a fundraising or promotional event with another activity is a well-accepted principle (Stier, 1998b). For example, piggybacking the date and timing of a reverse raffle to coincide with an evening of viewing the televised national (NCAA Division I) basketball championship game on a big screen television. This enables the organizers of the reverse raffle to use the attractiveness and popularity of the basketball championship game so that the desirability of the reverse raffle (held just prior to the game and during half-time) would be enhanced.

Another example of the piggyback technique is obtaining permission from the electric company (or gas company or refuse company) to be allowed to insert advertisement or promotional materials about one's sports program in the monthly statements from the business or corporation. This piggyback approach enables almost every household to receive the mailing containing the sport promotional materials with little effort or cost to the sport program. The only cost to the sport entity is the expense for the printing of the promotional materials—and frequently even that can be absorbed by the business making the actual mailing (Stier, 2009).

Combining Two or More Fundraising Activities Together

A variation of the piggyback strategy that many promoters use in an effort to maximize their potential profits associated with any fundraising effort is to combine *two or more separate promotional/fundraising projects together*. For example, when an *auction* is planned, the addition of a *concession stand* at the auction site increases the potential profit for the total experience. Additionally, piggybacking yet another profit center, a *craft show*, held within the same facility and at the same time further increases the potential for profit.

Thus, fundraisers should always be on the lookout for ways to increase the profitability and enhance the exposure of any project through the staging of two or more different fundraising activities at the same time and site. Still another example is the introduction of a *free car wash* to be held in conjunction with the *auction/concession stand/craft show*. Those individuals driving to the auction/craft show might well be enticed to have their vehicles washed on a free basis, and to partake of the concession stand, thereby providing four possible distinct profit centers for the organizers.

In this attempt, the principle of synergism comes into play. That is, the attractiveness of both activities is greater than either single activity standing alone.

TAKING HOLIDAY SEASONS INTO ACCOUNT WHEN PLANNING

National holidays (Christmas, New Year's Eve, Halloween, President's Day, Thanksgiving, Independence Day, Labor Day, Memorial Day, Valentine's Day, Easter), seasonal activities, and special school events (Homecoming Weekend, Midnight Merry Madness, Alumni Day, Parents Day, etc.) provide natural opportunities for special promotional and fundraising events. Such sport activities or projects as a Christmas tournament, Octoberfest, Winter Sports Special, Spring or Fall Golf Outing, Fall Homecoming Weekend, etc., lend themselves to being repeated on an annual basis coinciding with the annual holiday, season or special event. And, of course, repeated fundraising events are easier to implement in succeeding years and tend to become more successful as they are repeated annually.

> **PRINCIPLE # 213:** *Breakdown tasks into their basic components—assign tasks to individuals on the basis of both interest and ability*

Whenever an organization is attempting to plan and implement an involved fundraising or promotional project there is always a need for a well thought out division of labor among the people working the event. Generally speaking, there is a need to address specifically a number of different areas or tasks. The responsibility for these areas may fall to one individual or may be assigned to committees. The point is that careful thought needs to be given, in most cases, to each of these categories whenever a fundraising project is being planned.

A typical administrative or organizational structure includes an overall *project chairperson* for the fundraising event, whose responsibility it is to coordinate and supervise the entire operation and to serve as the motivating force, the spark plug for the event. Working with the project chairperson might be any number of committees, each with a chairperson, assigned to address a separate and distinct aspect of the project. Again, it is the responsibility of the overall project chairperson to coordinate the efforts of all of the various committee chairpersons and their specific committee members.

Some fundraising efforts will necessitate, merely by the very nature of the activities involved, more committees than others. However the work or tasks are assigned, it is important to break down the work to be done in an organized and logical fashion, keeping in mind the talents and time available of the individuals who will actually be doing the work.

Remembering the age old principle that *it is easier said than done*, the objective is to assign tasks to actual doers, individuals who are interested in completing assigned tasks successfully, on time, rather than assigning tasks to people who mean well but who are unable to produce when called upon. Possible breakdown of specific responsibilities for fundraising projects by committees are provided below (Stier, 1997a). Naturally, not all fundraising projects require the use of all of these committees; administrators must assess their own situation to determine which committees to form in support of their fundraising efforts.

1. Planning committee
2. Site selection committee
3. Theme or topic committee
4. Publicity
5. Promotion committee
6. Ticket and invitation committee
7. Program committee
8. Exhibitor or participant solicitation committee
9. Equipment and supplies committee
10. Finance committee
11. Decoration committee
12. Refreshments and hospitality committee
13. Trouble shooting (on-site) committee
14. Prize or gift committee
15. Security committee
16. Clean-up committee
17. Post event roundup and assessment committee

CATEGORIES OF PROMOTIONAL AND FUNDRAISING ACTIVITIES

On the following pages are a partial listing *and* a very brief description of some of the more popular and successful promotional and fundraising ideas that are applicable for the sport and recreation scene, figure 11.1 Most of these activities, with slight adaptations, are applicable at almost any sport level. For convenience sake, these fundraising and promotional ideas and projects included within this section have been arbitrarily classified within the following five categories:

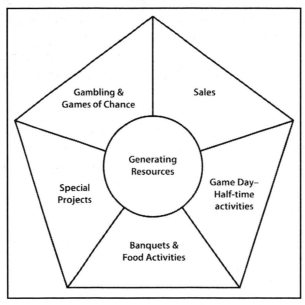

Figure 11.1 Types of fundraising and promotional activities generating resources

1. Sales
2. Gambling—contests of chance with prizes
3. Special fundraising and promotional projects
4. Pre-game, half-time and game day activities
5. Banquets and luncheon activities

SALES

The sale of any number of items and services is a traditional means of attempting to raise monies for sport purposes. *Almost anything* (as well as *any kind of service*) can be sold in almost any setting (Stier, 1992). Items such as books, plants, pizzas, candles, light bulbs, seasonal candy, items, trash bags, household cleaners, flowers, calendars and coupon book sales are just a few of the numerous items that can be sold on a door-to-door or group sales. Sales of these and other items are also possible while sitting in a mall, on a sidewalk or in a department store. Sales may be consummated prior to, during, and/or after athletic contests, special events, and school hours, etc. (Stier, 2000b).

Many of the strategies involving the *sale of items* or *services* can be linked with other *special projects, game day and half-time activities*, as well as with *banquet* and *luncheon-type activities*. Or, sales can be affiliated with special holidays, such as Valentine's Day, Christmas, Thanksgiving, Easter, the 4th of July, etc. Space itself for advertising may be sold within the sport facility, as well as within the sport publications and over the airways during, before and following athletic contests. Additional items that can be advertised, marketed and sold include, but are certainly not limited to, sales of souvenir sport publications, team programs, sport booklets, team photos, as well as various sports merchandise.

> *PRINCIPLE # 214: Sales can be linked with many other activities or events including special projects, game day and half-time activities as well as banquet/luncheon-type activities*

GAMBLING—CONTESTS (GAMES) OF CHANCE WITH PRIZES

Special note should be taken in terms of fundraising efforts that involve gambling or games of chance. While in some communities it is flat out impossible to legally hold a fundraising project involving any type of gambling activity, other locales permit such projects only after receiving permission from an appropriate licensing (local and/or state) authority.

Many states, counties as well as numerous individual communities have laws or ordinances on the books *prohibiting, restricting or regulating games of change and gambling activities.* Thus, sport and recreation leaders interested in generating money via gambling type events must be cognizant that such activities might very well be strictly regulated and enforced by law or ordinance. The best advice to potential fundraisers is to check with the organization's legal counsel before attempting to organize a fundraising project based on gambling or games of chance.

In some instances in which the fundraising efforts of sport and recreation organizations involve gambling type activities, the organizers indeed attempt to secure permits when the law provides for such. However, in other situations no actual effort may be made to apply for licenses or permits. Rather, the organizers merely overlook or ignore the local ordinances or state laws while planning and implementing the gambling project or game of chance anyway. And, in some situations, no real effort is made by the law enforcement agencies to enforce such ordinances or laws currently on the books in light of the fact that it is the local athletic or recreation organization attempting to generate much needed support for the local program or activity. However, there is no guarantee that this will be the case in your locale.

Those fundraising organizers who abide by the philosophy of "forgiveness is easier to obtain than permission" need to be aware of the possible negative consequences when it comes to illegally conducting gambling type activities. Individual fundraising leaders need to be aware that conducting games of chance or gambling projects without securing the appropriate permits or licenses, when such are required, can result in serious legal and punitive actions being taken against them personally and professionally as well as against the sponsoring organization. These consequences can be severe not only in terms of legal penalties but also in respect to negative publicity and tarnished image. It is strongly recommended that organizers take the time and expend the effort to comply with all local and state regulations when and where they apply. In this instance, "an ounce of prevention is indeed worth a pound of cure."

Restrictions on Gambling Activities in the State of New York

In the state of New York, for example, organizations wishing to conduct such games of chance or gambling projects must secure advance permission from both the *New York State Racing & Wagering Board* and from the local municipality (through the Town Clerk) where the event will take place. New York State provides two different kinds of permits, one for *Bingo* (now close to a $50 million dollar-a-year industry) and one for what is referred to as *Games of Chance*. The cost of conducting a bingo game is one amount per event while Games of Chance cost an additional amount per day. An further requirement is that a financial statement must be submitted to the state within a specified number of days following the conclusion of the event. And, there is a limit in terms of how much prize money can be awarded to a single individual in a game of bingo.

Overcoming Major Obstacles and Objections to Gambling and Games of Chance as Fundraisers

The two major stumbling blocks to successfully employing gambling or games of chance as a means for generating additional funds for a sport or recreation program rest upon (1) local and statewide legal restrictions and (2) the local mores of the community that determines acceptable levels of behavior by various organizations, including sport programs (Stier, 2000c). If these two obstacles can be overcome, there are many very effective fundraising projects based on games of chance. Some of the more productive contests of chance are outlined below.

50/50 Drawing

Often referred to as one of "the easiest fundraising projects," this fundraiser is frequently utilized at sport contests or gatherings. The 50/50 drawing is very simple, takes little effort or time, and has a down side risk of zero. Specifically, this technique involves the selling of tickets (say for example, $1). Half of all of the monies generated from the sale of tickets on a given night or at a specific event is given away via a drawing of some type with the remaining half of the money reverting to the coffers of the athletic program. If a single drawing would result in some $500 tickets being sold—the actual amount of money given away will be $250 (either to a single winner or split among multiple recipients), with the remaining $250 going to the sport or recreation entity.

> **PRINCIPLE # 215:** *An ideal fundraising project, the 50/50 raffle/drawing, can generate significant monies during a year with little downside risk and minimal effort*

Over a number of games throughout a season, this can amount to a sizeable amount of money for athletics. Additionally, the excitement of the drawing and the possibility of positive public relations and publicity enhance the effectiveness of this specific project. Winners can be publicized in the local paper or in school or athletic publications, as well as via the public address system at subsequent drawings.

Raffle

A raffle is a lottery in which a number of individuals purchase chances to win a prize or prizes. Anything that can be sold can be raffled, automobiles, trips, wine and cheese at Christmas, cash, savings bonds, free weekends at a hotel, items of food (beef, turkeys), game balls, athletic equipment, vehicles, etc.

The raffle project can be either very simple or very complex, depending upon the structure of the raffle itself. Usually the raffle is time consuming in its organization and planning respects and has significant down side risks in terms of effort expended and the negative consequences of failure. Many raffles are organized so that the actual raffle activity takes place with another type of activity (piggyback), either a dinner or luncheon. Usually, various contributors will donate the items to be raffled off, as well as other resources needed for the raffle. However, this necessitates that these potential contributors be contacted and donations be successfully solicited in a timely fashion.

In many situations in which money is part of the raffle winnings, the money to be given away is generated from the income realized from the sale of raffle tickets. Thus, a risk associated with this type of raffle centers around the need to sell a sufficient number of tickets to cover the expenses of the raffle itself, including any cash awards to be distributed. This means the use of a suitable sales force and adequate publicity for the raffle.

Finally, the downside risk is notable in that the failure of the raffle project not only means the loss of time and effort spent on the project but also creates negative publicity towards the sponsoring organization and upon the sports program itself. The general public takes due notice of any such failure. Hence, it is important that such projects become successful—it would be better not to have attempted the raffle than to try to pull it off only to fall on one's face, in full view of the public and various sport constituencies (Briggs and Duffy, 1987).

Reverse Raffle

The reverse raffle is a variation of the time proven raffle project in which the winning tickets pulled from the so-called bowl are those that are pulled last, in reverse order of the regular raffle. In a reverse raffle, with some 200 tickets sold and with five prizes, the first 195 tickets pulled would receive nothing. The 196th ticket would receive the 5th prize, the 197th ticket pulled would receive the 4th prize, the 198th ticket would earn the 3rd prize, and the 199th ticket garners the 2nd prize, while the GRAND PRIZE would be reserved for the 200th or last ticket pulled.

> **PRINCIPLE # 216:** *In the reverse raffle the last ticket(s) pulled is(are) the big winner(s)*

The advantage of the reverse raffle, in addition to its uniqueness, is that the excitement generated through the awarding of prizes in reverse order is significant. Every ticket purchaser will have his/her ticket actually pulled. When the number of tickets remaining becomes smaller and smaller there tends to be greater excitement among all in attendance. Finally, when there are just a handful of tickets remaining, all eyes are on the bowl and the final drawing of the winning tickets. This is in contrast to the regular raffle in which the 5 winners are known after the first five tickets are pulled.

The reverse raffle works best when there are 200 or less tickets to be selected from the bowl. With a potential of some 5000 winning tickets, it would be foolish to attempt a reverse raffle. There would not be sufficient time to pull all 4999 tickets before reaching the grand prize; the people in the audience would have long ago fallen asleep or left for home.

Pseudo Give-A-Way

This contest is ostensibly a raffle but without the actual selling of tickets. Rather, the item to be given away will be given to the holder of a ticket stub sometime during the contest, most preferably at half time. There is nothing for the potential winner to buy other than a ticket to the athletic contest. Usually, the items to be given away are donated for this purpose. Naturally, suitable publicity for the event and appropriate credit to the individual or organization responsible for donating the item or items is required. *In some states and communities, this pseudo give-a-way falls under the gambling classification and must be treated as such by meeting all of the requirements, including record keeping and truth-in-advertising regulations.*

Lottery/Sweepstakes and Sport Pools

Lotteries and sport pools provide opportunities to generate both small and large sums of money depending upon the structure of the lottery or sport pool, as well as upon the successful efforts of the promotional team behind such a program. Frequently, the determination of winners for lotteries or sweepstakes of sport programs are the actual numbers of state lottery winners (either in one's own state or in an adjacent state). However, any method of selecting numbers, which will be determined in the future, will suffice. Sport pools, those associated with professional contests, are most popular during the championship contests, i.e., the SUPER BOWL, the WORLD SERIES, the STANLEY CUP FINALS, the NBA CHAMPIONSHIP, etc. Again, the use of sport pools, like the lottery or sweepstakes, can result in financial gain by the amateur sport program with a minimum of risk, save the effort to sell tickets for the pool or the lottery.

Casino Nights

The so-called casino nights are modeled after the casinos in Las Vegas and Atlantic City. Casino nights provide opportunities for a wide array of gambling games from *craps* to *black jack* to *roulette* to *poker* to *baccarat* to *backgammon*, etc. Dealers can be athletic staff, as well as members of the booster organization, who have undergone indoctrination in terms of the various rules and regulations of various games. The gambling is not conducted with actual cash. Rather, cash is exchanged at the "bank" for play money, which in turn is used at the various gambling tables. Prizes, which are donated to the charitable event, may be exchanged at the end of the evening's festivities for the play money won at the various gambling tables. Whether a cover charge is in effect or not is up to the organizers of the event.

Sometimes a professional card manipulator/teacher can be hired to provide both demonstrations and lessons to participants on how to play the different gambling games and to perform various card tricks. This lends an atmosphere of professionalism to the evening's festivities and enables all in attendance to have an authoritarian source to answer any questions that may arise. Of course, such an experience is also great entertainment.

Bingo

> **PRINCIPLE # 217:** *Bingo is popular among all ages and can generate big dollars over a period of time if organized and planned properly*

One of the most popular games of chance in the United States and Canada today, bingo, is a game in which players place markers on a card with a pattern of numbered squares in the order that the numbers are drawn and subsequently announced by the caller. This game has significant potential for both public relations and monetary benefits accruing to the sport program on a recurring or isolated basis. Whether the bingo games are organized and sponsored exclusively by the sport organization or are co-sponsored by another organization, the potential for significant profits are very real. Naturally, local and state laws must be adhered to with appropriate licenses or permits obtained. One potential problem might be in the competition provided by various church groups and professional bingo organizations in some communities. A company that claims to be the *largest distributor* in North America of bingo and other fundraising supplies, equipment and related merchandise is Bazaar & Novelty, Toronto, Canada.

A SAMPLING OF SPECIAL FUNDRAISING AND PROMOTIONAL PROJECTS

Providing premiums to fans to encourage excitement and support for one's team

The following are examples of special activities that are social, recreational, educational, or athletic in nature and are planned and implemented for the purpose of raising funds and/or promoting and marketing the sports program. There are literally thousands and thousands of such fundraising projects that sport and recreation organizations can initiate in an effort to obtain needed resources as well as increased positive publicity and public relations (Stier, 1999a(.

1. Creating **discount cards** (small credit card sized plastic cards) that enable the purchaser to secure financial discounts at a variety of retail stores, fast food restaurants and other establishments (Stier, 2001a).

2. **Coupon Booklets** [involving many more special deals then discount cards] can also be used instead of **discount cards** to enable purchasers to take advantage of "specials" for the goods and services advertised in the coupon booklet. (Stier, 2000d).

3. Using **scratch cards** to generate sizeable profits with minimal investment and effort. Cardboard cards with special rub-off "spots" are used to solicit donations from individuals who scratch off one or more of the "spots" revealing an amount (varying from 50¢ to one or more dollars) that the person is to donate (Stier, 2001b).

4. **Athletic contests** scheduled against a variety of opponents, such as varsity against alumni or against students, media versus athletic staff, faculty versus general students, members of various community organizations versus one another, All-Star games, etc.

    These contests may be held as stand-alone events. They may also be associated with a regular sporting contest by serving as a preliminary game to a varsity or regular season sporting event.

5. Selling **fake "tattoos"** (of your school or organization's logo/mascot) to students, fans, spectators and anyone else who is willing to place temporary (and safe) tattoos on their face, hands, and/or arms. (Stier, 2001c).

6. Similar to fake tattoos, **pins and buttons** can also be sold to fans, spectators and community people as part of a fundraising project (Stier, 1999b).

7. **Coaches' clinics** and **workshops** dealing with coaching strategies for any number of sports may be sponsored by the booster group or by the sport organization itself.

8. **Youth sport camps** or **clinics** may be very attractive and profitable, especially if the needed facilities (practice facilities and dormitory space) may be secured without costing the sponsoring organization an arm and a leg.

9. **Fun nights** are all night (12-24 hour) gatherings staged within the athletic facilities and are supervised by school or athletic staff. (Stier, 1998c).

10. **Team** and **individual athlete photos** may be obtained on a donated or reduced cost basis and displayed in a prominent place within the school, as well as sold to parents and friends of athletes.

11. **Flea markets** and **consignment sales** involve resale of donated merchandise or items placed on consignment. The profit is generated through the sale of the donated items or from a percentage of the sales price in the situation involving items left on consignment.

12. Create your own professionally prepared and bound **cookbook** for your organization and sell copies to a wide audience (Stier, 1999c).

13. **Car washes** are a perennial fundraising project and merely require access to water, a high traffic location.

14. **Free car washes** are a variation in that the car washes are *FREE*. The profit comes from the advanced planning in which the organizers of the *free car wash* obtain pledges ranging from 10¢ to $1 *per athlete, per car washed* (Stier, 1998d)

15. **Invitational tournaments sponsored by businesses and corporations**.

16. **Novelty athletic events** involving specialized programs can have special appeal to the general public. Two examples are the *Harlem Globetrotters in basketball* and the *King and His Court in softball*.

17. **Craft and hobby shows or sales** can be very popular annual or one-time fundraising projects.

18. **Rummage, white elephant,** or **garage sales** can be organized in a similar fashion to the craft and hobby shows, in that donated items are offered for sale, with suitable advance advertisement, in a high traffic location. The major distinction, however, is that the items for sale have all been donated by individuals and organizations rather than being on consignment. (Stier, 1998e; Stier, 2000e).

19. Other types of specific **shows** and **exhibitions**, such as art shows and antique shows, have potential for significant income if sufficient interest can be created on behalf of both exhibitors and potential viewers or purchasers.

20. **Bazaars, festivals, fairs**, and **carnivals** have all been utilized as successful fundraising projects for sport programs. Potential profits are generated from the booth fees, entrance fees (if any), and concession sales. Usually **bazaars** are associated with a variety of food items tastefully displayed in booths, as well as a variety of entertainment, such as **music**, and **exhibitions**. **Festivals** are frequently organized around a particular season in which the event will be implemented or around national holidays, i.e., Summerfest, Octoberfest, Springfest, Winterfest, etc. **Fairs** and **carnivals** often involve music, entertainment, games of chance, amusement rides (merry-go-around, ferris wheel), animal rides, etc.

21. **Rodeos** are similar to fairs and carnivals in that professional organizers of such events may be secured to conduct the rodeo under the auspices of a sponsoring organization, such as a local athletic program or educational entity.

22. **Donkey baseball** is the sport of baseball played where all players, except the pitcher and catcher, play the game while sitting upon donkeys. This is crowd-pleasing entertainment. One of the leading donkey ball organizations that accounts for the majority of the donkey baseball contests that are staged within the United States is the *Buckeye Donkey Ball Company*.

PRINCIPLE # 218: *With any fundraising or promotional project involving animals be sure not to run afoul with the society for the prevention of cruelty to animals (SPCA)*

---

23. Sport teams and organizations can now sign up with one of several firms that provide **cash back bonuses on credit card purchases** made by the sport entity's patrons, fans and/or members. Supporters apply for and receive a special credit card and for all purchases made with that credit card, the sport entity receives a small percentage in the form of a cash back bonus.

24. A variation of the *cash back theme* is the fundraiser that involves having the sport entity's fans, patrons and supporters log onto a specific web site, and once registering as representing the sport organization, any purchases made by the supporters at that web site generates a small cash back rebate to the sport organization (Popke, 2000).

25. **Celebrity golf tournaments** as well as **regular golf tournaments** are traditional spring fundraising events. The "holes," as well as the "tees," may be "sold" to individuals or corporate sponsorships for $100 to $500, or whatever the market will bear.

26. Card and board games such as chess, checkers, backgammon, as well as card games such as bridge, canasta, and pinochle, can be very popular components of a fundraising project when combined with other activities.

27. Selling **flowers** within the community involves purchasing the flowers, such as tulips and mums, from a wholesaler and then reselling them to anyone and everyone within the community (Stier, 2000f)

28. **Excursions** to sporting events or places of interest for sightseeing experiences or shopping sprees can be perennial fundraising successes. Typically, buses are hired to take individuals to away sites for either sight seeing purposes or combined with viewing sporting events.

29. **House tours** or **garden tours** of stately homes in nearby geographical areas are low risk projects. The profit comes from the sale (contributions) of tickets that are promoted, publicized and marketed well in advance.

30. **Fashion Shows** have proven to be popular and profitable annual or biannual events in many communities (Stier, 1999d).

31. **Staging professional** or **special sporting events** such as professional wrestling matches or sponsoring the Harlem Globetrotters can result in big money profits provided that there exists drawing power for a sufficient number of spectators.

32. Establishing temporary **haunted houses** for Halloween involves construction work to convert a suitable vacant structure into a scary (but safe) haunted house for which a modest admission charge is established and refreshments sold

33. Building a **Christmas and Santa Claus workshop** for children is similar to the haunted house project explained above.

34. Providing a **holiday gift-wrapping service**, especially around the Christmas season. Reserving space or a booth in a mall or shopping center and offering quality, on the spot, holiday gift-wrapping for gift buyers can be a great annual fundraising project. (Stier, 2000g).

35. **Ghost dinners** are an intriguing fundraising project. In this situation, invitations for a "dinner" are sent to selected individuals specifying a certain date, time, exotic location of the *make-believe, ghost dinner* as well as the amount of contribution requested. However, *in reality, there is no actual dinner* and the prospective donors are apprised of that fact during the initial communication attempt. Rather, the money is collected from the donor/purchaser as if the dinner was indeed going to be held.

36. A similar idea to ghost dinners is the **ghost (stay-at-home) event**, in which an invitation to sent to a predetermined special event (whether it be musical, sporting, political, educational, drama, etc.) asking the recipients to contribute/donate *what it would have cost them* to attend (sitter, parking, dinner, gas, etc.) a specific event.

37. **Dances**, based upon unusual and fun themes, can be very successful in providing for great entertainment, as well as financial benefits to the sponsoring organization. Possible themes include the "Big Band Era," the "Roaring Twenties," the "60's Dance

Marathon," the "50's Rock and Roll," "Country and Western," as well as a host of others (Stier, 2000h).

38. **Mall promotions** provide excellent opportunities to get the message of the sport organization (marketing effort) before the general public. The objective is to secure permission from a manager of a mall to allow a display table to be set up within the mall over a weekend or on a Saturday and/or Sunday afternoon. The mall traffic can be significant over a weekend, providing the sport program with potential exposure to some thousands and thousands of people, if not tens of thousands. Finally, means should be available for collecting names, addresses and phone numbers of those interested in the program for use in a database.

39. Combining major **televised athletic events** such as the Super Bowl, NCAA Basketball Championship, the Kentucky Derby, the Indy 500, various boxing spectacles, and the World Series with a local sport organization's fundraising project, has proven successful in many, many instances.

40. The **"selling" of part of the sport facility** is an exciting project. This *make-believe sale of part of the sport facility* can be organized around several variations. The general idea, however, is to "sell" a piece of the facility, a field or a building, to local fans and boosters. The actual item to be "sold" might be a square inch of the football field or part of the field house. Of course, there is no actual sale, but the *pseudo-sale* nevertheless can be enticing to the general public and sport fans.

41. **Actual selling of discarded parts of athletic facilities** (segments) can be a source of much needed funds. In this case, actual physical items are sold, with accompanying "certificates of ownership." When a facility becomes slated for demolition, the administrators arrange to secure the bricks of the old field house and market (sell) each brick for $15 to $20.

42. **Selling personalized engraved bricks** for use in a paved walkway or wall commemorating a special event, an organization or individual(s) (Stier, 2001d).

43. **Rental of advertising space** within a facility can be a steady source of income for the recreation or sport entity.

44. **Rental of the athletic facility to outside groups**, when the facility is not being used by the sport organization, can reap big benefits for both athletic-oriented organizations and non-athletic entities.

45. **Sponsoring camping, boating or recreational equipment shows** at the athletic or recreation facilities can be productive in exposing a wide range of publics to the organization's facilities, as well as provide monetary benefits through the charging of fees by the exhibitors and the profits from concessions.

46. **Athletic Hall of Fame** luncheons, brunches or dinners, honoring past sports greats of the organization can raise sizeable monies for the sponsoring group through ticket sales.

47. Purchasing and then **reselling tickets to various public performances** to the general public can generate sizeable profits. For example, tickets for a special event on a specific date are secured at greatly reduced prices to theater shows, sporting events, museums, musicals, etc. Thus, this specific date becomes the team's sponsored event and tickets are resold with that theme to the public under the auspices of the sport organization.

48. **Solicitation of equipment** and **souvenirs** from other organizations, such as pro teams or colleges, for resale or use as give-a-ways in a wide variety of fundraising and promotional efforts. Almost any item of equipment or apparel can be solicited and used as a tool within some type of promotional and/or fundraising project.

49. **Personal appearances by public figures** can enhance any athletic function. Such personal appearances might be part of a greater overall fundraising or promotional scheme, such as a fundraising luncheon or end-of-season athletic team banquet.

50. **Auctions** are a special means of offering a variety of goods for public sale. An auction involves a process of bidding to dispose of accumulations of unused, as well as used, yet serviceable, items for the sport program's benefit. It is important to have a professional auctioneer to work the auction, as it is essential to have authenticity.

51. In a **silent auction**, a card providing a brief description of the item, indicating the donor and approximate value, accompanies each item or lot that is set out. Bids are submitted by indicating a bid amount and signing one's name on the card, raising the price with each successive bid. After a specific period of time, bidding is closed and all cards are collected. The final bidder (highest bid amount) on the card is the purchaser of the item for the amount specified on the card.

52. A **raffle-auction** is a combination of a raffle and a silent auction. Individuals purchase "chances" consisting of two-part tickets, identically numbered for a set price. To make a selection, the purchaser ("bidder") drops half of one or more of the tickets purchased into the container adjacent to the desired item. The item to be sold is marked with a minimum bid value. At the conclusion of the "raffle-auction," the winning ticket is drawn from each container and the person holding the corresponding number wins the specific item.

53. The **blind auction** features blind bidding for items wrapped in paper bags or the items otherwise disguised so the content(s) can't be identified.

54. The **people auction** is, as the name implies, an auction of individuals (students, athletes, administrators, staff, fans, parents, etc.) to the highest bidder. This auction involves the "selling" of individuals for a specific purpose and/or time frame. For ex-

ample, the auctioning off of the athletic director or other dignitaries for a dinner for two at a local restaurant (Stier, 2001e).

55. **Road races** (10 K race or 5 K) have become more popular (often with sponsors) with the advent of acceptance of the need for fitness among the general public.

> **PRINCIPLE # 219:** *Be sure to anticipate safety issues when planning fundraising projects such as road races and "thons"— make arrangements for protecting the health and welfare of the participants*

56. **"Thons"** are those fundraising projects in which individuals participate in a wide variety of physical activities usually associated with endurance or skill. Profits are generated from participants paying entry fees and/or having the participants solicit sponsors who pledge to pay a specific sum based upon the nature of the activity (Stier, 1999e).

57. **Professional fundraising company selling advertisements** for team calendars, sport programs, and other printed items can generate profits for sport programs. In this situation, the sports program receives free 100 or 200 calendars, programs, schedule cards, etc., to sell, to give away, or to display within the community. The company makes it profit from the sale of advertisements minus the cost of producing the printed items.

Be careful of cheering stunts lest accidents occur

58. Colleges and universities may set aside ("sell" or lease) buildings and/or portable tents and parking spaces adjacent to major stadiums and gymnasia *as rental facilities* for exclusive "tail-gate gatherings" that include reserved parking spaces (Regan, 1992).

59. The *"selling"* (reserving) **of so-called luxury box seating** or **special reserve seating** to businesses or corporations can be implemented in any facility that enjoys the advantages of an attractive sporting activity in conjunction with seating arrangements that can be divided and segregated to provide an atmosphere of exclusivity.

PRE-GAME, HALF-TIME AND GAME DAY ACTIVITIES

The day of an athletic contest or recreation activity can serve as a base of operations or a foundation for a wide variety of promotional, marketing and fundraising activities. From the traditional tailgate party preceding the athletic contest to numerous half-time activities, the objective remains the same, i.e., to promote the sport program or a specific team and/or to generate additional funds and support. Whatever is accomplished is done to enable people to find the athletic event enjoyable and satisfying so that they will return again and again to participate and to support the sport entity. Some of the pre-game, half-time or day-of-game activities that may be used to help promote the attractiveness of the sport are provided below.

> *PRINCIPLE # 220: Take advantage of advances in technology in equipment and supplies when planning one's promotional and fundraising efforts*

1. Use the "**hot dog blaster**" (hot dog launcher), a machine [costing in the range of $6,500 to $8,000] that can blast a hot dog in a bun (wrapped accompanied by mustard and ketchup packets) far into the bleacher section from the ball field or court, to help provide some excitement as well as promote the concession stand (Hiestand, 1999).

2. Have **parachutists** jump into the stadium or onto any game field. This type of promotional event attracts significant attention from fans and helps increase gate receipts.

3. Provide a variety of **contests of skills** involving selected spectators at half-time. In the sport of basketball, chances are sold to fans prior to each home contest. A specific number of tickets are subsequently drawn prior to half-time with the winners having an opportunity to make a basket from varying distances. Donated prizes as well as cash can be awarded to each winner.

4. Construct a temporary "**jail**" at a home athletic contest or recreation event. People (teachers, administrators, students, fans, parents, anyone and everyone) can be temporarily "placed" in jail by donating money and the persons placed in jail can bail themselves out by making a suitable donation (Stier, 1999f).

5. **Special dress up activities** are those promotional programs that center around a common theme and involve suggested special clothing or dress requirements by those who choose to participate. For example, in a **red freak out night** for a basketball game, the objective is to encourage those in attendance to wear outlandish RED outfits or costumes. Even faces, arms and hands are painted. A contest is held at half-time to determine who has the most outlandish red costume and body paint (the school's colors being red and white). Winners are awarded prizes.

6. **Outside organizations, companies** or **corporations can compete** against one another in an athletic event prior to the school's regularly scheduled athletic contest, coupled with a $500 donation to the sport program by both companies. Excellent publicity, suitable awards, coupled with a little advanced planning, can insure success if there are interested organizations willing to participate and to donate a specific sum of money for the privilege of being involved.

7. **Special announcements** made over the public address system prior to, during, and following athletic contests should never be overlooked as promotional tactics. These timely messages can play a large role in communicating with a whole host of constituencies in attendance at the contest and can promote anything and everything related to the sport organization.

8. **Exhibitions, demonstrations** or **contests** by outside schools, sport organizations and other groups on the day of the BIG GAME and/or during rest periods (half-time) of THE CONTEST.

9. **Alumni** or **faculty contests** associated with a regularly scheduled contest or event. Inviting alumni to return to the school to play in a preliminary game or during an extended half-time continues to be a popular event. Similarly, involving the faculty and administration at a school in a contest with students can reap many benefits, both in financial and public relations terms.

10. Athletic contests can also serve as the vehicle for **conducting drawings** or **contests** before, during and following the games. This is an excellent way to create excitement and attract the attention and interest of those in attendance.

11. **Special invitations to area groups** to attend athletic events on a full pay basis, on a free basis or a reduced admission basis. With empty seats available, it hurts no one to give tickets away or to discount tickets to any number of charitable and non-charitable organizations, groups and individuals.

12. The use of **Special DAYS** designations **based on the group of individuals being honored or highlighted**. For example, the use of a *family day, Scout day, alumni day, youth day, parents' day*, etc., can be successful in attracting a specific audience to a specified athletic event and in so doing sets the stage for a common theme for the day in question.

13. The use of a **Special DAY** designation *may be based on the promotional activity itself*, for example, special souvenir give-away items [to a specific number of attendees] such as *bat night, ball night, hat night, shirt night*, etc. A study conducted by Friedman (1989) found that free give-a-way items were most popular among the 18-24 years of age and those in the $20,000 to $29,000 income range.

14. Providing **fireworks** prior to a contest or at the intermission is certainly a way to attract attention, especially around the 4th of July. Fireworks can be effectively used at any time of the year.

15. **Bovine Drop** (also referred to as the **Cow Drop** or **Cow Chip Bingo**) is an excellent fundraising project that can be connected with an athletic or recreational event. A cow is turned loose in the fenced field with squares marked on the grounds and the squares having been "sold." Wherever the cow "does its business" on the field, on whichever square, the "owner" of that square wins the big (usually cash) prize (Stier, 1997b).

16. Special **THEME nights/events** (An Evening with Big Bird, Community Night, Fan Appreciation Night, Boosters Night) hold unlimited potential for the promotion of the sports activity and can be combined with other promotional activities, such as *give-aways* and *reduced admission prices*.

17. Establishing a "**Stuff the Arena**" or "**Stuff the Stadium**" or "**Stuff the Gymnasium**" contest with prizes given away to groups with the largest representation provides entertainment for everyone. Prizes could be money, pizzas, tickets, hats, t-shirts, miniature basketballs or footballs, etc. A variation of this theme could revolve around counting life size cardboard cutouts or "stuffed animal" in addition to real people in determining the winning group.

18. Involve teachers or special boosters by extending invitations to them to be **guest coaches** for the week or for a specific home and/or away game(s). This would involve having the individual guest coach attend practices/contests over a specific number of days.

19. **Tailgate parties** and related activities can always be used at home contests to generate excitement on the day of the game for the home team, as well as providing a small, but nevertheless stable flow of revenue through the sale of food and merchandise during the time of such gatherings. The sale of merchandise (apparel and souvenirs) during this period of time prior to and following the actual game should not be overlooked.

BANQUETS AND LUNCHEON ACTIVITIES

Kick-off (preseason) luncheons or banquets have often been used to generate enthusiasm and support for the upcoming sport season. The use of post season dinners, banquets or gatherings may be used as vehicles for honoring athletes as well as athletic staff and volunteers for their efforts, as well as thanking boosters and sponsors for their support.

In addition, these preseason and post-season activities revolving around food and beverages have the potential for serving as a means for generating additional revenue (in the form of additional contributions), for increasing the number of supporting boosters, as well as for publicizing positive facts and accomplishments to the general public (Stier, 2000i).

> **PRINCIPLE # 221:** Take advantage of opportunities to thank individuals or to honor people by structuring a fundraising activity or project around an appreciation gathering

In planning the food-oriented event, there are three essential ingredients in the successful implementation of such a gathering. These include providing (1) an excellent speaker (pitchman or pitchwoman), (2) establishing a professional atmosphere, and (3) exhibiting patience.

Food and Beverage Related Fundraising and Promotional Activities

Professionally created signs can do wonders for selling food items

The breakfast/brunch/luncheon/dinner gathering has proven, over and over again, to be an effective way of enhancing the visibility of the sport program as well as generating sizeable income. The actual *solicitation of donated* or *reduced cost food* and *beverages*, from local merchants for any athletic sponsored event involving food and beverages, is the key to enhancing the profitability of such sponsored events involving food and drink.

There are numerous specific fundraising and promotional activities and strategies that revolve around the world of *food* and *beveages*. Some examples are *Traditional Fundraising Dinners* organized around a specific theme that dictates the decorations and the type of food that will be served. Some of the possible themes and/or food categories from which to choose include such events as: Bar-B-Q Evening, Buffet Supper, Chicken Fry, Chinese Banquet, Clambake, Fish Fry, German Evening (Sausage & Sauerkraut), Grecian Evening, Harvest Festival, Hawaiian Luau, International Evening, Italian Evening, Kish Kebob Supper, Lobster Night, Malaysia Satay, Mexican Meal, Patio Party, Smorgasbord Supper, Spaghetti Supper, Steak Dinner, Turkey Dinner. Western Party, Wienie Roast, etc.

Other food related fundraisers include *Wine and cheese gatherings, Ice cream socials, Progressive dinners, Wine-tasting parties, Pancake breakfasts, Adult dinner dances, Meet the coaches' breakfasts, luncheons or dinners, Monday night football, Reunion of championship teams and Celebrity Roasts.*

REFERENCES

Briggs, J. Jr., & Duffy, J. (1987). *The official soccer fundraiser's guide*. North Palm Beach, Florida: Soccer Industry Council of America.

Friedman, A. (1989, March). Consumer indicates discounted tickets. *Team Marketing Report*, 5.

Give & take. (1996, September 27). *Chronicle of Higher Education, 43*(5), A-37.

Hiestand, M. (1999, June 3). Airborne hot dogs taking off. *USA Today*, 2-C.

Madden, B. (1989). Going once, twice . . . sold. *College Athletic Management, 1*(1), 54–56.

Popke, M. (2000). Out There. *Athletic Business, 24*(9), 14.

Regan, T. H. (1992, May). Parking Condos. Unpublished manuscript, University of South Carolina, Department of Sports Administration.

Stier, W.F., Jr. (1992). Understanding fundraising in sport: The conceptual approach. *Sport Marketing Quarterly, 1*(1), 1992, 41–46.

Stier, W.F., Jr. (1996). Fundraising—Arts & sciences 101. *Athletic Management, VIII*(3), 10.

Stier, W.F., Jr. (1997a). Avoiding major mistakes in fundraising. *Athletic Management, IX*(1), 220-21.

Stier, W.F., Jr. (1997b). Bingo with Bessie. *Athletic Management, IX*(5), 19, 21.

Stier, W.F., Jr. (1998a). The perfect fit: Finding the right moneymaker. *American Cheerleader, 4*(1), 70, 72–73.

Stier, W.F., Jr. (1998b). Sport promotions, sponsorships and resource generation for the 21st Century. *Applied Research in Coaching and Athletics Annual 1998, 13*, 191–210.

Stier, W.F., Jr. (1998c). Marathon party night. *American Cheerleader, 4*(5), 94, 96, 97, 98.

Stier, W.F., Jr. (1998d). 217. The free car wash. *American Cheerleader, 4*(2), 95–97.

Stier, W.F., Jr. (1998e). The annual garage sale. *American Cheerleader, 4*(4), 63–65.

Stier, W.F., Jr. (1998f). Post game mini-auction. *American Cheerleader, 4*(6), 90–92.

Stier, W.F., Jr. (1999a). A fundraising and promotion primer for sport: Part One. *Applied Research in Coaching and Athletics Annual 1999, 14*, 219–242.

Stier, W.F., Jr. (1999b). Cute as a Button. (1999, December). *American Cheerleader, 5*(6), 72, 73.

Stier, W.F., Jr. (1999c). A Recipe for Profits. (1999, June). *American Cheerleader, 5*(3), 98, 100, 101.

Stier, W. F., Jr. (1999d). Fashioned for Profits. *American Cheerleader, 5*(4), 87, 89, 91.

Stier, W.F., Jr. (1999e). Bowl-a-thon Marathon. *American Cheerleader, 5*(5), 98, 100, 103, 104.

Stier, W.F., Jr. (1999f). On the Jail and Bail Trail. *American Cheerleader, 5*(1), 75–77.

Stier, W.F., Jr. (2000a). The new paradigm of sport marketing, promotions and fundraising in the 21st century. *PROCEEDINGS*—The 2000 Seoul International Sport Science Congress—New Paradigms of Sport & Physical Education in the 21st Century, Seoul, Korea.

Stier, W.F., Jr. (2000b). Sales, sales, and more sales—How to be successful in the fitness and the sport industry. *PROCEEDINGS*—Aerobic Fitness & Health Association of *R.O.C.*, Taiwan, Taipei.

Stier, W.F., Jr. (2000c). Fund-Raising and Promotion Secrets for the Busy Athletic Director. *PROCEEDINGS*—National Athletic Business Conference. Wisconsin: Madison. Athletic Business.

Stier, W.F., Jr. (2000d). Clipping coupons for cash. *American Cheerleader,* 6(4), 83, 84, 86, 87.

Stier, W.F., Jr. (2000e). The annual garage sale—How to turn a fundraising mainstay into a truly fab source of funds! In *Best of the Children's Market,* published by The Institute of Children's Literature.

Stier, W.F., Jr. (2000f). Watch your funds blossom. *American Cheerleader,* 6(3), 87–88, 90–91.

Stier, W.F., Jr. (2000g). That's a wrap! American Cheerleader, 6(5), 95–96, 98–99.

Stier, W.F., Jr. (2000h). Dancing for dollars. American Cheerleader, 6(6), 86, 88–89.

Stier, W.F., Jr. (2000i). A fundraising and promotional primer for sport: Part two. (2000, July). Applied Research in Coaching and Athletics Annual, 15, 12–147.

Stier, W F., Jr. (2001a). It's in the cards. (2001). *American Cheerleader,* 7(1), 82, 84–86.

Stier, W F., Jr. (2001b). It's in the cards. *American Cheerleader,* 7(5), 101–102, 104, 105, 107.

Stier, W.F., Jr. (2001c). "Fake it"—Boost school spirit and raise permanent funds selling temporary tattoos. *American Cheerleader,* 7(4), 101, 103, 105, 107.

Stier, W.F., Jr. (2001d). Set in stone. *American Cheerleader,* 7(2), 118, 120, 122.

Stier, W.F., Jr. (2001e). Going once, going twice, sold. *American Cheerleader*, 7(6), 84–86.

Stier, W.F., Jr. (2001f). Take a hike. *American Cheerleader,* 7(3), 93, 95–97.

Stier, W.F., Jr. (2002). Shooting Baskets for Bucks *American Cheerleader.* 8(1), 71–72, 74–75.

Stier, W.F., Jr. (2009). *Fundraising projects for sport, recreation, leisure and fitness programs.* Boston, MA: American Press.

Tailgate partybook. (1985). Redford, Michigan: Tailgator Enterprises, Inc.

DISCUSSION QUESTIONS

1. Explain how community standards can play a role in an organization's fundraising efforts. Provide examples.

2. Explain the "piggy-back" concept of fundraising and provide examples of successful such efforts.

3. Explain several gambling type fundraising efforts and outline strategies and tactics in their successful planning and implementation.

4. Describe how to utilize the committee process in fundraising and provide examples.

5. What are the so-called "ghost" type fundraisers and how do they operate? Provide examples.

12 ORGANIZING SPECIFIC FUNDRAISING PROJECTS THROUGH THE USE OF A TEMPLATE

The wiener dog racing contest

CHAPTER HIGHLIGHTS

This chapter will emphasize:

- The purposes of the *Fundraising-Planning Template*
- The advantages of using a template in the organization and creation of a fundraising project
- The advantages of using a template in the implementation a fundraising project

- The *Fundraising Planning Template* as an aid in the planning and organization of a fundraising project
- The categories associated with a *fundraising template* for use in fundraising
- The importance of examining potential fundraising projects in light of one's own situation and circumstances
- Eleven questions that will aid the fundraiser in one's thinking and planning efforts regarding a potential project

This chapter introduces the strategy of utilizing a **Fundraising-Planning Template** in the planning, organizing and implementing of any fundraising project. In addition, **The Fundraising-Planning Template** is presented to aid the reader in identifying and examining any number of possible fundraising efforts that organizers might find helpful within a variety of organizations and with various constituencies.

USING THE FUNDRAISING-PLANNING TEMPLATE IN PLANNING A FUNDRAISING PROJECT

The **Fundraising-Planning Template** is nothing more than a pattern or outline that serves as a guide for the sport fundraiser in organizing and planning a potential money-raising project. The template contains *key words* or *phrases* that remind the planner/organizer of the essential elements that are necessary in the organizing and carrying out of any type of fundraising project, whether the goal is $1,000 or $100,000.

Two Purposes of the Fundraising-Planning Template

> **PRINCIPLE # 222:** *The* **Fundraising-Planning Template** *serves as a blueprint to organize the project*

The template can serve two very important purposes for organizers of fundraising projects. *First*, it can be extremely helpful in the planning process of a potential fundraiser. If you are able to complete or fill out the template with all pertinent information pertaining to a particular fundraising project, the template can serve as a *blueprint* or *guideline* for the implementation of the project. *Second*, the completed template can be most helpful in securing permission to actually start the fundraising project from the individual or individuals who have the final say in approving any fundraising activities sponsored by your organization. If a well-organized and adequately planned project is clearly and succinctly outlined within a template, the template becomes an excellent educational, selling, promotional or marketing tool within your organization in your quest to gain formal approval or permission to actually begin the effort (Stier, 2009).

CREATING A TEMPLATE CONCEPTUALIZING IN DETAIL THE COMPLETE FUNDRAISING PROJECT

All fundraising projects can be viewed by means of a single, identical format (using the template) for ease of comparison and understanding. The **Fundraising-Planning Template** is described in detail below with an explanation of the essential components (key words and phrases) that make up the template (Stier, 1994).

The Fundraising-Planning Template

TITLE OF THE PROJECT: This is the descriptive name of the specific fundraising project that will be explained in detail.

POTENTIAL NET INCOME (GAIN): An estimated net profit is provided for each individual fundraising project. Of course, this can vary from event to event and from community to community. A ballpark idea of the net profit that can be generated from the event is provided.

COMPLEXITY/DEGREE OF DIFFICULTY: Complexity is indicated by the adjectives or descriptive terms *low*, *moderate* or *high*. The terms are indicative of the amount of work, effort and time that are generally involved in bringing the fundraising project to fruition. This includes both the planning and the actual implementation of the project. Of course, the difficulty of any event is dependent upon the resources, restrictions and the community climate that exist for the sponsoring organization. What might be of great difficulty for one group might not be as difficult for another organization in a different community or under different circumstances.

DESCRIPTION OF PROJECT: Under this category is a detailed explanation of exactly what the project is all about. The details of the event, which must be addressed if it is to be successful, are presented here. Naturally, individual fundraisers need to take into account individual differences and circumstances that exist within their own sport or recreational organization and in their communities when planning, organizing and implementing any fundraiser.

SCHEDULING STRATEGIES: The information provided in this area are those techniques and strategies that might prove to be helpful in the scheduling of the project for a certain date, at a specific time and at a particular location.

RESOURCES NEEDED: This general heading is further broken down into those categories listed below to provide a detailed glimpse into those resources, tools and assets that are needed in order to successfully conduct the fundraising project under consideration.

Facilities: A listing is provided of what facilities, if any, are needed and the type of facilities that would best be suited for the fundraising event. Also, suggestions are made as to whether the use of the facilities might be secured on a paid, reduced cost or free basis when appropriate.

Equipment & Supplies: Most fundraising efforts involve some type of equipment and supplies. Those items deemed necessary will be listed and information will include suggestions on how to obtain and best utilize such items, preferably on a reduced cost basis, or better yet, donated free.

Publicity & Promotional Activities: Suggestions regarding the use of specific publicity strategies and promotional tactics are presented for the fundraising project. Additionally, the timing of such promotional efforts is given, when appropriate.

Time Requirements: Here information is presented in terms of how long each fundraising event actually lasts. Additionally, a time reference is made in terms of the planning and implementation stages of the specific project.

Money Expenditures: It costs money, in most instances, to make money. Suggestions as to the areas of financial expenditures are presented to give the reader an idea of how and where money might have to be spent in order to conduct the particular fundraiser. Ideas on how to save money, when appropriate, are also shared. Generally speaking, organizers of fundraisers should avoid spending money at retail prices whenever possible. Rather, they should always attempt to obtain on a free or reduced basis those tools, assets and resources that are needed in the implementation of the project. If poster boards are needed, have them donated. If signs need to be painted, have someone donate their time and expertise. Of course money will have to be spent in many projects. When fundraising projects involve the selling of items the organizers will frequently need to purchase (reduced cost basis) that which is to be sold. This is part of the *cost of sales*. Finally, there is no magic formula or fixed percentage that can be used as a benchmark in all situations in terms of how much money should be spent in the effort to raise a specific dollar amount. Naturally, the less money spent the better. But this will depend upon the specific situation and circumstances which the organizers and planners of the event find themselves.

Personnel (Staff/Volunteers): Every fundraising effort is dependent upon personnel, both paid staff of the sponsoring recreation or sport organization as well as volunteers or boosters. Under this category are suggestions of the approximate number of people involved with the event as well as their principle areas of responsibilities and tasks.

> **RISK MANAGEMENT:** This category deals with (1) *legal risks*, such as liability concerns and insurance matters, (2) *public relations risks*, such as very public embarrassments, as well as (3) *financial risks*, which might prove to be disastrous for the would-be fundraiser. For example, there can be public relations hazards, financial exposure as well as legal exposure (downside risks) for both the sponsoring group and organization and for individuals involved in many fundraising schemes. The topic of risk management involves the tactic of examining the *worse case scenarios* and then making plans to take steps to avoid or minimize, as much as is possible, such negative consequences.
>
> **PERMITS/LICENSES/PERMISSIONS:** This category refers to permits or licenses (or permissions) that might have to be obtained from a variety of sources. The reader is instructed where to go to secure possible permission and permits in order to carry out the project without dire legal and/or financial consequences.
>
> **HINTS AND SUGGESTIONS:** This final category is reserved for those specific suggestions that might be of real help in planning, executing and evaluating the fundraising event. Additionally, hints are shared in terms of providing insight into different or alternative ways to conduct the specific event. These suggestions and hints need to be taken by the reader with a "grain of salt," so to speak, in light of individual resources and limitations in one's community and within the sponsoring group itself.

EXAMINING POTENTIAL FUNDRAISING PROJECTS IN LIGHT OF ONE'S OWN SITUATION AND CIRCUMSTANCES

Those involved in fundraising will find that their individual situations are usually somewhat different, sometimes radically different, from the situations in which others must operate. Sometimes specific resources (facilities, personnel, equipment & supplies, money, image, etc.) are not available or conducive to effectively run a particular project. Frequently there are limitations (financial, programmatic, public relations, image, reputation, competition, location, etc.) that exist and that in turn restrict the fundraiser from performing in a way that other fundraisers in other communities and under different circumstances have been and are able to act.

Thus, with a critical eye the reader must look at the specific assets as well as limitations of each fundraising project being considered to see if these suggestions can indeed help simplify and/or improve some aspect of the fundraising process, if not the total project itself. But it is up to the directors and coordinators of the various fundraising projects to determine what will work and what will not work in their own communities *in light of the resources available and the limitations that exist.*

Mascots are an indispensable element in contest promotion

It is suggested that the reader glean through all of the potential projects under consideration to develop a clearer understanding of the differences as well as the similarities between the various methods of raising money for sport and recreation organizations. Many projects contain information and suggestions that can be applicable in many other types of fundraising efforts.

Certainly it is advisable to examine carefully a variety of potential projects that use similar ideas or ways of generating money. Take, for example, the *auction method* of raising resources. If the reader is thinking of using some type of auction at the local level it would be of great help to think about all of the fundraising projects that use the auction method as the basic technique of fundraising. Similarly, there are a variety of fundraising efforts that use the *raffle c*oncept. And, there are numerous activities that involve the use of *food* or a *concession operation* in the fundraising plan. Examining the projects that are dependent upon the same concept or idea only enhances the understanding and competency level of the reader in terms of creating, developing and implementing one's own successful fundraising program using the concepts and ideas presented herein.

There Is More than One Way to Do Anything

There is an old fundraising axiom that states that there are *a thousand ways to skin a cat*. This implies that there is no one, single way to conduct any specific fundraising project. If fifty different organizations conducted a fundraising event that involved a raffle, there could easily be fifty different ways to actually organize and implement such an event.

> **PRINCIPLE # 223:** *There are a 1000 ways to "skin a cat"*

Thus, it is up to you, the potential fundraiser, to decide to what extent you wish to copy any particular project you are considering and to what extent you might want to make changes and adapt the ideas or adjust the strategies and tactics presented here to suit your particular situation and circumstances.

Questions to Ask Yourself in Assessing and Planning a Potential Fundraiser

Although there are many different ways to plan and organize any fundraising project, there are some questions that might help you in your thinking and planning efforts. The author outlined eleven such questions that appeared in a journal in 1998 (Stier, p. 72). These questions, which are provided below, are directly related to the categories that make up the **Fundraising-Planning Template** described above. The answers to these questions will go a long way toward helping to outline the details of a potential fundraiser and to determine, with some specificity, what possible courses of action will be necessary to make the project successful.

Signage on athletic fences can be a source of money on an annual basis

1. How much money do you need and when? The answer to this question alone will eliminate many possible projects from further consideration.

2. What projects are reasonable, feasible, suitable and "doable" in terms of the standards of the community and the school? Some projects might be inappropriate due to its very nature. For example, fundraising efforts involving gambling, use of alcohol, card playing and even dancing might be frowned upon in some communities.

3. How complicated or difficult is the proposed fundraising project? Is the project considered complex, moderately complex or simple? Can the organization successfully tackle such a project?

4. What are you going to name the fundraising effort? Remember, a fancy or distinctive name often helps in the promotion and publicity of the effort. In some situations there is a very real advantage in having a name that is clearly descriptive of the project.

5. How would you describe the proposed project to others? Being able to succinctly explain and justify the project to others helps planners to (1) clearly understand the idiosyncrasies of the total effort and (2) secure permission from higher authorities to begin the project.

> **PRINCIPLE # 224:** There is only so much discretionary income *available to the average family; therefore, schedule your fundraising project at a time when there is little or no competition from other fundraisers within the community*

6. When would be the best time for the fundraiser to be scheduled? You don't want to schedule your project so as to be in conflict or competition with other fundraisers? Also, should the project be tied in to an official holiday? The timing of the event is critical if the maximum benefits are to be realized in terms of money raised, positive public relations and publicity.

7. What resources are needed in order to have a successful project? Resources such as facilities, equipment and supplies, time, money, and finally, people, must be considered prior to initiating any project. Are such resources currently available or can they be secured for the proposed project at a reasonable cost?

8. What type of promotional and publicity efforts are required or desirable? When should they be implemented? Every fundraiser desires positive and timely publicity. Every project should be adequately promoted. The challenge is to decide what is needed and when is the optimal time to promote the event and communicate publicly with the potential patrons and constituencies.

> **PRINCIPLE # 225:** *Fundraising is not without risks, sometimes significant risks*

9. What risks are involved and how can they be avoided or minimized? What are the downside *financial risks*? What are the *legal liability risks*? What about *public relations risks*? In order to plan to avoid problems it is imperative that you are aware of what could go wrong and what risks are involved in any fundraising effort. Good planners anticipate the *worse case scenario* and then make appropriate plans to prevent discord and disaster.

10. Are there licenses, permits or permissions that must be obtained in order to go ahead with the proposed fundraising project? Permission may have to be obtained from your own organization to even initiate the project. Permits may have to be secured from city, county or state governmental agencies. Licenses may have to be obtained from a health department or from city hall.

11. Finally, what final comments or suggestions might you add to help clarify any aspect of the proposed fundraiser that has not been covered by answering the questions above? Is there something peculiar or unique to this particular effort that needs further clarification or explanation in order to be clearly understood by all? Some fundraisers are such that special comments, suggestions or instructions are appropriate to help planners and their helpers understand fully what is involved in the effort.

REFERENCES

Stier, W.F., Jr. (1994). *Fundraising for sport and recreation.* Champaign, Illinois: Human Kinetics.

Stier, W.F., Jr. (1998). The Perfect Fit: Finding the Right Moneymaker. (1998). *American Cheerleader, 4*(1), 70, 72–73.

Stier, W.F., Jr. (2009). *Fundraising projects for sport, recreation, leisure and fitness programs.* Boston, MA: American Press.

DISCUSSION QUESTIONS

1. Explain the advantages and purposes of the *Fundraising Planning Template* in the planning of fundraising projects.

2. Explain the principle # 223 *There are a 1000 ways to "skin a cat"* in terms of fundraising and the *Fundraising-Planning Template* and provide examples.

3. Describe the various types of resources that can be delineated within the template.

4. Discuss the fact that there is only so much discretionary funds available to the average family and how this impacts the sport/recreation fundraiser.

5. What kind of risks do fundraisers expose themselves to and how do they go about dealing with these risks? Be specific.

Appendix A

SAMPLE BY-LAWS GUIDE FOR BOOSTER CLUBS

Adapted from the Official Handbook, (1981), of the Boosters Clubs of America, North Palm Beach, Florida, pp. 22-28.

ARTICLE 1—ORGANIZATION

This organization shall be a non-profit, unincorporated association, unless state laws require differently.

The name of this organization shall be:

_____
Booster Club Name

_____
School Name or Organization Name

_____
Street Address

_____
City   State   Zip Code

ARTICLE II—PURPOSE

Section 1

The booster club exists for the purpose of broadening the involvement of students, student families, and the school, through support for all female and male activities of the inter-school athletic programs. The booster club works to achieve this through active participation of as many parents as possible in booster club programs and in concentrated support for individual sports, working closely with the coaches, athletic director, activities director, and the principal of the school.

(1) To support, promote, and maintain a high standard of integrity and good sportsmanship in all athletic activities of high school.
(2) To foster and promote good will and fraternal spirit among the members.
(3) To promote and encourage better attendance at all sports activities by the parents, and friends of athletes, the students, and faculty of the school.
(4) To promote and encourage more young men and women to become involved in athletics, either as an active participant or as a volunteer assistant such as statistician, etc.
(5) To raise funds to assist all athletic programs through the school's athletic fund. The athletic director may help to create smaller booster club committees to directly support each coach's program or support a strong revenue producing program to raise the funds to assist all athletic programs and supported volunteers working for the operation of concession stands, selling of advertisements, tickets, and donations for any other legitimate purpose that the Board of Directors shall determine.
(6) To assist in holding down expenses of the athletic department by volunteering services to provide people to serve as parking lot attendants, chain gang crew, admission ticket takers, timers, judges, as well as other similar activities approved and sanctioned by the athletic department.
(7) Budgets are to be established at the beginning of each year. The coaches will submit to their respective committee their list of needs, prepared and approved by the athletic director and the school principal. The committee chairperson will then present the budget requests for approval by a 2/3 majority vote of the general membership in attendance.
(8) All money raised by special fund raising projects to meet the athletic department's requests, will be presented to the school administration in a manner of general agreement with the school administrator and club officers. The agreed plan is as follows:

_____

_____

_____

ARTICLE III—MEMBERSHIP

Section 1

Parents and friends of all past or present student athletes, and such other sports-interested persons who desire membership shall be eligible for membership in the association.

Section 2

There will be yearly membership dues of $ _____ per person for regular active members. Dues shall be payable at the beginning of each school year. Dues may be increased or decreased by the Executive Board and by a majority vote of the general membership.

Section 3

A special sustaining membership may be established for persons unable to volunteer their efforts but who can support the school athletic program through what may be a tax-free membership gift. There are three levels of contributions and memberships are to be renewed each year for non-participating supports. The three levels of contribution are as follows:

- (A) Gold level membership: $ _____
- (B) Silver level membership: $ _____
- (C) Bronze level membership $ _____

Section 4

All active coaches, the Principal, the Activities Director, and the Athletic Director shall automatically be considered ex-officio members of the association. The Principal, or a representative of the Principal, shall be a member of the Executive Board of the association.

ARTICLE IV—OFFICER ELECTIONS

Section 1—Officers

Officers shall consist of a President, Vice President, Treasurer, Recording Secretary, and Corresponding Secretary. There shall be such additional officers, committee chairpersons, and other officials as the President shall appoint from time to time.

Section 2—Election of Officers

Election of officers shall take place at the meeting of the Association to be held in April of each year or as near there to as is reasonable (the election meeting). The slate of officers should be presented to the membership at the March meeting or a meeting preceding the election meeting (the Nomination Meeting). The proposed slate of officers shall be nominated by a nominating committee, hereafter defined, and the committee may nominate more than one proposed officer for each position. The proposed nominations may be accepted by the nominating committee in their sole consideration from the floor during the Nomination Meeting or the nominating committee may generate nominations itself. The full slate or slates as nominated by the nominating committee must be accepted by the Executive Board and will be presented and voted upon during the Election Meeting.

Section 3—Nominating Committee

The nominating committee shall consist of five members; two shall be elected by the Executive Board; two shall be elected from the floor at a general meeting of the Association to be held preceding the Nomination Meeting; and one shall be the Principal of the school.

Section 4—Term of Office

Officers shall serve for one year and not for more than two consecutive years.

Section 5—Eligibility

Only members in good standing shall hold office or vote in elections, unless this provision is waived by the Executive Board.

Section 6—Voting

Voting shall be by secret, written ballot at the Election Meeting. There shall be an election committee of three, appointed by the President of the Association on the day of the election of officers.

The duty of the election committee shall be to pass out the ballots, collect the ballots and count them. The chairperson of that committee shall read the final account to the Association. In the event there is more than one person nominated for any one office, the winner of the majority of votes cast shall be deemed the winner of the election.

In the event there is one nominee for any particular office, and that nominee does not receive the majority of votes cast, the executive Board shall then appoint an eligible member to serve in that office, and hold that office until next regular election, or in the alternative, the Executive Board may determine to hold another election for that particular office. The President, with the consent of the nominating committee, may forgo the secret balloting and call for election by voice vote if the President deems that the electors are clearly in favor of such a procedure.

Section 7--Installation of Officers

Installation of officers shall be at the May meeting or final meeting of the school year, at which time the new officers shall take over their duties in all matters affecting the next subsequent school year.

Section 8—Annual Meeting

The annual meeting of the Association shall be the last meeting of the school year that, ordinarily, will be held in May. At the annual meeting, all annual reports shall be received and the new officers, retiring board, and the newly elected officers and new board, if organized, shall hold a joint session. At the joint session, the retiring officers and board shall transfer all books and papers in their possession and belonging to the Association to the new administration, and otherwise advise the new administration as to the status of affairs of the Association.

ARTICLE V—DUTIES OF OFFICERS

Section 1—President

It shall be the duty of the President to preside at all regular and special meetings and all Board meetings. The President shall perform all of the duties of the office; shall appoint all committees and committee chairpersons and shall be an ex-officio member of all committees, except the nominating committee. The President shall also sign all contracts, checks and disbursements, subject however, to the approval or ratification of the Executive Board. The President shall be able to disburse funds up to $ _____ with the approval of one other Board member. The President shall have regular meetings with the school Principal and the Athletic Director, as determined by the three individuals.

Section 2—Vice President

The Vice President shall act as President in the event of the President's absence, death, or incapacity and shall assume such duties for the balance of the term, unless replaced by the Board. The Vice President's line of succession shall be as designated at the time of elections.

Section 3—Recording Secretary

It shall be the duty of the Recording Secretary to keep a record of all regular and special meetings, and all Board meetings. It shall also be the duty of the Recording Secretary to maintain a procedure book that is a record of the activities of the Association compiled into a permanent form.

Section 4—Corresponding Secretary

It shall be the duty of the Corresponding Secretary to conduct the correspondence of the Association, keep a list of the membership's current addresses, send out all notices when not hereinafter provided for, and send special letters, unless provided for in the standing rules. A sustaining membership program shall be maintained and regular reports will be given to the Treasurer.

Section 5—Treasurer

It shall be the duty of the Treasurer to receive all monies due to the Association and deposit same in a place approved by the Association. The Treasurer shall disburse the funds of the Association only for purposes approved by the Association, from time to time. The Treasurer shall present a statement of account at all regular meetings and at other times when requested to do so by the President and shall make a full, written report at the annual meeting. The accounts of the Treasurer may be audited by a committee approved by the President.

ARTICLE VI—EXECUTIVE COMMITTEE

Section 1

The Executive Committee shall consist of the elected officers.

Section 2

The duties of the Executive Committee shall be to transact emergency vbusiness in the interval between Executive Board meetings.

Section 3

The majority of the Executive Committee shall constitute a quorum.

Section 4

Meetings of the Executive Committee shall be held as needed.

ARTICLE VII—EXECUTIVE BOARD

Section 1

The Executive Board shall consist of the officers of the Association, the chairpersons of the various standing committees, and the Principle of the school or a representative appointed by the Principle. The chairpersons of the standing committees shall be selected by the officers of the Association and the Principle of the school or the Principle's representative. The members of the Executive Board shall serve until the election and qualification of their successors.

Section 2

The duties of the Executive Board shall be to:

- (A) Transact necessary business in the intervals between association meetings and such other business as may be referred to it by the Association.
- (B) Create standing committees as well as hoc committees.

Appendix A: Sample By-Laws Guide for Booster Clubs 297

    (C)   Approve the plans of work of the standing committees.
    (D)   Present a report at the regular meetings of the Association.
    (E)   Prepare and submit to the Association for approval a budget for the fiscal year.
    (F)   Approve any bills within the limits of the budget.

Section 3—Meetings

Regular meetings of the Executive Board shall be held monthly during the school year, the time to be determined by the board at its first meeting of the year. A majority of the Executive Board members shall constitute a quorum. Special meetings of the Executive Board may be called by the President or by a majority of the members of the board.

ARTICLE VIII—GENERAL MEETINGS

Section 1

Regular meetings of the Association shall be held on the _____ (day of month and hour) each month during the school year, unless otherwise provided by the Association or by the Executive Board, (number)_____ days notice having been given.

Section 2

Special meetings may be called by the Executive Board with (number) _____ days advance notice having been given.

Section 3

The annual meeting shall be in the month of _____.

Section 4

A quorum shall exist when _____ members are present for the transaction of the business in any meeting of this association.

Section 5

QUORUMS: A quorum shall consist of not less than tow-thirds of the Executive Board and not less than 25-five members of the general membership. It is noted, however, that at times, due to other commitments of the members, it may not be possible to obtain a quorum. Under such circumstances, such action which are taken at this meeting at which there is not a quorum shall be subject to review by a full quorum within sixty days of such action having been taken, at which time the full quorum may reverse the action taken at the meeting which failed to have a quorum.

ARTICLE IX—STANDING AND SPECIAL COMMITTEES

Section 1

The Executive Board may create such standing committees as well as ad hoc committees as it may deem necessary to promote the objectives and carry on the work of the Association. The term of each chairperson shall be one-year or until the election and qualification of the person's successor.

Section 2

The chairperson of each standing committee shall present a plan of work to the Executive Board for approval. No committee work shall be undertaken without the written consent of the Executive Board.

Section 3

The power to form special committees and appoint their members rests with the Association and the Executive Board.

Section 4

The President shall be a member ex-officio of all committees except the nominating committee.

ARTICLE X—PROPERTY RIGHTS

Membership in this Association shall not title or vest any of the members with any property rights or rights having monetary value of any kind whatsoever, including, but not limited to, property rights or monetary rights in the school or in the Association.

ARTICLE XI—AMMENDMENT

These by-laws shall be approved by a meeting of the regularly called general membership, by a majority vote of those members eligible to vote and actually casting their vote at said meeting. The by-laws may be amended by a two-thirds vote of the members present at any regularly called meetings. Such amendments may only be recommended by the Executive Board, and shall be presented in writing and read at the regular meeting prior to the time of voting.

ARTICLE XII—RELATIONSHIP WITH THE SCHOOL ADMINISTRATORS AND ATHLETIC DEPARTMENT

The booster club shall operate in full support of the school Administrators Athletic Director, and coaches. At no time shall the booster club make recommendations or become directly involved in the day-to-day operation of the school athletic program. The booster club serves only to support and facilitate the school athletic program and has no role in deciding the direction of policy established by the school Principal or by the Athletic Director.

Appendix B

Membership Plan for an Athletic Support Group

The College at BROCKPORT — State University of New York

Friends of Brockport Athletics

BENEFITS / CLUBS	Green $30	Gold $50	Century $100	Flying Eagles $150	Varsity $250	Coach's $500	University $1000
Membership Card	1	1	1	2	2	2	2
Bumper Sticker	1	1	1	2	4	6	10
Eagle "Stick On"	1	1	1	2	4	6	10
Periodic Newsletter	1	1	1	1	1	1	1
Hospitality Lounge Privilege	1	1	1	2	2	2	2
Socials		1	1	2	2	2	2
All Year Sports Pass			1	2	4	6	10
Booster Hat			1	2	4	6	10
"Eagle Pin"			1	2	4	6	10
T-shirts				1	2	4	6
Family Sports Pass (Children 18 & Younger)				Yes	Yes	Yes	Yes
Recognition Plaque (Home/Office)					1	1	2
Recreation Pass for Family					Yes	Yes	Yes
Annual Recognition Plaque in Tuttle N						Yes	Yes
Folding Stadium Seats						2	4
Corporate Benefit Package	— Contact Athletic Director						

APPLICATION FORM (please print)

Name: _____ Phone: _____

Address: _____ City: _____ State: _____ Zip: _____

Type of Membership Selected: _____ Date: _____

Name(s) and Age(s) of Children: _____

Method of Payment (circle one):   Check   Cash   Bill Me

Appendix C
Athletic Fundraising Request Form

(1) Name of person making request and assuming responsibility of fundraising activities

_____

                                    Home Phone _____

                                    Office Phone _____

(2) Team or organization raising funds _____

(3) Nature of FUNDRAISING ACTIVITIES (please be specific) _____

_____

_____

(4) Amount needed to be raised _____

(5) Length or duration of solicitation/fundraising activities _____

_____

(6) Who will be solicited (please be specific)? _____

_____

_____

(7) Where will solicitation/fundraising activities be conducted? _____

_____

_____

(8) Purpose of fundraising efforts (what will funds be spent for)? _____

_____

_____

(9) Other _____

_____

_____

_____

NOTE

(1) No solicitation or fundraising activities may take place without this form being filled out and written approval being given by the Director of Athletics, and Dean and the Vice President.

(2) The individual responsible for the approved fundraising activities shall be required to provide to the Athletic Director a full, typed fiscal accounting for the fundraising activities within three (3) weeks following the close of the fundraising activities. This will be shared with the Dean and Vice President.

(3) All funds raised shall be placed in the special athletic income account prior to a team attempting to expend funds raised through fundraising activities; it is necessary for the Athletics Director to sign off.

(4) Approval by the Athletics Director, Dean, and Vice President may contain specific restrictions that must be strictly adhered to by the individuals attempting to raise funds. For example, specific individuals, groups and organizations may be "unapproachable."

(5) Approval by the Athletics Director, Dean, and Vice President may be removed at any time.

(6) Periodic reports to the Athletics Director (by the person responsible for the fundraising activities) are expected and appreciated (this is to keep the Athletic Director aware of the progress of various outside and inside fundraising activities by different teams/groups, etc).

Appendix C: Athletic Fundraising Request Form

A. _____ Approved

   _____ Disapproved

   _____ Approved, with the following restrictions

   _____

   _____

   Signed _____
          Director of intercollegiate Athletics

B. _____ Approved

   _____ Disapproved

   _____ Approved, with the following restrictions

   _____

   _____

   Signed _____
                   Dean

C. _____ Approved

   _____ Disapproved

   _____ Approved, with the following restrictions

   _____

   _____

   Signed _____
                Vice President, Development

Appendix D: Individual Sport Mascots for a Single Athletic Program

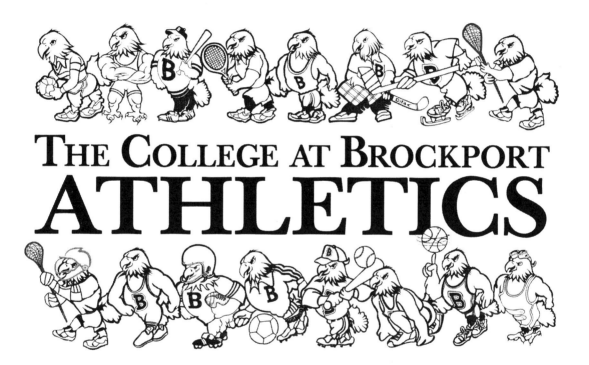

PHOTO CREDITS

Photos pages 244, 273 courtesy of the College at Brockport, State University of New York, Sports Information Office, Photo by Mike Pratt

Photos pages 150, 207 courtesy of the College at Brockport, State University of New York, Sports Information Office, Photo by Janelle Feuz

Photo Illustration page 47courtesy of the College at Brockport, State University of New York, Sports Information Office, Photo illustration by Adam Kendrick

Photos pages 11, 221, 266, 286 courtesy of the College at Brockport, State University of New York, Sports Information Office, Photo by Angelo Lisuzzo

Photos pages 1, 28, 59, 99, 105, 138, 166, 188, 227, 255, 276, 287 courtesy of Veronica Martin

Photos pages 6, 19, 75, 127, 161, 173, 181, 273, 286 courtesy of the College at Brockport, State University of New York, Photo by James Dusen

Photos page 36 Courtesy of Will Rumbold, Rochester (NY) Red Wings

Photos pages 68, 87, 197, 211, 233 courtesy of Western Illinois University Intercollegiate Athletics Media Services

Photos pages 83, 115, 281 courtesy of Western Regional Off-Track Betting Corp , Batavia, New York

Front cover photos courtesy of courtesy of Veronica Martin; courtesy of the College at Brockport, State University of New York, Photo by James Dusen; Western Regional Off-Track Betting Corp , Batavia, New York;

INDEX

Abuse of power 70
Accountability 37, 120
Act of God 87
Advanced ticket sales 185
Advertisers 115, 217
Advertising 187, 200
Alcohol 92
Alumni outreach EFFORTS 164
American Red Cross 101
Annual fundraising projects 107
Appeal model 130
Art 4
Assets 27, 28, 133
Associates 35
Athletic handbook 137
Atmosphere 34
Attendance 182
Attitudes 4

Banquets 273
Benefits 244
Benefits of membership 67, 68
Beverages 218
Billboards 200
Board members 63
Bobbleheads 115
Booster clubs 50
Booster(s) 48
Brand recognition 229
Brochure(s) 238
Budgeting 26
Business investment 248
Business partnerships 207
Business revenue approach 129
Buying 130
By-laws 63

Car wrapping 200
Cash flow 182
Categories of giving 107
Centers of Influence 83, 165
Change 56
Characteristics of donors 112
Charitable approach 249
Charitable requests 100, 104
Chicken Little syndrome 131
Circumstances 285
Clearinghouse 137
Clearinghouse 141
Climate 34
Cold calls 164
Commission 87
Community standards 138
Competencies 9
Computer software 173
Conceptual approach 128
Concessions 189
Consecutive terms 65
Constituencies 6
Consumers 185
Continuity 64
Contributors 115
Cool, calm and collected 119, 122
Coordinating 24
Corporate giving 103
Corporate Olympics 211
Corporate partnerships 212
Corporate sponsorships 162
Cost of raising money 102
Cost of sales 193
Creativity 10
Credibility 101
Cultivating major donors 164

Cutting edge knowledge 10
Cutting one's loses 118

Data 95, 239
Database 173
Decision making 24, 95
Decisions 3, 123
Deferred giving 110
Direct mail appeal(s) 171, 174
Directing 23
Discretionary income 287
DNA 14
Donors 176
Door-to-door solicitation/sales 166

80-20 rule 114
Effectiveness 214
Endowment outreach efforts 164
Endowments 108
Environment 34
Evaluating 26, 123
Exchange of benefits approach 249
Exchanges 157
Exclusivity 203, 211, 212

Facilitation 26
Facilities 30
Factors affecting fundraising efforts 162
Failure(s) 76, 124
Feasibility study 94, 147, 149
Financial considerations 243
Financial transactions 66
Firing line 3
5-P handbook 137
Flexibility 70
FOBA 55
Follow-up efforts 168
Food 218
Franchisers 232
Franchises 232
Fundraising 3
Fundraising-Planning Template 282

Gambling 261
Game day activities 273
Games of chance 91, 261
Gate receipts 53
Gifts-in-kind 246
Gifts 68, 177
Goals 85
Good taste 139
Goods 4, 212
Grants 104
Group rates 186
Guilt and Glitter Syndrome 117

Hard data 95
Hard sell 156
Hawking 91
Heavy hitters 141
Hindsight 121
Holiday seasons 258
Hot button 146

Image 32
Incorporation 67
Inflation 50
Information 240, 241
In-service education 10
Insurance considerations 89
Inventory 193, 194
Investment 249
IRS 67

Kick-off activity 62

Laws 90, 140
Leadership 42
Level of competition 33
Liability considerations 86
Liability insurance 51
Licenses 90
Life insurance 110
Logo(s) 198
Lost avenues 185
Luncheon activities 273

Index 313

Luxury boxes 203

Mailing lists 173
Major donors 165
Managing by being seen MBBS 158
Market research 147
Marketing 187
Mascots 198
Media 230
Medical insurance 51
Medical services 51
Menu 190, 193
Merchandise 197
Merchandising model 129
Micro manage 235
Mini-businesses 182
Models of fundraising 162
Money 4, 33, 212
Murphy's Law 80

Naming 220, 247
Naming rights 221, 235
NASCA 209
National matching gift program 144
NCAA 12
Needs 84, 97, 147, 241
Negative influences 70
Negligence 87
Net profit 193
Network 81
New blood 64
Non-Major (Olympic) sports 248
Non-profit organizations 169

Objectives 85
Officers 63
Omission 87
One-shot effort 79
One-Third Rule 114
One-time fundraising projects 106
Open door policy 145
Opinion research 96
Opinions 4

Optimist 16
Organizing 23
Outside influences 70
Overhead 193

Packaging 237
Pareto Principle 114
Parking 201
Parking condos 204
Peddling 91
Perceptions 41
Permission(s) 90, 135
Permits 90
Persona non grata 139
Personnel 29
Person-to-person 238
Pessimist 16
Philanthropy 10, 100, 248
Phon-a-thons 176
PIA 78
Piggy-back strategy 175, 257
Pilot study 94
Pitfalls 62
Planning 22, 76
Point of sale method 167
Potential contributors 155
Power person 232
PPPOSDDCORRRFEB
Preferred seating 203
Premium retail prices 168
Premiums 8
Prescreening 177
Pre-selling merchandise 200
Prevention 87
Pricing merchandise 199
Pricing schedule 193
Pricing structure 222
Pricing of tickets
Principles 16
Prioritizing 22
Priorities 154
Prizes 261
Problem Solving 22

Processes 20
Product 121, 218
Product sales 197
Product(s) 7
Professionalism 36
Profit centers 8, 162, 182
Program Evaluation Review Technique PERT 80
Program Sales 196
Promotions 3
Prospect lists 176, 188
Prospect pool 156
Prospects 171
Public relations 3, 5
Publicity 5
Publics 6

Quality 191

Reality 41
Record keeping 120
Recording 25
Records 240
Recreation support group RSG 59
Reduced costs 133
Rejection 156
Renaissance person 44
Renewing agreements 250
Repeatable fundraisers 106, 143
Reporting 24
Reputation 31
Resources 19, 27, 28
Restrictions 91
Restrictive philosophies 139
Results 94
Rifle approach 80
Ringers 152
Risk management 88, 285
Risk taking 25
Risks 288

Safe practices 51
Sales 260

Sales approach 165
Sales piece 174
Sales tax 169,
Sales team 168
Science 4
Scripts 176
Seating 203
Security 120
Self promotion 157
Service 191, 218
Services 4, 35, 212
Shotgun approach 80
Single person appeals 162
Sizzle 147
Skills 38
Sky boxes 203
Slippage 250
Soft data 95
Software applications 31
Solicitation kit 165
Solicitation model 130
Soliciting support 111
Solicitors 177
Sound fiscal management 134
Sources of money 85, 135
Special fundraising projects 162, 256, 266
Spectators 185
Sponsors 217
Sponsorship agreements 234
Sponsorship proposal 236
Sponsorships 207
Sport support group SSG 58
Squad concept 117
Staff (Staffing) 29
Staffing 23
Steak 147
Strategic planning 77
Success 94, 183
Supermarket approach 129
Supervision 88, 177
Support groups 49, 55, 60

Index

Take-order method 167
Tax collector 169
Tax laws 170
Team concept 117
Technology 13, 185, 203
Telephone solicitation 175
Television 215
Ten Commandments of Fundraising 82
Term limits 64
Three o'clock wonder 71
Ticket sales 184
Timing 143
Timing of fundraising efforts 106
Tip-off club 56
Title IX 52
Tradeouts 245

Training 191
Turnstile scanners 185
Types of consumers 146
Types of donations 105

Urgency 130
User fees 201

Vending machines 202
Volunteer(s) 29

Why people contribute 115
Wide Web 7, 30, 166
Worse case scenario 152
Worthy cause(s) 102